face2face

Advanced Student's Book

Gillie Cunningham & Jan Bell
with Chris Redston

CAMBRIDGE
UNIVERSITY PRESS

Contents

Listening	Extended Speaking	Accurate Writing	Preview
People discussing a book	Getting to know you	**connecting words**: addition (*also, as well, too, besides, what's more, not only*); **spelling**: homophones (*whose/who's, there/they're/their, of/'ve, you're/your*) p15	**Preview 1** p6 Past Simple and Present Perfect **Preview 2** p15 relative clauses; gradable and non-gradable adjectives; adverbs; verb+*ing* and past participles
Interviews: Who do you confide in?	Discussion: What makes a good friend?		
Favourite sayings	A panel game: Bluff		
			Reading and Writing Portfolio 1 WB p54
Radio programme about a painter	Deciding which people should win an award	**connecting words**: time (1) (*the moment, as soon as, first, ever since, originally, from then on, while, as, afterwards, then, meanwhile*) **punctuation**: apostrophes p25	**Preview 3** subject and verb inversion p25
People talking about memorable holidays	Describing places you love or hate		
Interview about tourism **Song** *Little Wonders*	Recommending places to visit in your country		
			Reading and Writing Portfolio 2 WB p57
Interview with people about 'impostor syndrome'	Giving both sides of an argument	**connecting words**: contrast (1) (*although, even though, whereas, however, but*); **spelling**: one word, two words or hyphenated (*everyday* v *every day*; *a hundred years old* v *a hundred-year-old*, etc.) p35	**Preview 4** future verb forms p35
Conversations about how to cheer yourself up	Persuading people to try your ideas		
People being tactful in different situations	Short role plays		
			Reading and Writing Portfolio 3 WB p60
Discussion about TV programmes	Predicting the future of the media	**connecting words**: contrast (2) (*despite, but, in spite of, although, nonetheless, nevertheless, however, even though*); **punctuation**: capital letters and full stops p45	**Preview 5** reflexive pronouns (1); verb + infinitive with *to* or verb+*ing* (1) p45
Radio programme: How *Star Trek* changed the world	Describing and discussing strange inventions		
Interview with the sub-editor of a national newspaper **Song** *Summer in the City*	Creating a front-page news story		
			Reading and Writing Portfolio 4 WB p63
Interview with TV/film 'extras'	Role play	**connecting words**: time (2) (*instantly, at once, previously, immediately, straightaway, following, subsequent, eventually, at the end, lately, finally, up until, prior*, etc.); **spelling**: *ie* or *ei* (*patience, receive*, etc.) p55	**Preview 6** ways of comparing; adverbs p55
Interview with three 18-year-olds	Discussion about how to improve schools		
Discussion about work issues	Extending and role-playing dialogues		
			Reading and Writing Portfolio 5 WB p66

Listening	Extended Speaking	Accurate Writing	Preview
Four friends talking about quirky behaviour	Talking about unusual habits	**connecting words**: purpose (*so as, in order, so that*, etc.);	**Preview 7** conditionals: basic forms; passive forms
People talking about advertising campaigns	Discussing effective advertising campaigns	**punctuation**: colons and semi-colons p65	p65
Professor John McRae talking about short stories; A short story extract **Song** *Chasing Cars*	Telling a story		
Interview with a science journalist	Discussing open and closed prisons	**connecting words**: condition (*unless, in case, as long as, unless, otherwise, providing, imagine, whether, supposing*);	**Preview 8** *wish, if only …* p75
People discussing 'state intervention' in their countries	Reporting and giving opinions on news headlines	**punctuation**: commas p75	
Extract from a play	Role play		
Eddy Canfor-Dumas talking about an environmental campaigner	Choosing a famous person to spend an evening with	**connecting words**: comment adverbials (*obviously, personally, frankly, fortunately, quite honestly, surely, in fact, surprisingly*, etc.);	**Preview 9** simple v continuous; *a/an, the* or no article (-) p85
A radio programme about emotions	Discussing things that frighten you	**spelling**: commonly misspelled words (*necessary, acquaint, business, accommodate*, etc.) p85	
People discussing whether it's better to be a man or a woman **Song** *You Gotta Be*	Class survey about gender		
Can money buy you happiness?	Discussion about experiences v possessions	**connecting words**: reason and result (*due to, because, because of, so, as a result, consequently, since, as, therefore, owing to*);	**Preview 10** modal verbs (1): functions p95
A radio programme about Satish Kumar	Evaluating how long you could survive without money	**spelling**: *-ible* or *-able* (*edible, understandable*, etc.) p95	
A lecture describing the importance of economics	Giving a two-minute talk		
A radio programme about inventions	Prioritising useful inventions		
People discussing the secret of success	Discussing achievements		
People talking about their language-learning strategies	Discussion about your future language-learning strategies		

1 Let's talk

1A Make a good impression

Preview 1 Past Simple and Present Perfect

1 **a)** Use these prompts to make questions with *you*. Use the Past Simple or Present Perfect.

1 / learn / English for a long time?
Have you been learning English for a long time?
2 How old / be / when / have / first English lesson?
3 / see / any films in English recently?
4 When / be / the last time / speak / English outside class?
5 / have to / write anything in English last month?
6 / ever / read / a novel that was written in English?
7 How long / come / this school?

> Have you been learning English for a long time?

> I first learned it at school, actually. But I forgot most of it so I decided to do this course.

b) Work in pairs. Ask and answer the questions. Ask follow-up questions. Check in Language Summary 1 **G1.1** p118.

> **Vocabulary** communicating
> **Grammar** time expressions with Past Simple and Present Perfect

Vocabulary Communicating

2 **a)** Tick the words/phrases in **bold** you know. Check new words/phrases in **V1.1** p117.

a) It's essential to **make eye contact** when you're speaking to someone.
b) On average, I **come into contact with** about twenty people a day.
c) On the whole, women **gossip** more than men.
d) In general, men **butt in** more than women, which women find very annoying.
e) If you **overhear** people **having a row** in public, you should intervene.
f) Politicians generally **witter on** without ever answering the interviewer's questions.
g) Elderly people have reason to **grumble** about the youth of today.
h) Adults spend more time **chatting** on the phone than teenagers.
i) Couples who constantly **bicker** should split up.
j) Women **chat up** men as often as men chat up women.

b) Tick the sentences you agree with. Then change the other sentences to make them true for you.

Perhaps it's not essential to make eye contact, but it might seem rude if you don't.

c) Work in pairs. Compare ideas. Do you agree?

Listening and Grammar

3 **a)** Think of someone (not in your class) who is popular. Write five personal qualities that make him/her popular.

b) Work in pairs. Tell your partner about the person you chose. Are any of the personal qualities the same?

c) Agree on the three most important qualities. Tell the class.

4 **a)** Look at the book cover and read the introduction. What did the author and his publishers initially think about the book?

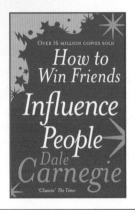

How to Win Friends and Influence People, first published in 1937, has become an all-time international best-seller. The first print run was limited to 5,000 copies, which was an indication of how small a readership the author and the publishers were expecting. However, from the very beginning the book's runaway success meant the publishers had difficulty keeping up with demand.

OVER 16 MILLION COPIES SOLD
How to Win Friends Influence People
Dale Carnegie
'Classic' *The Times*

b) R1.1 Listen to Ann, Sy, Dean and Amy at their book club meeting. Which of Carnegie's suggestions do they mention?

Amy   Ann

Sy

Dean

c) Listen again. Answer these questions.

1 a) Why did Ann suggest the book to the group?
   b) Why wasn't she very impressed with it at first?
2 a) Does Sy usually read books like this?
   b) Which of Carnegie's points does he strongly agree with?
3 a) Did Dean expect to enjoy the book?
   b) Why does he talk about his friend, John?
4 a) Which of Carnegie's suggestions did Amy try out?
   b) How did the man in the ticket office react?

d) Work in pairs. Which of Carnegie's suggestions do you think is the most important and why?

Help with Grammar
Time expressions with Past Simple and Present Perfect

See Preview, p6.

5 **a)** Look at these sentences. Are they talking about a definite time in the past or time up to and including now? Which verb form is used?

1 I've bought quite a few self-help books <u>over the past few months</u>.
2 I've read about 150 pages <u>so far</u>.
3 <u>During the last couple of weeks</u> I've actually been trying out some of Carnegie's suggestions.
4 <u>Up until now</u>, I've never really had any contact with the guy in the ticket office.

b) <u>Underline</u> the time expression in each sentence in **5a**).

c) Sometimes we can use the Present Perfect or the Past Simple with the same time expression. Compare these pairs of sentences. Why did Speaker A use the Past Simple? Why did Speaker B use the Present Perfect?

1 A I **told** at least ten people about it at work <u>this week</u>. *the speaker considers the working week finished*
   B I**'ve told** at least ten people about it at work <u>this week</u>. *the speaker considers the working week unfinished*
2 A I **read** it <u>during</u> the summer holidays.
   B I**'ve read** a lot of books <u>during</u> the last month.
3 A <u>Since</u> Ann **suggested** this one, I've read a couple of his other books.
   B I've read lots of his books <u>since</u> I**'ve been** unemployed.
4 A <u>As soon as</u> I **finished** reading it, I gave it to my brother.
   B <u>As soon as</u> I**'ve finished** reading it, I'm going to give it to my brother.

d) Check in G1.2 p118.

6 **a)** Are both verb forms possible? Why?/Why not?

1 I *spoke/'ve spoken* to him this morning.
2 I *saw/'ve seen* her during the last few months.
3 I'll call you as soon as she *arrived/'s arrived*.
4 She *came/'s been* here a lot last month.
5 During last night's performance, several people *walked/have walked* out.
6 There have been a lot of changes since I *worked/'ve worked* for them.
7 Once I *met/'ve met* her, I really liked her.
8 I've been skiing twice since I *saw/'ve seen* you last.

b) Work in pairs. Compare answers.

Reading

7 **a)** Work in pairs. Give examples of what you consider to be good and bad service in shops, restaurants, etc.

b) Read the article. Why do very friendly, chatty shop assistants and waitresses annoy the writer?

c) Read the article again. Tick the true sentences. Correct the false ones.

1 The writer was in a hurry when she went into the shop. ✓
2 She wondered why the shop assistant's behaviour had upset her.
3 She enjoyed the food she had at the restaurant.
4 She told the waitress what she thought of the food.
5 No psychological studies have the same view as hers.
6 She wouldn't object to assistants who were naturally friendly.

8 **a)** Look at the words/phrases in **bold** in the article. What words are missing from each phrase?

b) What types of word can we miss out in informal written and spoken English?

9 Work in groups and discuss these questions.

1 Would you have responded to the shop assistant and the waitress in the same way as the writer of the article? If so, why? If not, what would you have said?
2 How would you describe the service in shops and cafés in your country? Has it changed over the years?

Get ready ... Get it right!

10 **a)** Write three topics you would like to talk about, e.g.

● films/TV/music ● sport ● clothes ● pets
● work/studies

b) Work in pairs. Swap papers. Choose one of your partner's topics and write six questions to ask him/her.
How many films have you seen during the last six months?

Work in pairs. Take turns to ask and answer your partner's questions. Tell the class one thing you've learnt about your partner.

fake nice

TEN DAYS AGO, on the way to a meeting, I remembered that I was running low on face cream. There was a chemist's across the road so I ran in and grabbed the first cream I saw.

"**Having a good day?**" asked the girl at the till, smiling blissfully.

"Um, yes thanks," I replied.

"That's great." She ran the scanner over the jar, and made eye contact.

"**Been shopping all morning?**"

Not having the time to take her through my diary, I simply went, "Mmm."

"Yeah? Lucky you!" She told me the total and said, "**So, got anything planned for this afternoon?**"

"Oh, you know," I said, aware of time ticking by. "This and that."

As I hurried on my way I found myself thinking about the girl and the amount of niceness I had just experienced. Why did it make me feel so bad? Was it impolite not to chat back? Or was this sort of pushy friendliness, in its way, every bit as rude? I was reminded of this after the meeting, when I met a newish friend for lunch. I had the fishcakes. They were perfectly disgusting.

"**Everything all right with your meal?**" asked the waitress, interrupting our conversation.

"**Fine,**" I said. What else could I have said even if I'd wanted to? It might have made my new friend uncomfortable.

On the way home that afternoon I thought about manners. As a society, we do not take manners, by which I mean how we behave towards strangers, very seriously. If you are entering a bank or shop, the person just ahead of you is sure to let the doors swing back in your face. Middle-aged men drive into disabled spaces, teenagers slump in their seats on the bus, pretending not to notice the pregnant woman standing in front of them. And yet

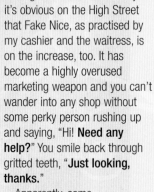

it's obvious on the High Street that Fake Nice, as practised by my cashier and the waitress, is on the increase, too. It has become a highly overused marketing weapon and you can't wander into any shop without some perky person rushing up and saying, "Hi! **Need any help?**" You smile back through gritted teeth, "**Just looking, thanks.**"

Apparently, some psychological studies have shown that if the assistant treats you as a friend, there's a psychological effect – the customer will return. Or will they? Other studies suggest that this sales technique is a turn-off. Perhaps the solution is to appoint people who are genuinely interested in people, not those who are trained to be insincere robots.

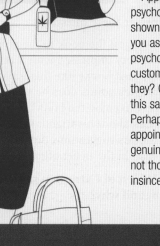

Adapted from the Independent
29/04/06

Vocabulary prepositions and phrases
Grammar cleft sentences: *what* and *it* clauses
Review time expressions with Past Simple and Present Perfect

Listening and Grammar

 Check the meaning of the phrases in **bold**. Then work in pairs and discuss these questions.

1 As a rule, do you tend to **unburden yourself** to friends or to members of your family?
2 By and large, is it men or women who find it easier to **unload** their worries **on to** other people?
3 Broadly speaking, do adults in your country **bottle up** their feelings or let them out?
4 Do you think, in the main, that teenagers would rather **confide in** their parents or their friends?

TIP! ● Notice the underlined expressions, which are used to make generalisations.

Dave   Helen   Andrea   Alex

 a) Work in pairs. Who would you expect men, women and teenagers like the ones in the photos to confide in: a) their friends? b) both friends and family? c) somebody else? d) no one?

b) R1.2 Listen and check.

c) Listen again. Tick the true sentences. Correct the false ones.

1 Dave and his friends tend to talk about only serious issues.
2 Dave thinks men make friends with people who enjoy the same things.
3 Helen sees her friends every day.
4 Helen's friends are very patient with her.
5 Andrea trusts her hairdresser to be discreet.
6 Andrea enjoys listening to her hairdresser's problems.
7 Most of Alex's conversations are about everyday events.
8 Alex confides in people of his own age.

d) Work in pairs. Which things that the speakers talked about do you identify with? Do you think people confide in each other about different things at different ages?

Help with Grammar Cleft sentences: *what* and *it* clauses

● Cleft sentences divide a message into two parts, using *what* or *it* clauses. They can focus attention on new, more important or contradictory information.

(I can get a bit stressed by work.) **What** *I do if I get stressed* **is** *talk to my friends.* (new information)

(I get on well with my parents.) However, **it's** *my friends* **that** *I talk to if I have a problem.* (contradiction)

 WHAT CLAUSES

a) Look at this example and answer the questions.

(We'll have a drink and talk afterwards.) **What** *we talk about* **isn't** *deep and meaningful, though.*

1 Underline the clause that gives new information in the cleft sentence.
2 Which verb joins the two clauses?

● To focus on an action we can use *what … do … .*

(**What** *I do if I get stressed*) **is** (*talk to my friends.*)

● To focus on a whole sentence we can use *what happens … .*

(Men don't unload on to other people.)

(**What** *happens*) **is** (*we bottle things up.*)

TIP! ● When we use *who, why, whose, when, where,* etc. instead of *what,* we usually use an expression such as *a person, the reason,* etc., with or without the *wh-* word.

A person (who) I tend to confide in **is** *my hairdresser.*

IT CLAUSES

b) Look at these cleft sentences with *it.* Answer the questions.

a) **It'd** probably **be** my parents **who** I'd talk to first.
b) **It wasn't** until he broke up with his girlfriend **that** my hairdresser started to confide in me.

1 Does the speaker emphasise the information in the *it* clause or in the *who/that* clause?
2 What verb follows *it*?

c) Check in G1.3 p119.

4 **a)** Complete sentence b) so it has the same meaning as sentence a).

1 a) Lucy's coming to help me out.
   b) The reason _Lucy's coming is to help me out_ .

2 a) After leaving my last job, I began to work freelance.
   b) It …

3 a) You should write a letter and refuse to pay.
   b) What …

4 a) Tim is the problem, not Jo.
   b) It's …

5 a) I wanted to speak to Ben.
   b) The person …

6 a) This is what happened. I forgot the map.
   b) What …

b) **R1.3** Listen and check.

c) Listen again and practise.
The reason Lucy's coming is to help me out.

 5 **a)** Complete the following sentences about yourself.

1 What I find really boring … .
2 It's … that really irritates me.
3 It wasn't until … .
4 The year that … .
5 What amuses me … .
6 A place I really love … .

b) Work in groups. Say your sentences. Ask follow-up questions.

Reading and Vocabulary

 6 **a)** Work in pairs. Make a list of the different types of friends you could meet at different stages of your life, e.g. school friends. Will they always be important to you?

b) What do you think 'friendship overload' means? In what ways might it be a problem?

c) Read the article. Does the writer agree with your ideas in **6b)**?

d) Read the article again. Answer these questions.

1 Why are families often no longer available to do the things they used to?
2 In what ways do people living locally feel like family?
3 According to the writer, what are 'second division' friends?
4 Why do people these days seem to have so many more friends than before?
5 What does the writer say about some of the people you see often?
6 Why does the writer suggest a real friend is one you hardly ever see?

e) Work in pairs. Which of the opinions in the article do you agree or disagree with? Give reasons.

Friendship overload

Old college friends, Internet chat room mates, work colleagues, neighbours … we collect friends as if they're going out of fashion, says _Mary Killen_

Friends are the new family. We've no choice any more because the jobs that used to be done by family members on a regular basis, such as confidant, babysitter and someone to watch the TV with, have gone for good. More often than not, we now live too far away for this to be practical, which means that our friends – the people we actually come across most regularly – have to help us out. Naturally, they have to be on the same wavelength as well, but living nearby, having kids at the same school and so on means that we tend to have a lot in common. This is why they often end up as substitute family, either by chance or on purpose!

But what about the friends we are not so close to? There was a time when people tended to have a small group of 'best' friends and then a second division of twenty or more friends we acquired along the way. They could be people we were on good terms with at work, and since a British 25-year-old has, on average, experienced three different jobs, that soon adds up! Or perhaps we made friends with them at school or university and kept in touch. Maybe they are neighbours, people we know through hobbies, nightclubs or holidays, or even friends of friends.

At times it feels as if the numbers in the second division are getting out of control as we travel more and move jobs or houses increasingly frequently – either by choice or out of necessity. It sounds ungrateful, but many of us have collected too many friends and with only so many hours in the day it's impossible to keep in contact with all of them So, let's be honest here. Perhaps one in five of our friendships is purely email, or text-based. You like each other, but realistically the friendship is not going to last in the long run. Another fifth is the people you only phone but barely ever meet. Next are the friends you do see sometimes, just out of habit. Finally, the last two-fifths are split between the people you see a lot in phases and those you see regularly, which include some you like a lot less than some of the people you only speak to on the phone, but who happen to live very close. Add to this lot your partner's friends, your work colleagues and the parents of your children's friends, and you're soon feeling out of your depth. It's a huge commitment, the kind that can keep you awake at night.

The Americans call it 'obligation overload'. It's the very 21st-century condition of collecting friends as if our life depended on it and then worrying how on earth to keep track of them all. Having so many friends is making us miserable and funnily enough it's your real best friends that won't put pressure on you to see them because they know that life is stressful enough already!

In fact, it could be argued that perhaps the definition of a really close friend is one you hardly ever see!

Adapted from the _Express_ 17/09/99

Help with Vocabulary Prepositions and phrases

- Make a note of words/phrases together with their prepositions and try to learn them as 'chunks' of meaning.

7 **a)** Look at the phrases in the word map. Then look at the phrases in **bold** in the article. Check their meaning in context then match them to definitions 1–6.

on — the same wavelength
— purpose

in — phases
— the long run

out of — habit
— your depth

1 intentionally, not by accident
2 something you do often, without thinking about it
3 after a very lengthy period of time
4 with similar views/opinions
5 for short, irregular periods
6 without the knowledge or skills to deal with something

b) Match these words/phrases to the prepositions in the word map. There is sometimes more than one possible answer.

| control   fashion   necessity   good terms |
| a regular basis   touch   average   common   contact |

c) Work in pairs. Look at the phrases from **7b)** in blue in the article. What does each phrase mean?

d) Check in **V1.2** p117.

8 **a)** Complete these sentences with one or two prepositions.

1 Who is the friend you have most .... common with?
2 Do you keep .... touch with any of your old school or college friends?
3 What kind of things do you do .... habit, but which you would like to stop doing?
4 Do you ever do things .... phases and then stop altogether?
5 What sports do you do .... a regular basis?
6 What clothes did you use to wear but which are now .... fashion?
7 In what subject have you always felt .... your depth?
8 Have you ever broken something .... purpose?

b) Work in pairs. Take turns to ask and answer the questions in 8a). Ask follow-up questions.

Get ready ... Get it right!

9 Tick the sentences you agree with. Change the other sentences to make them true for you. Then complete sentences 7 and 8 with your own ideas.

1 What you're looking for in a friend is someone who is very different to you.
2 You need to have interests in common if a friendship is to last.
3 Friends are people who will always stick up for you, whatever happens.
4 You can't really be 'just friends' with someone of the opposite sex.
5 A real friend is someone who will tell you the truth even if it's something you don't want to hear.
6 Women form closer friendships than men.
7 It ...
8 What ...

10 **a)** Work in groups. Discuss what you have written and give reasons.

b) Tell the class three things that you agreed on.

By and large, we agreed that what we tend to be looking for is someone who is loyal and ...

1C Favourite sayings

Vocabulary sayings; idioms
Real World explaining and paraphrasing
Review prepositions and phrases

QUICK REVIEW ● ● ●
Write five sentences using phrases with *in*, *on* and *out of*. Work in pairs. Say one of your sentences but don't say the preposition(s). Your partner says the sentence with the correct preposition(s): A *I'm ... good terms ... my in-laws.* B *I'm on good terms with my in-laws.*

1 **a)** Match the first half of sayings 1—8 to their endings a)–h).

1 Rome wasn't ————	a)	before mouth.
2 Don't make a mountain	b)	built in a day.
	c)	nothing gained.
3 Once bitten,	d)	louder than words.
4 Actions speak	e)	is another man's
5 One man's meat		poison.
6 Engage brain	f)	out of a molehill.
7 Nothing ventured,	g)	than never.
8 Better late	h)	twice shy.

b) Work in pairs. Compare answers. What do you think the sayings mean? Check in V1.3 p117.

c) Choose a saying from your country. How would you explain what it means to a British person?

2 **a)** R1.4 Listen to five people talking about sayings that they like. Put the sayings in pictures A–E in the order they talk about them.

b) Work in pairs. Try to match the sayings to these meanings.

1 You shouldn't worry about things that might or might not happen in the future.
2 It's important to choose the right person for the right activity.
3 It's pointless doing something yourself if you know someone who can do it for you.
4 If you mix with a bad crowd, you'll be judged the same way as the crowd.
5 If you don't offer people enough money to do a job, you won't get the best person.

c) Listen again. Check your answers.

d) Work in pairs. Which of the sayings in **1a)** and **2a)** do you like the best and why? Tell the class.

Ⓐ *If you fly with the crows, you get shot with the crows.*

Ⓑ *Let's cross that bridge when we come to it.*

Ⓒ *If you pay peanuts, you get monkeys.*

Ⓓ *Why have a dog and bark yourself?*

Woof
Woof
Woof

Ⓔ *Horses for courses.*

Real World
Explaining and paraphrasing

● When we need to clarify, simplify or explain something we have already said, we often use phrases which signal to the listener that we are going to say the same thing again in a different way.

3 **a)** Fill in the gaps with *what* or *which*.

1 .... simply/just/basically means ...
2 And .... it/this/that means is ...
3 .... I mean by that is ...
4 By .... I mean ...
5 .... I'm trying to say is ...
6 .... is to say ...

b) Fill in the gaps with these words.

| that   simply   other   way |

1 To put it ...., ...
2 .... is to say, ...
3 Or to put it another ...., ...
4 In .... words, ...

c) Look at R1.4, p148. Listen again and notice how the speakers explain and paraphrase their ideas.

d) Check in RW1.1 p119.

4 **a)** Fill in the gaps with one word. Then match 1–6 with endings a)–f).

1 ...*What*... I'm trying to say is we should
2 She's quite a closed person. What I mean .... that is you can never tell
3 There are roadworks on the motorway, ... basically means
4 This is a difficult situation, by .... I mean we need
5 We urgently need to reduce our costs. In other ....,
6 It's a hard-drive back-up system, or to put it ....,

a) what she's thinking.
b) you have to allow an extra hour for the journey.
c) it ensures that you won't lose what's on your computer.
d) cross that bridge when we come to it.
e) to think about it more carefully.
f) we have to make some people redundant.

b) Work in pairs. Take turns to say a complete sentence from **4a)**. Do you have the same answers?

SHE'LL BE APPLES

5 **a)** R1.5 You are going to play a game called *Bluff*. Listen to two teams playing the game and answer the questions.

1 What is the game about?
2 What does each person on the first team have to do?
3 What does the second team have to do?

b) Work in pairs. Which do you think is the true definition of the Australian expression 'She'll be apples'?

c) R1.6 Listen and check.

6 Work in two groups. Group A, try to guess the meaning of idioms 1–3. Group B, try to guess the meaning of idioms a)–c).

Group A	**Group B**
1 rave about something	a) be up for something
2 hit the roof	b) talk shop
3 lose your bottle	c) call it a day

7 Group A → p108. Group B → p111. Follow the instructions.

1 a) Replace the words in **bold** with these words/phrases. Use the correct form of the verb. **V1.1**

have a row   bicker   overhear   come into contact with   chat   butt in

1 Do you often hear people **arguing** in public? *having a row*
2 Do you think it's rude to **interrupt** when someone's talking?
3 Do you ever **talk in a friendly and informal way** to strangers when you're on public transport?
4 Do you know any couples who continually **argue about unimportant things**?
5 Do you **meet and communicate with** many English-speaking people on a day-to-day basis?
6 Have you ever **accidentally heard** people talking about you or a person you know?

b) Work in pairs. Take turns to ask and answer questions 1–6 in **1a).**

2 Choose the best ending, a) or b), for each sentence. **G1.2**

1 **Did you go to rock festivals**
2 **Have you been to any rock festivals**
a) in the last few months?
b) in your teens?

3 **So far this morning**
4 **This morning**
a) three people phoned about the job.
b) three people have phoned about the job.

5 **I read three of his books**
6 **I've read four of his books**
a) last summer.
b) during the last few weeks.

7 **When I've sold my car**
8 **When I sold my car**
a) I'll just use public transport.
b) I just used public transport.

3 Fill in the gaps with the correct form of the verbs in brackets. Use the Past Simple or the Present Perfect. There is sometimes more than one possible answer. **G1.1** **G1.2**

The flat above mine [1] *has been* (be) empty ever since I [2]............... (move) in six months ago. But a few people [3]............... (see) it recently. And three more people [4]............... (already come) to see it this morning. I [5]............... (bump into) one of them as I was going out. She [6]............... (work) in Dubai over the last few years. Apparently, up until now she [7]............... (always prefer) working abroad, but she [8]............... (recently offer) a great job here. Anyway, this is the first time she [9]............... (try) to buy a flat. I hope she gets it. Then after she [10]............... (move) in, I'll invite her round for dinner.

4 Rewrite these sentences to emphasise the words in **bold** starting with the words in brackets. **G1.3**

1 I am very close to **my older sister**. (The person)
   The person who I'm very close to is my older sister.
2 They **sold the house**. (What they did)
3 **We** were responsible. (It)
4 She's tired **because she didn't go to bed until 2 a.m.** (The reason)
5 I didn't start exercising **until I reached 40**. (It)
6 I can't stand **fried food**. (It)
7 It really annoys me **when people talk during a film**. (What)
8 **Julie** was brought up in Scotland. (It)

5 Choose the correct prepositions. **V1.2**

1 My sister and I don't have much *in/on* common.
2 I'm *on/out of* very good terms with all my neighbours.
3 My brother's dog is completely *on/out of* control.
4 She lives in that area *out of/in* necessity, not because she likes it.
5 Are you still *on/in* touch with your ex-girlfriend?
6 It may seem hard now, but *out of/in* the long run you'll see the benefits.

6 Complete these sayings with one word. **V1.3**

1 Rome wasn't built in a ....
2 Once bitten, twice ....
3 Actions .... louder than words.
4 One man's .... is another man's poison.
5 Nothing ventured, nothing ....
6 Better .... than never.

Progress Portfolio

a) Tick the things you can do in English.

☐ I can describe different ways of communicating.

☐ I can talk about the present and the past using a variety of time expressions.

☐ I can understand an article in which the writer expresses a specific point of view.

☐ I can use various structures to emphasise important or new information.

☐ I can use circumlocution and paraphrasing to clarify what I mean.

b) What do you need to study again? See **CD-ROM ●1A–C**.

Accurate Writing

CONNECTING WORDS: addition
SPELLING: homophones

1 Fill in the gaps with these connecting words/phrases. Sometimes there is more than one possible answer. **AW1.1** p119.

> also   as well   what's more   besides   too   not only

1 She's been running the company since November. She's got three children to look after, ...
2 Chinese food is very tasty. It's quite cheap, ...
3 The problem we were set was extremely difficult to solve. .... , we didn't have much time to do it.
4 The traffic is really heavy at this time of day. The roads are .... extremely icy, so be careful.
5 The village is .... remote but totally inaccessible by road.
6 I haven't got any change on me. .... , you already owe me money from last time.

2 Choose the correct spelling. **AW1.2** p119.

1 I think it's her brother *whose/who's* the difficult one in that family.
2 I'm not entirely convinced *there/they're* up for the challenge, are you?
3 He might *of/'ve* forgotten my mobile number.
4 It's not unusual for you to forget *you're/your* own telephone number!
5 We must make sure that they check in *they're/their* luggage on time.

3 **a)** Read the extract from a student's work. Correct the underlined mistakes using connecting words of addition. There is more than one possible answer.

b) Find and correct five common spelling mistakes.

> I've got two friends in particular who I've been really close to for much of my life. What I like most about them is how kind they are. ¹<u>As well</u>, I can trust them completely – there the kind of people you feel you can phone up at any time of the day and night if you need to talk about you're problems.
>
> They're names are Jess and Olivia. We might of lost contact for a while but when we see each other it's as if we've never been apart. It's Jess whose my oldest friend – we only met Olivia when we went to college but all three of us have always got on really well together. I think we're very supportive to each other ²<u>also</u> and I'm determined never to lose contact with them in the future.

Preview 2

1 RELATIVE CLAUSES

a) Find and correct one mistake in each sentence. Sometimes there is more than one possible answer. **G2.1** p121.

1 The singer what you admire so much is giving a concert next month.
2 I'd love to go and see that show who everyone's talking about.
3 That's the café at where we met last time.
4 Have you met the woman her daughter babysits for us?
5 Do you know the man whose his house was broken into?
6 I'm meeting Michael Jones who is joining our firm very soon.
7 I didn't buy his latest book, that was unusual for me.

b) In which of the corrected sentences can the relative pronoun be left out?

2 GRADABLE AND NON-GRADABLE ADJECTIVES; ADVERBS

Choose the correct adjective for each adverb. They may both be possible. **V2.1** p120.

SUE I saw a programme on crocodiles last night. It was very ¹*interesting/fascinating*.
BEN I'd be absolutely ²*scared/terrified* if I saw one.
SUE Me too. What I was extremely ³*amazed/surprised* by is how fast they can run.

CARL Are you going to the concert tonight?
KEN No, it's really ⁴*difficult/impossible* for me to get to Birmingham without a car.
CARL I could give you a lift.
KEN That's very kind, but I'm also fairly ⁵*tired/shattered* so I'll give it a miss, I think.

3 VERB+*ING* AND PAST PARTICIPLES

Fill in the gaps with the correct form of these verbs. Use verb+*ing* (e.g. *writing*) or a past participle (e.g. *written*). **G2.3** p122.

> ~~frighten~~   write   leave   spoil   bore   open   build   try

1 We found the prospect of giving a talk rather <u>*frightening*</u> .
2 People .... early should do so very quietly.
3 Despite .... very hard, I didn't finish the job.
4 She can't resist .... her grandchildren.
5 According to the manual, that switch is for .... the boot.
6 The castle, ... in the tenth century, is just round the corner from where we're staying.
7 That report, ... by Ted, is on my desk.
8 Karen was soon .... out of her mind by the guided tour.

2 Remarkable!

2A Exceptional people

QUICK REVIEW ● ● ●
Work in pairs. Give the beginning of four English sayings. Your partner completes them and explains what they mean: A *We'll cross that bridge …* . B *We'll cross that bridge when we come to it. What this means is …* .

Vocabulary intensifying adverbs
Grammar relative clauses with prepositions
Review sayings

Reading and Grammar

1 **a)** Work in pairs. Look at the title and introduction. Think of questions you would like to ask about Kim Peek.

b) Read the article to see if your questions were answered.

c) Read the article again. Tick the correct sentences. Then correct the mistakes.

1 Kim Peek is famous for his appearance in a well-known film.
2 His extraordinary brain has still not been fully explained.
3 He is unable to look after himself on a day-to-day basis.
4 Kim's parents have always followed medical advice about him.
5 He has always been extremely friendly and outgoing.
6 Fran thinks that working with people on the film was very good for Kim.

d) Match these meanings to the words in **bold** in the article.

1 changed
2 frightening
3 at the same time
4 watches carefully
5 a way of walking
6 moves quickly

e) Work in pairs. Discuss these questions.

1 Is a person's intelligence determined before birth?
2 Is academic brilliance more important in life than emotional intelligence, or being creative or practical?

The cleverest man on earth

Kim Peek was labelled 'mentally deficient' at birth. By the age of four, he was reading encyclopedias for fun. Today he can play the piano like Mozart and recall any fact from more than 9,000 books.

There is something familiar about this man in the hotel lobby, who is muttering to himself about airlines and heavy snow. He gives a bellow of laughter and people turn round in surprise, then smile as they recognise the **shuffling gait** and large bespectacled head of Kim Peek. Something of a local hero here in Salt Lake City, it's Kim's life on which an Oscar-winning film was based. *Rain Man* was a film about an autistic* savant* with astounding mathematical skills, although Kim himself is developmentally disabled, not autistic. Most savants possess remarkable expertise in one to three subjects; Kim, an expert in at least 15 different subjects, is known as a mega-savant, although he has a lot in common with *Rain Man*, such as the lightning speed at which he can memorise facts.

Recently dubbed 'the living Google', no one in the world is thought to possess a brain quite like Kim Peek's. As soon as he was born it was immediately clear he was different. His head was so huge that his neck muscles couldn't support it and a later brain scan revealed he had one solid brain hemisphere instead of two. It is

possible that, because the two sides of the brain were unable to communicate with each other, the brain may have turned into one mega-computer. However, this is one of many theories, none of which have yet been proved.

The analysis of Kim's brain does, however, explain the reason for his severe motor deficiencies. He is looked after by his father, Fran, on whom he totally depends. 81-year-old Fran, although not in the best of health himself, takes care of his son full-time, helping him to wash and dress and checking on him in the night. Doctors believe it is Fran's unconditional love and belief in his son that are partly responsible for Kim's exceptional brilliance. However, it obviously runs in the family; Kim also has a brother and a sister, both of whom, along with Fran himself, are exceptionally clever and are classed as geniuses.

When Kim was a child, doctors advised putting him in an institution, at which point his parents took him home instead and introduced him to books. By four and a half, although no school would accept him, he had sought out encyclopaedias, atlases

Kim is a local hero in his home town.

and telephone directories, all of which he memorised. It has recently been discovered that each of Kim's eyes can read a separate page **simultaneously**, taking just ten seconds, rather than the average three minutes. These days, he spends most afternoons in the local library, where he is a much-loved figure.

It's hard to hold a conversation with Kim, whose mind **flits** from one subject to another with confusing speed. Physically, he can be a little **intimidating**. A big man, he rises suddenly out of his chair to distribute bear hugs; his mild, kindly father **keeps an eye on** him and tries to explain what he's talking about. However, although Kim is charming and affectionate, he hasn't always been socially confident. Until a chance meeting with the screenwriter led to the making of *Rain Man*, Kim seldom dared look another person in the face. It was Dustin Hoffman, the actor who played Kim in the film, who urged Fran to take Kim out into the world. The way in which social contact has **transformed** Kim's life is immeasurable. It has developed in him a marked sense of humour and he loves meeting people. "It is only since *Rain Man* that Kim's mind became connected to his heart," says Fran. "Now I think his heart is even bigger than his brain."

Adapted from the *Sunday Telegraph* 06/02/05

*autistic = having a mental condition that makes people unable to communicate well
*savant = someone who has unusual abilities or knowledge

Help with Grammar Relative clauses with prepositions

See **Preview, p15.**

2 **a)** Look at these pairs of sentences. Which sentence, 1 or 2 in each pair, is an example of a) more formal, usually written English? b) less formal, usually spoken English?

1 He is looked after by his father Fran, **on whom** he totally depends.
2 He is looked after by his father Fran, **who** he totally depends **on**.
1 It's Kim's life **on which** an Oscar-winning film was based.
2 It's Kim's life **that** an Oscar-winning film was based **on**.

b) Fill in the gaps in this rule with the correct words from the pairs of sentences in **2a).**

● In more formal, usually written English, *who* changes to _____ after a preposition and *that* changes to _____ .

c) Look at this sentence and choose the correct answer in the rule.
This is one of many theories, (*none of which*) *have yet been proved.*
● Determiners (*both, all, one, neither, most, none*, etc.) combine with *of which* or *of whom* in non-defining relative clauses. They refer to words/phrases in *the previous clause/the following clause*.

TIP! ● When we are speaking informally we can use *both of them, all of them*, etc.: *This is one of many theories – none of them have been proved yet.*

d) Change the informal phrases in **bold** in these sentences to a more formal written style. Check with the phrases in blue in the article.

1 Kim also has a brother and a sister, **who are both** exceptionally clever.
2 He had sought out encyclopaedias, atlases and telephone directories **and memorised them all**.

e) Check in G2.2 p121.

3 Rewrite the phrases in **bold**, using a preposition and *which* or *whom*.

1 This is the name **that he was known by**.
This is the name by which he was known.
2 She should consult the students **who she is responsible for**.
3 He embarked on a long journey **which he never returned from**.
4 Mahler is the composer **that he is always associated with**.
5 I'm impressed by the speed **that he runs at**.
6 The artist eventually finished the picture **that he'd been working on**.

4 Combine these two clauses, using *of which* or *of whom*.

1 She had lots of ideas, but most of them were impractical.
She had lots of ideas, most of which were impractical.
2 She has two children, but neither of them look like her.
3 Tim interviewed several people, who were all unsuitable.
4 She gave me four tops, but I only wore one of them.
5 There were only two flights that day but they were both full.
6 I studied German at school, but remember none of it.

Listening

 a) Look at the photo of Tommy McHugh, a builder who became a painter. What do you think of his paintings?

b) R2.1 Listen to the radio programme. Why did Tommy become a painter?

c) Listen again and complete these sentences with one word.

1 Tommy hadn't done any painting at all until he reached his ....
2 He compares his mind to a ...., which generates bubbles full of creative ideas.
3 After leaving hospital, Tommy and his wife received no ....
4 Tommy's life changed when Marion Kalmus told him that he was an ....
5 Changes to the temporal lobe tend to increase people's ....
6 As well as painting, many people with Tommy's condition tend to .... a lot.
7 Being very productive can often result in work of variable ....
8 Although Tommy's lifespan is uncertain, he regards his life as an ....

Vocabulary Intensifying adverbs

See **Preview, p15.**

 a) Which adverb does <u>not</u> go with these adjectives or verbs? Check in V2.2 p120.

1 I *utterly/thoroughly/really* enjoy ...
2 I'd be *deeply/strongly/totally* frustrated if ...
3 It's *highly/vividly/extremely* (un)likely that ...
4 I *strongly/firmly/highly* believe that ...
5 I *bitterly/deeply/perfectly* regret ...
6 I was *bitterly/utterly/extremely* disappointed when ...
7 I *completely/entirely/highly* agree ...
8 I *vividly/distinctly/perfectly* remember ...

b) Use five of the adverbs and verbs or adjectives in **6a)** to make true or false sentences about your life and views.

c) Work in pairs. Take turns to say your sentences. Guess which of your partner's sentences are false.

Get ready ... Get it right!

7 Think of someone who you think should win an award for being exceptional. It could be somebody famous or a person you know. Write five reasons why he or she should win it.

I firmly believe my cousin Julia should win the award. She was ill for a while and made redundant, neither of which put her off starting her own business.

8 **a)** Work in groups. Take turns to tell each other about the person you have chosen. Try to be as persuasive as possible. Then vote for the person you think should win the award.

b) Tell the class about the person your group voted for.

2B Memorable places

Vocabulary adjective word order
Grammar participle clauses
Review relative clauses with prepositions; intensifying adverbs

QUICK REVIEW ● ● ●
Think of two famous people and two famous places. Write descriptions using relative clauses with prepositions, and intensifying adverbs if possible. Work in pairs. Swap papers. Your partner tries to guess who or what you're describing:
A *I thoroughly enjoy visiting this Spanish city, in which you can find Gaudi's famous cathedral.*
B *Is it Barcelona?*

Reading and Grammar

1 Work in pairs. Which three reasons are most important to you when choosing a holiday, and why?

- the climate
- the tourist facilities
- the landscape
- the local culture
- the accommodation
- the cost of the holiday
- the nightlife

2 a) Read the article. Why did the writer fall in love with Kerala?

b) Read the article again. Answer these questions.

1 Why did the writer choose January to visit Kerala?
2 What did the writer find surprising about Kerala?
3 What does the writer predict will happen to Kerala soon?
4 Which is the best way to travel if you want to see the 'real' Kerala?
5 What is unusual about the way people fish in Cochin?
6 Why are some famous people attracted to Kerala?

c) Work in pairs. In which place, if any, have you 'lost your heart'? What made it so wonderful? How would you spend a perfect day there?

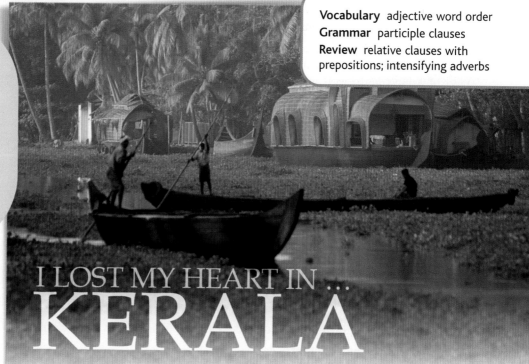

I LOST MY HEART IN ...
KERALA

WHY?

It's incredibly beautiful and hypnotic, with lush vegetation, white beaches and vividly green countryside. Entire communities live along the canals and lagoons, which stretch over 1,900 km, [1]**acting as a vital means of communication** between remote villages and crowded towns. In order to avoid the monsoon season, I went in January. At that time of year the weather is great and you are normally guaranteed warm days and cooler, comfortable nights.

I didn't expect to find it still so unspoilt given that it's relatively close to Goa. People don't seem to have worked out yet that Kerala is a lot nicer and much less touristy. So you feel as if you're discovering somewhere entirely new, like you're on a totally different planet. However, now that it's been nominated one of *National Geographic*'s '50 must-see destinations of a lifetime', it's only a matter of time before all this now changes.

WHAT SHOULDN'T I MISS?

Take a trip along the backwaters. [2]**Gliding silently along in a canoe**, you get to see a rural Kerala preserved through the ages and completely hidden from the road. You'll pass locals doing their laundry in the river, schoolteachers taking classes on the banks and so on, which is an enchanting experience. Make sure you take lots of batteries for your camera. A stopover in the fascinating capital, Cochin, is also a must. A cluster of islands surrounded by a network of rivers and lakes, Cochin is home to a unique culture. There's extraordinary fishing on the coast there; people hang from their boats into the water and pick up fish with their teeth, before chucking them into enormous nets. In the evenings, go to a restaurant and try the wide variety of fish Kerala is so famous for. [3]**Caught locally every day**, it's always wonderfully fresh.

A PERFECT DAY

I would probably wake up around 10 a.m. and tuck into a delicious Indian breakfast of pancakes with lots of curry powder. Then I'd take to the backwaters for three or four hours. Later on, [4]**having had an indulgent lunch**, I'd lie in a hammock, sipping fresh coconut milk through a straw and reading a good book. I might follow in the footsteps of the Hollywood stars, who come to Kerala in search of Ayurveda, the natural Indian healthcare which dates back more than 3,000 years. The treatments use herbal oils made from the exotic spices that are so plentiful here. [5]**Poured very slowly across your forehead, the oil feels like a cow is licking you**; this may sound revolting but is actually very enjoyable and is supposed to be good for people suffering from the stresses and strains of modern life.

After supper, totally relaxed, I'd head for bed, putting on an eye-mask in order to avoid seeing any of the local spiders!

Adapted from the *Guardian* 22/06/02

19

Help with Grammar Participle clauses

See Preview, p15.

- Some participle clauses give more information about a verb or idea in a sentence. They are often used to make a piece of writing more varied and sophisticated.

 a) Look at participle clauses 1–5 in bold in the article. Which one uses a) a present participle? b) a past participle? c) a perfect participle?

b) Compare a)–e) with 1–5 in the article. What grammatical changes occur when we use participle clauses?

a) … **so** they act as a vital means of communication between remote villages and crowded towns.

b) **While** you glide silently along in a canoe, you get to see a rural Kerala preserved through the ages.

c) **Because** it's caught locally every day, it's always wonderfully fresh.

d) **After** I'd had an indulgent lunch, I'd lie in a hammock.

e) **If** it's poured very slowly across your forehead, the oil feels like a cow is licking you.

c) Match the words in **bold** in a)–e) in 3b) to meanings 1–4.

> 1 cause   2 result   3 condition   4 time

a) result

d) Check in G2.4 p122.

 4 Rewrite sentences 1–5 using the words in brackets.

1 Not knowing my way round Kerala, I headed straight for the Tourist Information office. (because)
2 The rain was very heavy at that time of year, causing flooding everywhere. (so)
3 Visited out of season, Kerala is not full of tourists. (if)
4 Having saved up for ages, Lauren finally went out and booked her flight. (after)
5 Surfing through the channels, I came across a really good programme on India. (while)

Come face to face with massive, 100-year-old tortoises and swim in the clear, tropical waters of the Galápagos Islands

5 Rewrite these sentences. Use the correct participle form.

1 Even after I had read the instructions, I still couldn't understand how to use the camera.
   Even having read the instructions, I still couldn't work out how to use the camera.
2 Now that I have spoken to them, I feel much happier about the situation.
3 I didn't want to arrive late, so I called a taxi.
4 As I flicked through his address book, I noticed something strange.
5 As he comes from Brazil, he's not used to such cold weather.
6 You'll annoy people if you talk like that.

Listening

 a) R2.2 R2.3 Look at the photos and captions and check any new words. Then listen to two conversations. Did Bruce enjoy his holiday in the Galápagos Islands? Did Melissa enjoy her holiday in Ireland?

b) R2.2 Listen again. Tick the correct sentences. Then correct the mistakes.

1 The Galápagos Islands are just off the coast of Ecuador.
2 Bruce went to the Galápagos on his own.
3 He remembers the islands as being very green.
4 The warm seas were a big attraction for him.
5 He was very impressed by the wildlife there.

c) R2.3 Listen again and answer the questions.

1 Why had they decided to go to Ireland on holiday?
2 Why did Melissa decide to stay in this house?
3 How long did it take to get to the house?
4 What was the weather like when they arrived?
5 What was the problem with their local beach?

d) Which of these places would you like to go to? Why?

Spend summer in Ireland – stay in charming, rustic stone cottages and sunbathe on its beautiful, white sandy beaches

Help with Vocabulary Adjective word order

- When describing a noun, there is an order that adjectives usually follow. Notice that opinions come before facts, the general before the specific.

opinion	size	age	colour	origin	material	
beautiful			white		sandy	beaches
stark		modern			log*	cabins
	massive	100-year-old				tortoises
charming				rustic	stone*	cottages

*These are nouns used as adjectives.

7 **a)** Look at these adjectives in **bold**. Do they describe opinion, size, age, colour, origin or material?

1 **breath-taking, high, snow-capped** peaks
2 **delicious, Thai, fish and coconut** curries
3 **extravagant, white, marble** buildings
4 **picture-book, medieval Italian** villages

b) Look at these examples. When speaking we try not to put too many adjectives in front of the noun. How do we avoid doing this?

*rather stupid-looking, clumsy birds **with** blue feet **and** long necks*
*charming, rustic **cottages in** stone*
*delicious Thai curries, (**which were**) **made of** fish and coconut*

c) Check in V2.3 p120.

8 Put these words in order to make descriptive phrases.

1 idyllic / seas / Mediterranean / the / turquoise *the idyllic, turquoise Mediterranean seas*
2 leather / a(n) / box / old / interesting
3 modern / vibrant / the / capital / sprawling
4 that / French / fine / old / wine
5 small / 14th-century / a / castle
6 suede / that / jacket / expensive / black
7 Welsh / energetic / sheepdog / young / a(n)
8 armchair / velvet / a(n) / uncomfortable / antique

9 Join the extra information in brackets using a relative clause and/or *with*, *and* or *in*.

1 a delightful Victorian cottage (six bedrooms, quiet area)
a delightful Victorian cottage with six bedrooms in a quiet area
2 a spacious, modern flat (well-decorated, inexpensive)
3 a classic round-necked sweater (blue, cotton)
4 a funny, well-written contemporary drama (original, superbly-acted)
5 a scruffy young writer (dark hair, beard)
6 an Italian sports model (metallic grey, sun-roof)

Get ready ... Get it right!

10 Think about a place that you have been to that you either love or hate. Write as many adjectives as you can to describe it.

11 **a)** Work in groups. Take turns to describe your place. Ask follow-up questions.
The first time I visited this city I really disliked it because it was so noisy and chaotic, with a lot of traffic and pollution. But ...

b) Tell the class about the best or worst place you heard about.

2C Spoilt for choice

Vocabulary adjectives: describing places
Skills Reading: a tourist board website;
Listening: interview about tourism;
Speaking: talking about your country;
Writing: a guide to your country
Real World making recommendations
Review adjective word order

QUICK REVIEW ● ● ●

Work in groups. One person describes something, using one adjective. The next person adds an adjective in the correct order. Continue until someone in the group gives up or makes a mistake: A *an old man* B *a nice old man* C *a nice old British man*.

1 Work in pairs. Close your book and then list places in England that you have heard of or been to. How much do you know about each of the places?

NORTHWEST ENGLAND Whether it's for a night out, day trip or weekend away with the family, England's northwest has a wealth of attractions to inspire you. Museums, galleries, stately homes, **a host of** sporting events, and the **rural splendour** of the Lake District.

YORK One of the most intriguing cities in England; no other English city offers the history, beauty and sheer diversity of York. The superbly preserved walled city has witnessed more than 2,000 years of **vibrant** history. Combine quaint tea shops with **bustling** shopping streets, bars, cafés and fantastic attractions and you've got the perfect holiday destination.

SOUTHWEST ENGLAND A region of diverse contrasts, from the cosmopolitan appeal of Bristol and the beautiful countryside surrounding the Roman baths of Bath, to the wild and rugged coastal scenery of Cornwall. Quaint fishing ports, golden sandy beaches and medieval castles await your visit.

Map labels:
Newcastle
NORTH EAST
NORTH WEST
York
YORKSHIRE
Leeds
Manchester
Liverpool
EAST MIDLANDS
Wolverhampton
Coventry
WEST MIDLANDS
Birmingham
EAST OF ENGLAND
Cambridge
Oxford
LONDON
Bristol
Bath
SOUTH EAST
Canterbury
SOUTH WEST

2 Work in pairs. Look at the photos and read the website extracts. Which areas or cities would you like to visit? Put them in order. Then tell the class.

3 **a)** Look at the words/phrases in **bold** in the extracts. Match them to these meanings.

a) beautiful countryside   c) busy
b) many   d) energetic and exciting

b) Look again at the East of England and Southwest England extracts. Underline the adjectives the writer uses to make the areas sound interesting and attractive. Tick the ones you know.

c) Check new words/phrases in V2.4 p120.

4 **a)** R2.4 Listen to Kate Johnson, who works in tourism. What is the main point she is making about overseas visitors to England? What do these numbers refer to?

| 27.4 million | 3.5 million | 2 million | 1.7 million | 1.2 million |

b) Work in pairs. Compare answers. Did any figures surprise you?

5 **a)** R2.5 Listen to Kate talking about the diversity of what England has to offer as a holiday destination. Make notes on any additional information she gives about the places on the map.

b) Work in pairs. Compare notes. Then listen again and check.

6 R2.6 Listen to Kate talking about cities and food. Why is food in England so diverse?

7 Work in pairs. Tell each other about three people you know well who would choose different kinds of holidays. Which of the places Kate talked about would you recommend for each person and why?

8 **a)** Work on your own. Think of five places a visitor should see to appreciate the variety your country has to offer. Think about how you can tell other people about these places in an interesting and informative way. Make notes.

Real World Making recommendations

- If you have ever been to (Bath), you'll know why I included it in my list of 'must-see' places.
- To my mind it's one of the (best places) in the country/anywhere in the world.
- And you just have to go to (York).
- If it's (sports) you're after/into, …
- You can't beat/do better than (go to Cornwall).

b) Work in groups. Take turns to tell each other about the places you chose. Say why you chose them and what kinds of people would enjoy them. If you are from the same country, did you choose the same places? If not, why?

Writing Extension

9 Choose three of the places on your list and write a short piece about each, in the style of the website extracts.

R2.7 Look at the song *Little Wonders* on p106. Follow the instructions.

WEST MIDLANDS The West Midlands' appeal lies in both its timelessness and modernity. It is known as the 'Heart of England'. The cultural diversity and vibrancy of Birmingham reflect a very different England to the one of Shakespeare's Stratford-upon-Avon. Don't miss the sleepy villages of Warwickshire and Herefordshire or the beauty of the Cotswolds.

EAST OF ENGLAND With its miles upon miles of unspoilt beaches, meandering rivers, ancient woodlands and, of course, the Norfolk Broads, this region has a unique character.

2 Review   Language Summary 2, p120

1 Fill in the gaps with one of these phrases. G2.2

~~by which~~ both of whom
none of which   on whose
all of which   with whom
for which   after whom

1 The date _by which_ all bills must be paid is the 30th of the month.
2 The person .... I discussed the issue denied all knowledge.
3 I've got two sisters, ... are younger than me.
4 There are seven Harry Potter books, ... I've read yet.
5 You have all been very co-operative, ... I'm deeply grateful.
6 My favourite singer is Kylie Minogue, ... my daughter was named.
7 I am grateful to Jack Terry, ... research I largely depended for this book.
8 I bought myself six computer games, ... were reduced by 10%.

2 Fill in the gaps with these intensifying adverbs. V2.2

~~deeply~~ bitterly vividly entirely

1 I get _deeply_ frustrated when I'm stuck in a traffic jam.
2 I .... remember my first day at school.
3 I always feel .... disappointed when my country loses an important football match.
4 I .... agree that men and women should have equal opportunities.

deeply highly firmly completely

5 It's .... unlikely that I'll ever learn another language.

6 I .... believe that life improves as you get older.
7 I .... regret some of the things I've done in my life.
8 I .... agree with my country's policy on green issues.

3 a) Complete these sentences with a present participle, a past participle or a perfect participle. G2.4

eat
1 _Eaten_ in moderation, chocolate is good for you.
2 .... in restaurants all week, Lucy prefers to cook for herself at the weekends.
3 .... such a big lunch earlier that day, I didn't feel like any dinner.

see
4 .... the film three times already, she decided to give it a miss.
5 .... her ex-boyfriend approaching, she ran and hid.
6 .... from a distance, she looks like a 20-year-old!

read
7 .... the instructions twice, I began to assemble the desk.
8 .... out loud, the poem sounded much better.
9 .... the report so quickly, I missed a lot of mistakes.

give
10 .... the chance, I'd love to learn how to ski.
11 .... the job to Fred, she immediately regretted her decision.
12 .... myself an extra day, I should be able to finish the job.

b) Work in pairs. Rewrite sentences 1–12 in 3a) using *if*, *because*, *after*, etc. Make any other necessary changes.

If it is eaten in moderation, chocolate is good for you.

4 Read the story. Tick the groups of adjectives 1–6 that are in the correct order. Correct the groups which are not. V2.3

When I was 14, my parents went on holiday for a week and I was sent to stay in a(n) [1]**big beautiful, old** house in the country with some distant relatives. My cousin Linda's best friend was a(n) [2]**16-year-old attractive** girl called Anna, who had [3]**wide extraordinary emerald-green** eyes and [4]**dark shiny long** hair. I remember wonderful evenings chatting around the [5]**wooden round** kitchen table. The following summer, I went back there again, but Anna had fallen in love with a(n) [6]**Italian tall dark-haired** pilot, so I had no chance! I was only 15, but I felt life would never be the same again!

5 Fill in the vowels in these adjectives which are used to describe places. V2.4

1 _nsp_ _lt
2 d_v_rs_
3 q_ _ _nt
4 v_br_nt
5 r_gg_d
6 _n_q_ _

Progress Portfolio

a) Tick the things you can do in English.

☐ I can define and give extra information in a formal and informal way.

☐ I can emphasise verbs and adjectives using a range of appropriate adverbs.

☐ I can identify points of detail in a complex newspaper article.

☐ I can write concise descriptions using complex clauses.

☐ I can describe places in detail using accurate adjective order.

b) What do you need to study again?
● 2A–C.

Accurate Writing

CONNECTING WORDS: time (1)
PUNCTUATION: apostrophes

1 Fill in the gaps with these connecting words/phrases. Sometimes there is more than one possible answer. `AW2.1` p123.

> the moment   as soon as   first   ever since   originally
> from then on   while   as   afterwards   then   meanwhile

1 .... I met him I decided he was the man I was going to marry.
2 .... he came to the school he's been nothing but trouble.
3 The cottage was .... used as a post office, but it was converted a hundred years ago.
4 I bought a new computer last month. .... , I've had nothing but trouble with it.
5 I caught a glimpse of Steve .... I was hurrying down the street.
6 I accepted their invitation to supper. .... , I regretted it.
7 He began asking the boss about his plans. .... he realised the mistake he'd made and changed the subject quickly.
8 I sat anxiously waiting for the call. .... , I tried to get on with some work, but kept looking at the clock.

2 Add one or two apostrophes to each of these sentences. `AW2.2` p123.

1 Theres a lot of mud on the cars wheels.
2 Are you absolutely sure its not hers?
3 Britains most popular pets are cats.
4 I really cant remember its name.
5 Wheres the students coffee bar?
6 I think its written by Charles Dickens.
7 Id listen carefully to the womens opinions if I were you.

3 **a)** Read this extract from a student's work. Correct the underlined words/phrases using connecting words of time. Sometimes there is more than one possible answer.

b) Find and correct six mistakes in the use of apostrophes.

> I vividly remember the first time I saw Venice because it's so beautiful and theres nowhere else like it in the entire world. ¹Ever since you come out of the station you see all the boat's going up and down the Grand Canal, which contributes to it's fairytale atmosphere. I think its one of Europes most romantic cities. I ²at first went there with my parents when I was ten, and I've been going there ³afterwards, for the last 20 years. ⁴Meanwhile I'm going along in the river bus, I still can't stop looking at the fantastic building's which line the canals. Its' unique architecture makes Venice a real open-air museum! I ⁵afterwards love wandering around the narrow streets and going window-shopping.

Preview 3

1 SUBJECT AND VERB INVERSION

a) Tick the correct sentences. Then correct any mistakes. `G3.2` p125.

1 A I need an eye test.
  B So do I.
2 A I didn't know there was sugar in this.
  B No, nor I did.
3 Look. Here the doctor comes.
4 Look. Here they come.
5 She's a doctor, isn't she?
6 Have you any idea where are my glasses?
7 Do you remember what did they say about taking vitamin C?
8 Which doctor is it am I seeing?
9 I don't know what is his problem.
10 I wonder what his diet's like these days.
11 He asked me am I taking any extra vitamins.

b) Rewrite these sentences using the words in brackets.

1 Where are the nail scissors? (you know)
  Do you know where the nail scissors are?
2 A I haven't been able to contact Harry.
  B I haven't either. (neither)
3 What are you planning to do this weekend? (he ask me)
4 Does he still work with Megan? (I wonder)
5 A John wants to find another job.
  B Leo does, too. (so)
6 Look. The traffic warden. (here come)
7 Where do you work? (is this)
8 Where does he live? (I not know)
9 When can he come? (he want know)
10 What would Jill like for her birthday? (you any idea)

3 Well-being

> **Vocabulary** connotation: positive and negative character adjectives
> **Grammar** introductory *it*
> **Review** intensifying adverbs

QUICK REVIEW ●●●
Complete these sentences about yourself: *I vividly remember ... ; I strongly believe that ... ; I was bitterly disappointed when ... ; I'm extremely unlikely to ...* . Work in pairs. Take turns to tell each other your sentences. Ask follow-up questions.

Vocabulary
Positive character adjectives

 1 **a)** Tick the words you know. Check new words in **V3.1** p124.

> courageous   determined   meticulous
> generous   trusting   thrifty   confident
> spontaneous   cautious

b) Write the names of people you know who have some of the characteristics in **1a**).

c) Work in pairs. Swap lists. Take turns to ask about the people on your partner's list.

Reading and Grammar

 2 Work in pairs. Answer the questions.

1 What is your idea of a successful person?
2 Which characteristics from **1a**) do you think are necessary to be successful? Why?
3 Do you think everyone would like to be successful? Why?/Why not?

3 **a)** Check the meaning of these words.

> self-awareness   a triumph   distress
> an accolade   dominate

b) Read the article. Match headings a)–e) with paragraphs 1–5.

a) Some like the spotlight
b) An unexpected result
c) What most people believe
d) Know yourself
e) A lack of self-awareness

Born to lose?
We all want to win – or do we?

1 THERE ARE certain things in life that are obviously beyond question and it is clear that one of these 'unquestionables' is that everyone wants to win. At the enjoyable end of the victory spectrum is the sheer exhilaration of crossing the finishing line first, coming top of the class or spraying champagne from the podium; at the other end lies that depressing, kicked-in-the-guts ache of being the loser. So surely we all hate it when we lose – or do we?

2 Professor Schultheiss from the University of Michigan carried out various laboratory experiments on 108 college students and it surprised him to discover that while some people became stressed after losing out to a rival in a laboratory task, others became stressed after winning. He concludes that people can be split into wolves, who are utterly driven to win and find it difficult to cope with losing, and sheep, whose triumphs over others bring distress.

3 Dr Michelle Wirth, a colleague of Professor Schultheiss, says it's difficult to know whether sheep consciously feel stressed because, when people are asked if they prefer to win or lose, everyone says they'd rather win. Similarly, people are not always conscious of where they sit on the power spectrum. "If you ask people if they like being in a position of power, they usually say no." Dr Wirth believes it's not an aspect of their personality that they are conscious of.

4 Dr Wirth also says that the attention generated by winning might be part of the effect. "People with high power motivation like to be the centre of attention,

 4 Read the article again. Find evidence in the article to support these statements.

1 The writer finds it hard to believe anyone would prefer to lose.
2 Dr Schultheiss expected that everyone in the experiments would find losing stressful.
3 Most people aren't aware of which group they belong to.
4 Some people feel stressed when their success is made public.
5 Job satisfaction isn't necessarily determined by how much power you have over others.

Help with Grammar Introductory *it*

- The phrases in pink in the article show introductory *it* as the subject of the verb. The phrases in blue in the article show introductory *it* as the object of the verb.

INTRODUCTORY *IT* AS SUBJECT

- If the subject of the verb is a long and grammatically complex structure, we often put it at the end of the clause/sentence and use *it* as the subject of the verb at the beginning of the clause/sentence.

Whether sheep consciously feel stressed is difficult to know.

It's difficult to know whether sheep consciously feel stressed.

6 **a)** Match the five examples of introductory *it* as subject to these structures.

it + verb:
1 + adjective + (*that*) *It's clear that ...*
2 + (*not*) + noun + (*that*)
3 + adjective + infinitive with *to*
4 + *that* clause
5 + object + infinitive with *to*

INTRODUCTORY *IT* AS OBJECT

- We often use *it* as the object of a verb where *it* refers to a clause later in the sentence.

I hate it that she's so shy in public. not *I hate that she's so shy in public.*

b) Match the two examples of introductory *it* as object to these structures.

verb + it:
1 + *when*
2 + adjective + infinitive with *to*

TIPS! ● We don't use introductory *it* if the subject of the verb is a noun: *Their fears were completely unfounded.* not *It was completely unfounded their fears.*

● Common expressions with introductory it: *It's no good ... . It's no use ... . It's no wonder that ... . It's no coincidence that ... .*

c) Check in **G3.1** p125.

7 Rewrite these sentences using introductory *it* as the subject.

1 That we only had two applicants astonishes me.
   It astonishes me that we only had two applicants.
2 That she refused a promotion is strange.
3 To get this finished on time won't be easy.
4 To have a good working relationship with someone means a lot.
5 That we need people with more experience is obvious.

8 **a)** Use these prompts to make sentences about yourself or people you know.

1 prefer it when
   Most people I know prefer it when the weather's hot like this, but I don't.
2 can't bear it when
3 find it easy
4 consider it impolite
5 always enjoy it when
6 would love it if

b) Work in pairs. Take turns to tell each other your sentences. Ask follow-up questions.

---

so it follows that not winning is stressful." Apparently, these people find it hard to accept that someone else is getting the accolade that they feel should have been theirs. Dr Wirth also points out that for low-power individuals public recognition is equally stressful and they would do anything to avoid it.

5   Dr Wirth believes that knowing which category you fall into – wolf or sheep – can bring benefits. "If you can figure which one you are, you can tailor your working environment to suit you. There are some people who get pleasure and satisfaction from being in positions of power, and there are those who are less comfortable dominating others."

Adapted from *The Times* 31/08/06

5 Work in groups. Discuss these questions.

1 Are there people who really don't mind losing, for example when doing sport?
2 Is it possible to be both a sheep and a wolf? Why?/Why not?
3 Do even 'sheep' secretly enjoy success?

Listening and Vocabulary

 a) R3.1 Listen to the preview of a radio programme about 'impostor syndrome'. What is it?

Valerie   Richard   Miranda

b) R3.2 Listen to Valerie, Richard and Miranda talking about 'impostor syndrome'. Fill in the gaps in these sentences with their names.

1 .... knew about impostor syndrome before the interview.
2 .... has never experienced impostor syndrome.
3 .... works in TV.
4 .... is a garden designer.
5 .... is doing a postgraduate degree.

c) Listen again. Choose the correct answers.

1 a) Valerie *thinks/doesn't think* her clients realise she lacks confidence.
 b) She *experienced/didn't experience* impostor syndrome when she was a teacher.
2 a) Richard *makes/doesn't make* mistakes in his work.
 b) He says there *are/aren't any* people in the media who experience self-doubt.
3 a) Miranda *feels/doesn't feel* she's been very lucky.
 b) She *is/isn't* paying for her studies herself.

10 Work in groups. Discuss these questions.

1 Do you think that many people experience 'impostor syndrome'?
2 What advice would you give to someone who suffered from it?
3 Do you think impostor syndrome exists more amongst highly qualified people?
4 Do you think that everyone in very responsible positions feels this way sometimes? Why?/Why not?

Help with Vocabulary Connotation: positive and negative character adjectives

● Sometimes two character adjectives can describe similar traits, but one may have a positive and one may have a negative connotation.

11 **a)** Compare these extracts from R3.2. Answer the questions.

RICHARD   I don't want to sound <u>arrogant</u>.
INTERVIEWER   And you're generally quite <u>confident</u> that you can deliver what they want?

1 Do both of the <u>underlined</u> adjectives refer to someone who is very sure of himself?
2 Which adjective means the person thinks he is better than other people?
3 Which adjective has a positive connotation? Which has a negative connotation?

b) Match these negative character adjectives to the positive character adjectives in **1a)**.

| arrogant   reckless   tight-fisted   finicky |
| extravagant   gullible   obstinate   impetuous   timid |

arrogant – confident

c) Work in pairs. Compare answers.

d) Check in V3.2 p124.

12 **a)** Choose five adjectives from **1a)** and **11b)** that you would choose to describe yourself.

b) Work in pairs. Tell your partner which adjectives you chose and why.

Get ready ... Get it right!

13 Look at these sentences. Make notes on what you could say for and against each one.

a) It's impossible to be rich, powerful and nice.
b) Every employee in a company should have a turn at being a manager.
c) People should be allowed to wear what they want to at work.
d) Everybody should be taught to cook when they're at school.
e) People who are caught dropping litter should have to pick up litter from the streets for a month.

14 **a)** Work in groups. Discuss the sentences in **13**.

It's ridiculous to say ...

b) Tell the class which sentences your group agreed with.

Vocabulary phrasal verbs: health
Grammar inversion
Review introductory *it*

QUICK REVIEW ● ● ●
Think about things that are happening in the world at the moment and complete these sentences: *It amazes me that … ; I find it difficult to see how … ; It was good to hear that … ; I think it's terrible that … ; I hate it when … ; I love it when … .*
Work in pairs and tell each other your sentences. Ask follow-up questions.

Vocabulary Phrasal verbs: health

 a) Guess the meanings of the phrasal verbs in **bold**. Check in **V3.3** p124.

1 How long does it usually take you to **get over** a cold?
2 When you are bitten by an insect, does the area around the bite usually **swell up**?
3 Have you ever **picked up** a stomach bug when travelling?
4 Have you ever tried using steam when your nose **is blocked up**?
5 If you **go down with** flu, do you usually still go to work?
6 Do you usually catch bugs that are **going around**?
7 Does your doctor usually **put** people **on** antibiotics if they have a cold?
8 Have you ever **come out in** a rash because you were allergic to something you'd eaten?

b) Work in pairs. Take turns to ask and answer the questions.

Reading and Grammar

2 Work in groups of four. Look at the photos and read the headline and introduction. Try to predict the suggestions given in the article. Make a list.

3 Work in the same groups of four. Student A → p109.
Student B → p112.
Student C → p115.
Student D → p116.

Great ways to well-being

You don't have to follow a punishing diet or spend hours on the treadmill. The path to a healthier way of life may be easier than you think.

4 **a)** Work in groups. Discuss these questions. Give examples.

1 Which suggestions are common knowledge in your country?
2 Which research findings, if any, surprised you?
3 Would you disagree with any of the suggestions? If so, which one(s)?
4 Would you consider following any of the suggestions? If so, which one(s) and why?

b) Tell the class your conclusions.

> Most of us were surprised to hear that ...

> None of us agreed that it was a good idea to ...

> We couldn't agree on whether ... was good advice or not.

Help with Grammar Inversion

See Preview, p25.

● When we begin a sentence with a limiting adverbial (e.g. *seldom*) or a negative adverbial (e.g. *under no circumstances*), the subject and the auxiliary verb are inverted.

5 **a)** Look at the limiting and negative adverbials in **bold** in 1–6. Then <u>underline</u> the inversion in each sentence.

1 **Seldom** <u>do people associate</u> being married with being healthy.
2 **Not only** does dental hygiene save painful and expensive visits to the dentist, it may also prevent strokes.
3 **Not until** last week did he agree to stop smoking.
4 Very **rarely** do you hear anything negative about eating fish.
5 **Only recently** have experts come to appreciate the health benefits of eating curry.
6 **Under no circumstances** should you exercise immediately after eating a heavy meal.

b) Look at sentences 1–4 in **5a)**. What auxiliary is used when we invert Past Simple and Present Simple?

c) Look at the clauses in pink and blue. Which clause has the inversion?

1 Not until she learns to relax will things get better.
2 Only when we got the dog did we start going for long walks.

● Inversion *can* occur after another complete clause beginning with *not until*, *only when*, *only if*, *only after*.

TIP! ● Although inversion is usually found in literary and formal texts we also use it in less formal spoken and written English when we want to add emphasis or dramatic effect.

d) Check in G3.3 p125.

6 **a)** Read about two more ways to stay healthy. Find and correct five mistakes in the use of inversion.

1

Only recently experts have suggested that there are many health benefits from being exposed to sunlight. Not only it helps reduce depression and pain, it also reduces high blood pressure.

2

Seldom we hear anything positive about drinking wine. However, research suggests that not only drinking a moderate amount of red wine reduces the risk of heart attacks, it can also help protect elderly people from mental decline. But of course, under no circumstances people should drink and drive.

b) Work in pairs. Student A, read out your corrected version of paragraph 1. Student B, read out your corrected version of paragraph 2. Do you agree with each other's corrections?

7 Rewrite sentences 1–5 using these phrases. The meaning should stay the same.

> ~~only once~~   not until   not only
> under no circumstances   not for a minute

1 I've only seen him this happy once.
   Only once have I seen him this happy.
2 I never once thought I'd enjoy having a dog, but it's great.
3 I wasn't just stressed out, I was getting ill.
4 You should never agree to do overtime for nothing.
5 I didn't realise it was Jin till she spoke.

Listening

8 **a)** You are going to listen to six people talking about what they do to cheer themselves up. Try to predict some of the things they talk about. Make a list.

Fran and Ian

Alex and Helen

Rachael and Naomi

b) R3.3 Listen to three conversations. Were any of your predictions in **8a)** correct?

c) Listen again. Read the quotes and answer the questions.

CONVERSATION 1
a) Rachael says, "I'll open one of those." What does she open?
b) Naomi says, "It really does take you out of your down moment." What does?

CONVERSATION 2
a) Alex says, "I can do it any time I like." What can she do any time she likes?
b) Helen says, "It's impossible to feel stressed when you're zipping around like that." Zipping around on what?

CONVERSATION 3
a) Ian says, "… because it's great fun and colourful." What is?
b) Ian says, "I'll try to be cynical about it." Cynical about what?

9 **a)** R3.4 In spoken English the speaker often uses fillers (e.g. *you know*, *kind of*) or makes false starts (e.g. *I've got … I've kept all the letters*). This allows the speaker more thinking time. Look at this extract from one of the conversations. <u>Underline</u> different examples of redundancy that Fran uses.

FRAN Well, generally if I, um, if I'm not feeling, um, too happy then, um, I need something to work towards, so, um, I try and make contact with friends that I don't really see very often and, um, and I find that if I'm, I'm with them then I kind of forget about what's going on at the time and just remember the things I, you know, used to do with them, and, um, they just kind of, er, accept my personality so I don't have to, you know, that, that trivial thing that's usually making me not very happy. Doesn't really mean very much to them so …

b) Work in pairs. Compare answers.

c) Look at R3.4, p151. Check your answers to **9a)**.

Get ready … Get it right!

10 Make a list of things that you do to cheer yourself up when you're feeling a bit low. Think about all the positive effects associated with each activity.

go for a run and listen to music on an MP3 player → gets you out of the house, healthy, takes your mind off your problems

11 **a)** Work in groups. Take turns to try to persuade other students to try your ideas.

> Try it. Not only does it get you out of the house, but it's also very good for you physically.

b) Tell the class about your group's most unusual and most popular ideas.

3C # It's the way you say it

QUICK REVIEW ● ● ●
Complete these sentences for yourself: *Rarely ...* ; *Not until ...* ; *Not only ...* ;
Seldom ... ; *Under no circumstances ...* . Work in pairs. Swap papers. Take turns
to say your partner's sentences without inversion: *Rarely do I have time to
relax these days* → *I rarely have time to relax these days*.

Vocabulary euphemisms
Real World being tactful
Review inversion

1 a) How would you say the phrases in **bold** in
a more direct way? Check in V3.4 p124.

1 I think you were being **economical with the
truth** on that occasion.
I think you were telling a lie on that occasion.

2 You get a discount on public transport if
you're **a senior citizen**.

3 My dad's somewhat **behind the times**
when it comes to technology. He still
watches videos.

4 Rosie's car **has seen better days**. She could
really do with a new one.

5 You'll have to speak up – she's **getting on a
bit** and is **hard of hearing**.

6 I was feeling a little **under the weather**
yesterday, so I stayed in bed.

7 Your son can be **a bit of a handful** at times
and finds the work we're doing **challenging**.

8 It's **a bit on the chilly side** in this room.
Can we turn the heating up?

b) Work in pairs. Take turns to test each
other on the euphemisms in 1a).

> economical with the truth
>> That means 'telling a lie'.

2 a) Look at the pictures and read situations
A–D below. In which of these situations might
you complain, refuse an invitation, disagree or
give your opinion?

A Your partner has taken you to the first night
of a musical as a birthday treat. You didn't
like it but your partner did.

B Your boss asks you round for a meal but you
don't want to go.

C The waiter asks you if you liked your very
expensive meal. You are not happy with it.

D A friend is trying on some new trousers. You
really don't like them on him/her.

b) For each situation, think of ways in which
you could respond in a direct way and in a
less direct way. Why might you prefer to be
more tactful?

REAL WORLD • REAL WORLD • REAL WORLD • REAL WORLD • REAL WORLD • REAL WORLD • REAL WORLD • REAL WORLD

3 a) **R3.5** Listen to four conversations in which two people respond in different ways. Match each conversation to situations A–D in **2a)**.

b) Listen again. Which response in **3a)** do you think is more tactful, a) or b)?

1 a) b)
2 a) b)
3 a) b)
4 a) b)

Real World Being tactful

 4 a) Write these headings in the correct places 1–5.

> ~~using past forms~~ using adverbs of attitude
> using modals using vague language
> not sounding negative

1 *using past forms*

We **were planning** to go to the cinema tomorrow.

2 ....

They **could** do with being (a bit looser).
It **could** have been a bit hotter.
I'd go for black instead if I were you.

3 ....

We **must** all get together **some time**.
(They could do with being) **a bit** looser.
It was **sort of** interesting in parts.
The steak was **on the tough side**.

4 ....

I think darker colours **suit you better**.
I've seen better performances.

5 ....

Quite honestly, I've seen better performances.
Unfortunately, the steak was ... .

b) Check in **RW3.1** p126.

 5 **R3.6** Listen and practise the sentences so they sound tactful.

We were planning to go to the cinema tomorrow.

 6 a) Match each pair of phrases to situations A–D in **2a)**.

1
a) Tomorrow's not ideal for me, I'm afraid.
b) We'd hoped to go and visit Lisa's parents then.

2
a) Frankly, it wasn't quite up to your usual standard.
b) Well, I would have to say we've had better here.

3
a) It wasn't very gripping at times.
b) I wouldn't see it again but it had its moments!

4
a) I think I might choose something a bit less fussy.
b) I'm not over the moon about the style, personally.

b) Work in pairs. Can you think of anything else you might say in these situations?

 7 a) Work in pairs. Read conversations 1–4. Rewrite B's responses to make them more tactful. Use the ideas and language from **4a)** and **6a)**.

1
A Rick and I were hoping you and Harry could spend next weekend with us. Our kids would love you to.
B No sorry, we've made other arrangements.

2
A So, how do you think this holiday compared to previous ones then? I really enjoyed it.
B Did you? I didn't.

3
A So, what do you think of my new hairstyle?
B It looks ridiculous!

4
A I hope you're satisfied with your accommodation.
B Well, we're not. The room is too small.

b) Work in groups of four. Take turns to read out your conversations and suggest improvements to make the other pair's conversations as tactful as possible.

 8 a) Work in pairs. Read situations 1–3. Write a conversation for one of the situations and then role-play it. Try to write conversations of at least four lines for your situation.

1 Your elderly cousin invites your family to a party, but your teenage children really don't want to go.
2 Your friend is enthusing about a CD she's just bought, which you really dislike. Give your reaction.
3 Your brother has just moved into a new house, which you think is horrible. Give your opinion.

b) Swap papers with another pair. Try to extend the other pair's conversation.

3 Review

1 Match these adjectives to phrases 1–8. **V3.1**

> ~~courageous~~ cautious thrifty meticulous trusting confident spontaneous determined

1 doesn't let fear stop them from doing dangerous or difficult things *courageous*
2 usually believes that other people are good and honest
3 doesn't take risks
4 is very careful and pays attention to detail
5 suddenly decides to do something and then does it
6 is very sure of their own abilities
7 is very careful with money, and doesn't waste any
8 doesn't allow anyone or anything to stop them if they want to do something

2 Put the words in the correct order. **G3.1**

1 loves / My sister / I / to / when / it / read / her .
   My sister loves it when I read to her.
2 it / Holly / soon / a work permit / impossible / to get / realised / was .
3 would / wonderful / have / to / It / be / more / free time .
4 if / more / came round / love / it / I'd / you / to / visit / often .
5 the heating / could / appreciate / you / if / I'd / turn down / it .
6 concentrate / there's / I / find / to / difficult / it / when / music on .

3 Rewrite these sentences using introductory *it*. **G3.1**

1 Telling Janet to believe in herself is a waste of time.
   It's a waste of time telling Janet to believe in herself.
2 That Pat is after the top job is no secret.
3 To get there by public transport can't be that difficult.
4 That everyone is completely exhausted is obvious.

5 Asking him to help is no use.
6 Looking after young children all day isn't easy.

4 a) Fill in the vowels in these character adjectives. **V3.2**

1 r_ckl_ss   6 _bst_n_t_
2 _rr_g_nt   7 _mp_t_ _ _s
3 _xtr_v_g_nt   8 t_m_d
4 f_n_cky   9 t_ght-f_st_d
5 g_ll_bl_

b) Work in pairs. Take turns to test your partner on the meaning of the words in **4a**).

5 Complete the phrasal verbs with these prepositions. **V3.3**

> up (x3) over around on out down

1 Rachel's gone .... with flu, but the doctor hasn't put her .... antibiotics.
2 Jake's really unlucky. He seems to pick .... every bug that's going ....
3 I can't eat strawberries. My face swells .... and I come .... in a rash.
4 A You sound very blocked ....
   B Yes, I'm still trying to get .... a bad cold.

6 Fill in the gaps with the subject and the correct form of the verb in brackets. **G3.3**

1 Only once before *have I climbed* such a high mountain. (I climb)
2 Not only .... the film, I didn't enjoy the meal after either. (I hate)
3 Under no circumstances .... a car without insurance. (anyone should drive)
4 Not until she explained it again .... what had happened. (I understand)
5 Only by chance .... to get tickets for the concert. (we manage)

6 Rarely .... a plumber as good as Henry. (you find)
7 Only when Mark walked through the door .... I'd met him before. (I realise)
8 Only recently .... to play sport on a regular basis. (we begin)

7 Replace the words/phrases in **bold** with these euphemisms. **V3.4**

> a bit on the chilly side
> be economical with the truth
> bit of a handful   senior citizens
> challenging   getting on a bit

1 The work I'm doing at the moment is **very difficult**.
2 Al's a **naughty and difficult child to look after**.
3 Simon tends to **lie**.
4 My cat's **old**.
5 I think **old people** shouldn't have to pay for heating.
6 It's **cold** today.

Progress Portfolio

a) Tick the things you can do in English.

☐ I can describe people's character using a wide range of adjectives.

☐ I can read, understand and summarise information about health.

☐ I can recognise structures used for emphasis in more formal/literary language.

☐ I can understand some euphemistic expressions.

☐ I can express my ideas tactfully when necessary.

b) What do you need to study again? **3A–C** .

Accurate Writing

CONNECTING WORDS: contrast (1)
SPELLING: one word, two words or hyphenated

 1 **a)** Match an idea in A with one in B. Then join the ideas to make a sentence using *although* or *whereas*. **AW3.1** p126.

A	B
1 Mo still smokes,	a) I've had lessons.
2 They fell asleep,	b) I stopped playing ages ago.
3 I can't drive,	c) she knows she shouldn't.
4 Amy still plays tennis,	d) I'd been there before.
5 I got lost,	e) I was awake for hours.

Mo still smokes, although she knows she shouldn't.

b) Fill in the gap with these connecting words. Sometimes there is more than one possible answer.

> although   even though   whereas   however   but

1 .... I never bother to lock my car, I know I should.
2 I never bother to lock my car, ... I know I should.
3 .... Jane always helps, her brother never does.
4 .... Jane says she's willing to help, she rarely does.
5 .... I like cats, I prefer dogs.
6 I like cats. .... , I prefer dogs.
7 Frank is very athletic, ... his brother isn't.
8 Frank is very athletic. .... , his brother isn't.

2 Choose the correct spelling. **AW3.2** p126.

1 This isn't an *every day/everyday* occurrence.
2 *Every one/Everyone* of his jackets is handmade.
3 It's a *hundred years old/hundred-year-old* house.
4 Does *any one/anyone* know Pete's mobile number?
5 Is there *anyway/any way* I can help?
6 She *maybe/may be* coming tonight.

3 **a)** Read the extract from a student's written work. Then correct the <u>underlined</u> mistakes. There is more than one possible answer.

b) Find and correct five spelling mistakes. A missing hyphen counts as a spelling mistake.

> Every one I know feels low at times,
> ¹although I honestly don't. ²Whereas I do
> sometimes feel a bit low on energy, it's not
> something that happens everyday. May be
> it's related to the weather.
> Any way, when I do feel a bit low on energy
> I have a quick shower and that usually
> works. ³Even though, my brother is very
> different. If he's a bit low, he actually
> goes for a ten kilometre run. ⁴However he's
> actually 39, he sometimes behaves like a
> 20-year-old fitness fanatic!

Preview 4

1 FUTURE VERB FORMS

Look at the verb forms in **bold** in sentences 1–4 and 5–8. Match them to rules a)–d) and e)–h). **G4.1** p127.

1 The new airport tax **comes** into effect on Monday.
2 Who**'s meeting** you at the station?
3 I**'m going to stop** reading this paper, it's so right-wing.
4 Look at the time. We**'re going to be** late.

We use:
a) the Present Continuous for future arrangements. *2*
b) the Present Simple for a fixed event on a timetable or a calendar.
c) *be going to* for a personal plan or intention.
d) *be going to* for a prediction that is based on present evidence.

5 I think they**'ll have** an early election.
6 I**'ll be passing** the post office, so I can post it.
7 This time next week we**'ll be having** talks with the Prime Minister.
8 By the end of the year we**'ll have built** 10,000 new homes.

We use:
e) the Future Continuous for something that will be in progress at a certain time in the future.
f) the Future Perfect for something that will be completed before a certain time in the future.
g) *will* for a prediction based on opinion rather than evidence.
h) the Future Continuous for something that will happen in the normal course of events – not because you planned it.

2 Choose the best option.

1 A By the time Jon gets here, the meeting will *finish/have finished*.
  B I'll *try/I'm going to try* him on his mobile.
2 A I *call/I'm going to call* Jeff about getting tickets for Thursday's game.
  B Actually, I *see/I'll be seeing* him tomorrow. So I can ask him.
3 A The traffic's bad. We're not *getting/going to get* there on time.
  B I'm sure they *won't start/'re not starting* without us.
4 A I *start/'ll start* my new job next week.
  B I'm sure you *are enjoying/'ll enjoy* it.
5 A I hate driving in the dark so I *leave/'ll be leaving* around 4.30 this afternoon.
  B But it *gets/'s getting* dark at about 4 p.m.

4 Civilised

4A Society and the media

Vocabulary news collocations
Grammar phrases referring to the future
Review euphemisms

QUICK REVIEW ●●●
Make a list of six euphemisms (*getting on a bit*, etc.). Work in pairs. Swap lists. Take turns to make sentences with phrases from your partner's list.

Vocabulary News collocations

1 a) Match the verbs in A to the words/phrases in B. Check in V4.1 p127.

A	B
read	publicity
seek	a press conference
hold	the tabloids/glossy magazines

receive	the headlines
sue	for libel
hit	a lot of coverage

make	a press release
issue	the front page
run	a story

b) Fill in the gaps with a word from **1a)**.

1 Do you ever read .... magazines? If so, which ones?
2 Which celebrities in your country actually .... publicity?
3 What type of news regularly receives a lot of .... in your country?
4 What's the latest story to .... the front page of the newspaper you read?
5 Do you know of any famous people who have .... a newspaper for libel?
6 Do newspapers in your country often .... stories about TV celebrities?

c) Work in pairs. Ask and answer the questions in **1b)**. Ask follow-up questions.

①
The cost of an average family holiday abroad is likely to increase under current government plans. The Department of Transport proposals emerged at the height of the holiday season, when more than five million people a month fly from British airports. The Department is looking for ways in which aviation can meet its 'full climate change costs'. However, this decision is sure to annoy parents, particularly in the summer when they already pay a high premium for flying during school holidays.

Reading and Grammar

2 a) Work in pairs. Discuss these questions.

1 How do you find out what's in the news?
2 How much time do you spend each day watching, reading, listening to or discussing news stories?

b) Check the meaning of these words/phrases.

> a bugging device   go through the roof   axe something
> a lawsuit   a defendant   a spouse

c) Read news items 1–4. Then match four of these headlines to the news items. Which headline does not belong to any of the stories?

a) New airport 'green' tax due to be introduced
b) Driving age set to rise
c) Sale of bugging devices about to go through roof
d) New TV boss on the verge of axing reality TV shows
e) Dry cleaner's to face lawsuit over pair of trousers

d) Read news items 1–4 again. Then complete these sentences in your own words.

1 a) The government is bringing in a new airport tax because ...
  b) Parents will be upset about it because ...
2 a) The Chungs' story is extraordinary because ...
  b) Judge Pearson's basing his case on ...
3 a) The government is increasing the legal driving age because ...
  b) Another new restriction to be introduced is ...
4 a) Judge Benini concluded that the 22 defendants were ...
  b) The current law in Italy on invasion of privacy is restricted to ...

3 Work in groups. Discuss these questions.

1 What measures are being taken in your country to fight global warming?
2 What would happen in your country if a dry cleaner's lost or damaged an item of clothing?
3 At what age do you think people should be allowed to drive? Give reasons.
4 What legitimate reasons, if any, are there for using bugging devices?

Help with Grammar
phrases referring to the future

See **Preview**, p35.

4 a) Change headlines a)–e) in **2c)** into sentences by adding the correct form of *be* and using an article where necessary.

A new airport 'green' tax **is** due to be introduced.

TIP! ● Many newspaper headlines are not written as complete sentences.

b) Look at the words/phrases in pink in headlines a)–e) and in blue in news stories 1–4. Which group of words/phrases tells us:

1 that something is ready to happen, probably in the near future?
2 the speaker or writer's opinion of how certain they are that this will happen?

c) Look again at the words/phrases in pink and blue. Which phrase is followed by verb+*ing* (or noun)? What verb form follows the other phrases?

TIP! ● *due to* is usually used when we are talking about a particular time: *Building work is due to start in March.*

d) Check in G4.2 p127.

(2) An immigrant family from South Korea first went into business seven years ago and believed they had found their American dream. However, the Chungs, who own a dry cleaner's in Washington, are being sued for $65 million by Roy Pearson, a District of Columbia judge. The judge is suing the Chung family over a missing pair of trousers, despite the fact that they were later found! The family have been living with this legal nightmare for over two years and they are unlikely to stay in America if they lose their case. Much of Judge Pearson's lawsuit rests on two signs that Custom Cleaners had on its walls: 'Satisfaction Guaranteed' and 'Same Day Service'. Pearson claims the signs amount to fraud.

(3) The government has announced new measures aimed at reducing the number of road deaths. The minimum legal driving age is shortly to rise and ministers are proposing that learner drivers should undergo a training period of no less than 12 months; a measure which they claim is certain to reduce the number of accidents caused by young drivers. The same proposal, to be published this autumn, will also recommend a no-alcohol limit for newly qualified drivers of any age for a year after they pass their test.

From now on people in Italy would be wise not to use their cars for 'secret meetings'. According to a judge's ruling yesterday, married people can now legally bug their spouse's car if they believe their husband or wife is being unfaithful. When 22 of these bugging devices were recently found by police, the people involved were charged with 'invasion of privacy'. However, Lorenzo Benini, a judge in Brescia, ruled that installing bugging devices in a car "was not a criminal offence". He pointed out that the law forbidding bugging only applies to homes. Many fear the judge's ruling is bound to result in an increased use of these devices.

5 Fill in the gaps with these prompts. Use the correct form of the verb.

~~set / rise~~   verge / turn back   due / retire
about / sign   settle for

1 Interest rates *are set to rise* by a half a percent.
2 Liverpool's chief of police .... after 40 years of service.
3 Everest's youngest climbers .... because of poor weather conditions.
4 The singer, Migs, ... a new recording deal for £10 million.
5 The Workers' Union .... a 10% pay rise.

6 **a)** Complete the sentences with the words in brackets and the names of countries, people, etc. that you know or know of.

1 ... (likely / win) their next match against ...
Brazil is likely to win their next match against England.
2 ... (sure / do) very well this year.
3 ... (likely / get) married in the next five years.
4 ... (verge / make) an important decision.
5 ... (bound / spend) time playing computer games this weekend.
6 ... (about / sell) his/her ...
7 ... (due / retire) in the next couple of years.
8 ... (certain / do) something amazing with his/her life.

b) Work in pairs. Choose five of the sentences in **6a)**. Take turns to tell each other your sentences. Ask follow-up questions.

Listening

7 **a)** Make a list of what you think are the most popular TV programmes in your country. Tick the ones you watch.

b) Work in pairs. Compare lists. If you are from the same country, do you agree? If you're from different countries, are the programmes similar?

8 **a)** Read this news extract. What types of TV programme are likely to replace current reality TV shows on Channel 13, and why?

NEW TV BOSS ON THE VERGE OF AXING REALITY TV SHOWS

THE NEW HEAD of Channel 13, Millicent Davies, is about to make major changes to programming schedules.

"We believe people are ready for a change – a move away from the tired formulas of reality TV. Our research shows that viewers would like to see a return to more fact-based programmes – documentaries or wildlife films, for example. They would also like more drama, more comedy and this is what we intend to offer."

---

b) R4.1 Listen to Sue and Dan discussing television programmes. Answer these questions.

1 What programmes does Sue like and why?
2 Why doesn't Dan like the same programmes?
3 What programmes does Dan like?

c) Work in pairs. Who said the following, Sue or Dan?

1 It's intellectually bankrupt and it's just rubbish.
2 And actually sometimes you need to keep in touch with the youth of today, don't you? And they like this sort of thing.
3 It's fun to see people outside their normal environment, testing themselves.
4 It's there to create conflict. It's to see the worst in people.
5 There's enough sport on TV as it is, it's on all the time.
6 What about some costume drama?
7 What I want is some good comedy for me to relax.

d) Listen again. Check your answers to **8c)**.

9 **a)** Look at these quotes from R4.1. Match the words/phrases in **bold** in 1–5 to meanings a)–e).

1 it's **poking fun at people**
2 so reality TV is **fine by me**
3 they know **what they're letting themselves in for**
4 that's a bit **dull**
5 **each to their own**

a) making people seem ridiculous 1
b) I have no objection
c) what kind of unpleasant situation they're getting involved in
d) everyone likes different things
e) not interesting

b) Who do you agree with more, Sue or Dan? Why?

Get ready ... Get it right!

10 **a)** Look at these sentences. Think of reasons why you agree or disagree with them.

1 The Internet will replace television as the main form of home entertainment.
2 People won't go to the cinema to watch films but will simply download films onto their mobile phones or computers.
3 User-generated content* will continue to grow on the Internet.
4 CDs and DVDs will continue to exist.
5 People will still be able to see live performances by singers, bands, orchestras, etc.
6 People will continue to buy books and libraries will still exist.

*user-generated content = videos, photos, blogs, etc. that the general public produce and publish on the Internet

b) Work in groups. Discuss the statements in **10a)**.

c) Tell the class your conclusions.

Vocabulary near synonyms
Grammar future in the past
Review phrases referring to the future

QUICK REVIEW ● ● ●
Work in groups. Talk about stories that are in the news. Try to use future phrases like *set to*, *due to*, *about to*, *on the verge of*, etc. Tell the class about the most interesting news item you discussed.

Reading and Vocabulary

1 Work in pairs. Tell each other about cities that you particularly like and why. Say when and why you visited them.

 a) Look at sentences 1–5 and try and predict the missing information about the development of cities.

1 Originally humans didn't stay in one place because …
2 Trade and education began to develop once people …
3 Some cities didn't survive because of …
4 In the 1800s many people from the countryside came to cities because …
5 People in the country and in cities lived longer due to …

b) Read the article about how and why cities developed. Were your ideas in 2a) correct?

The world goes to town

The majority of people live in cities. Human history will increasingly become urban history, says John Grimmond.

WHEREVER YOU THINK the human story began, it is clear that <u>humans</u> did not start life as urban creatures. <u>Man</u>'s original habitat was governed by the need to find food; hunting and collecting things to eat were rural activities. Not until the end of the last ice age, about 11,000 years ago, did humans start building anything that might be called <u>a village</u>, and by that time man had been around for about 120,000 years. It took another six millennia for cities to grow to more than 100,000. Even in the 1800s only 3% of the world's population lived in cities. That figure has now risen to over 50%. So, wisely or not, human beings have become homo urbanus.

Living together meant security, but historians also point out that <u>a settlement</u> drew <u>people</u> to it as a meeting place where they could trade. Around 2000BC, metal tokens, the forerunners of coins, were produced as receipts for grain, and cities began to take shape at the same time

The city soon became the centre of exchange, learning, innovation and sophistication. It was life in the city that made it possible for man to acquire skills, learn from other people, study, teach and develop social arts that made <u>country folk</u> seem very uneducated.

Of course, not all cities were the same. As they developed some were known as the hub of an empire (Constantinople), for learning (Bologna), or commerce (Hamburg). Some were very successful, some died, depending on factors as varied as war, disease, misgovernment or economic failure.

Whatever the particular circumstances of a city, though, its success was likely to be governed by technological change. For example, it was <u>improvements</u> in transport that made the growth of trade possible. Then in the 19th century there was the invention of engines, which brought about a huge increase in technology

The industrial age was born. As more factories were built, multitudes of <u>rural inhabitants</u> left <u>the land</u> looking for work. By 1900, 13% of the world's population had become urban.

The latest leap, from 13% to over 50% (in little over 100 years), also owed something to science and technology. Improvements in medicine, including ways to avoid <u>disease</u>, meant that more and more people could live together without succumbing to diarrhoea, tuberculosis, cholera and other such <u>pestilences</u>. And these same <u>developments</u> in medicine also lengthened lives in <u>the countryside</u>, leading to a huge increase in rural population. As a result, even more <u>villagers</u> have been moving into the cities, and the speed and scale of current urban growth, particularly in countries such as China and India, are unlike any other big change in history to date; by 2050 an expected 75% of all human beings will live in cities!

Adapted from the *Economist* 05/05/07

3 **a)** Read the article again. What is the link between these numbers?

a) 11,000 and 120,000
b) 3% and 50%
c) 13%, 50% and 75%

b) Work in groups. Make a list of possible benefits and possible problems of having most of the world's population living in cities. Which list is longer?

4 Work in groups. Group A → p108. Group B → p111.

Help with Vocabulary Near synonyms

- We often avoid repeating the same words (particularly nouns, adjectives, verbs and adverbs) so that what we say or write sounds less repetitive and more interesting.

  *A **huge** number of <u>immigrants</u> arrive every year. To process this **large** number of <u>people</u>, the government ...*

5 **a)** Look at the <u>underlined</u> words in the article. Make six different groups of two or three words which show how the writer avoids repetition.

1 humans man people

b) Check in **V4.2** p127.

TIP! ● Not all near synonyms are interchangeable in all contexts. These are some of the reasons why:

1 **formality**: *kid* and *child* have the same meaning but *kid* is more informal. *How are the kids?* (informal) *There are 14.8 million children in the UK ...* (more formal)
2 **words that go together**: *A huge/large number.* *A huge/~~large~~ problem.*
3 **grammatical agreement**: *I like/enjoy travelling.* *I like/~~enjoy~~ to travel.*
4 **connotation**: *determined.* (positive) *obstinate.* (negative)

6 Work in pairs. Check you know the meaning of these words/phrases. Then replace the words in **bold** in the text with the correct form of the words/phrases in the box.

> be forced to   enjoy   urban   passers-by   vehicles   suddenly   standstill   exasperating   allow   gaze at

Personally, I like living in a city. I ¹**like** the bustle and sounds of ²**city** life and I love people-watching. In fact, I often sit in cafes just ³**watching** ⁴**people** in the street. I don't even mind all the cars. I know it's infuriating when you're driving along and ⁵**cars** unexpectedly come to a ⁶**stop** for no apparent reason. Then you ⁷**have to** wait for ages before anything moves. But let's face it, it can be equally ⁸**infuriating** when you're driving in the country and you ⁹**unexpectedly** have to stop to let a herd of sheep pass by. Then ten minutes later you have to stop again to ¹⁰**let** a herd of cows past!

Star Trek changed the world and we can prove it!

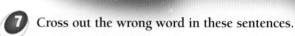

7 Cross out the wrong word in these sentences.

1 That's a *big/huge/~~large~~* mistake.
2 I love *watching/gazing* at TV.
3 I *enjoy/like/love* to learn languages.
4 Good evening, sir. I'd like to introduce you to my *mate/friend*.
5 I was very *cross/furious/angry*.
6 He's so *courageous/reckless*. It's such a good influence on the children.

Listening and Grammar

8 **a)** Look at photos 1–4 of props from *Star Trek*, a 1960s TV science-fiction series. What is today's equivalent of the technology in the photos?

b) **R4.2** Listen to four extracts from a *Star Trek* documentary and check your answers.

9 Listen again. Choose the correct answer.

1 Cooper made the first call to *a colleague/ someone working for another company*.
2 The first cell phones were roughly *10/50* times as heavy as modern phones.
3 Dr Raymon is *an astronaut/a scientist* involved in the exploration of space.
4 Voyager 1 is about to *leave the solar system/return to earth*.
5 Surgery used for diagnostic purposes before the 1970s *was/wasn't* safe.
6 Dr Adler *is working on/has produced* equipment that can destroy cancerous cells without surgery.
7 In the late 1980s, Steve Perlman *was working for/took his idea to* Apple Computers Inc.
8 QuickTime *followed/preceded* the iPod.

Help with Grammar Future in the past

11 **a)** Look at these sentences. In which one are we predicting the result? In which one do we know the result?

1 *We didn't know our ideas were going to be successful.*
2 *We believe our ideas are going to be successful.*

b) Match sentences 1 and 2 in **11a)** to these meanings.

a) talking about the future seen from now
b) talking about the future seen from a point in the past

c) Look at the verb forms in **bold** in speech bubbles A–D in **10** and complete the table.

the future seen from now	the future seen from the past
am/is/are going to + infinitive	*was/were going to* + infinitive
will + infinitive	
am/is/are supposed to + infinitive	
am/is/are about to + infinitive	
am/is/are to + infinitive	

d) Check in G4.3 p128.

12 Tick the correct sentences. Then correct the mistakes.

1 Kelly is going to come, but her car broke down.
2 I had no idea that it will be this exhausting!
3 You've finished! Wasn't Dave supposed to give you a hand?
4 I'm about to leave the house when I remembered you were coming.
5 I'm supposed to call my sister before she left, but I forgot.
6 We are to stay in a hotel near the beach, but it closed down.
7 That day he made a decision that he would regret till the day he died.

13 **a)** Complete these sentences with true and false information about yourself. At least two sentences should be true.

1 Yesterday I was about to …
Yesterday I was about to watch TV when there was a power cut.
2 Last summer I was going to … , but …
3 This time last year I had no idea I'd …
4 My best friend and I were supposed to …
5 When I was little I always knew I was going to …
6 Once, I made a promise to (myself, etc.) that I'd always …
7 I got up early last (Monday, etc.) because I was due to …

b) Work in pairs. Take turns to say your sentences. Your partner guesses which ones are true. Ask follow-up questions about the true sentences.

A We didn't know our ideas **were going to be** successful. In the original series nothing was based on scientific research. We just made it all up. Little did we know these gadgets were going to inspire a generation of young earthlings. And some of these young fans **would go on** to spend their lives trying to turn *Star Trek* fantasy
¹............................. .

B Years later we **were to find out** that many of the ²............................. in Silicon Valley had been *Star Trek* fans as kids. All these geeks in the 1960s decided they were actually going to make personal computers like those that Spock used, and that included pocket or palm computers. But it wouldn't happen overnight.

C We didn't realise that these bits of cardboard and plastic being used on set **were about to be** transformed into everyday ³............................. .

D And we thought that *Star Trek* **was just supposed to offer** ⁴............................. .

Get ready … Get it right!

14 Work in groups. Group A → page 109. Group B → p112. Group C → page 114. Follow the instructions.

10 R4.3 Listen and fill in gaps 1–4 in speech bubbles A–D with one, two or three words.

4C Making a splash

Vocabulary newspaper language
Skills Reading: stories from tabloid and broadsheet newspapers; Listening: an interview with a sub-editor; Speaking: creating a front-page news story; Writing: a newspaper story
Real World persuading
Review near synonyms

QUICK REVIEW ● ● ●

Think of as many near synonyms as you can for each of these words: *enormous*; *let*; *infuriating*; *enjoy*; *clever*; *unexpectedly*. Work in pairs. Tell each other your synonyms.

1 **a)** Look at the front pages of two different newspapers from the same day. Then work in pairs and answer these questions.

1 In what ways are these two newspapers different? Think about the size and content of the headlines, the page layout and what the main stories are.
2 Which paper is a tabloid and which is a broadsheet?
3 Which type of newspaper do you think sells the most?
4 What kind of readership do you think the different newspapers appeal to?

b) **R4.4** Listen to part of an interview with Andrew Cook, a sub-editor on a national tabloid newspaper. Compare your answers in **1a)** with what he says.

c) Listen again. Complete this information with one or two words.

1 Some broadsheets, like *The Times*, have changed their format and become ....
2 In papers such as *The Times*, the language is more .... and the presentation of the news is more ....
3 Tabloids try to control how you .... and ....
4 The broadsheet papers have a circulation of up to .... thousand.
5 The tabloids sell about .... copies.
6 Broadsheets often focus on .... stories.
7 'Downmarket' tabloids prefer stories about film stars, royals and .... stories.
8 Andrew describes 'his' paper as in .... of the market.
9 The people who buy Andrew's paper tend to be middle class ....

d) Work in pairs. Compare answers.

e) Read these extracts from the interview with Andrew. What do the words/phrases in **bold** mean?

1 … the so-called **quality press**, otherwise known as broadsheets …
2 … the tabloid papers tend to **shout at you** …
3 … something with a much sort of **brasher, instant appeal** …
4 … the downmarket so-called **red-top** tabloids …
5 … sometimes we'll decide that the **splash** should be a political story …
6 … the **heart of our circulation** …

2 **a)** Read the two different newspaper stories. What are the main differences in the kind of language used? Think about a) the length of sentences and paragraphs, b) the choice of vocabulary.

A

HERO PILOT SAVES FLIGHT BA038

Give him a medal as big as a frying pan

By MARTIN FRICKER & REBECCA EVANS

A HEROIC British Airways pilot averted catastrophe yesterday by gliding his jet into Heathrow after its engines failed.

Capt Peter Burkill kept Flight BA038 airborne over houses and schools before crash-landing in a field. Only 19 of the 136 people on board were hurt.

A witness said: "He deserves a medal as big as a frying pan."

The jet swooped in a few feet above cars heading for the airport – including one carrying Gordon Brown.

FULL STORY: PAGES 4, 5, 6&7

B

Heathrow escape for 150 passengers and crew as BA jet crash-lands before runway

More than 150 passengers and crew escaped disaster yesterday after a British Airways jet crash-landed short of the runway at Heathrow airport, just missing a nearby road. The Boeing 777, arriving from Beijing, struck the ground at 12.43pm on the grassy approach to the airport's south runway, crushing its undercarriage, which became detached, and skidding on its belly for several hundred metres.

The 16-strong crew and 135 passengers were evacuated via the emergency slides. Thirteen people including four crew were treated in hospital for minor injuries.

b) R4.5 Listen to Andrew talking about the language used in tabloids. Are these statements true or false, according to him? Find examples from story A.

1 Sentences in broadsheets are usually shorter and clearer than in tabloids.
2 The language of tabloids tends to have a dramatic feel.
3 Paragraphs are deliberately kept very short in tabloids.

c) Andrew uses these phrases to describe the language of tabloid newspapers. What do you think they mean?

1 snappier language
2 crisp sentences
3 a crash, bang, wallop style
4 in tune with the audience

d) Discuss these questions.

1 Were you surprised by anything Andrew said?
2 Does your country have the same distinction between the 'quality' and 'downmarket' press?
3 What kind of newspapers have the biggest circulation in your country?

3 R4.6 Listen to Andrew explaining how a story gets chosen for the front page of a tabloid and answer these questions.

1 Who do the reporters have to convince to choose their story?
2 How should the story be written?
3 Who makes the final decision about the main story?

4 Work in groups of three. Student A → p110. Student B → p113. Student C → p114.

Real World Persuading

- You've got to admit … .
- I'd have thought this story would make a better splash.
- Don't you think more people are interested in … ?
- This is just the kind of story people want to read.

Writing Extension

5 Write your story as it might appear on the front page of either a 'middle-of-the-road' or 'downmarket' tabloid.

 R4.7 Look at the song *Summer in the City* on p106. Follow the instructions.

1 Choose the correct words. `V4.1`

1 *read/receive* a lot of coverage
2 *hold/make* a press conference
3 *seek/issue* publicity
4 *run/read* tabloids
5 *run/issue* a story
6 *receive/hit* the headlines
7 *seek/sue* for libel

2 **a)** Choose the correct verb forms. Sometimes both are correct. `G4.3`

1 Mandy's *on the verge of retiring/going to retire* in five years' time.
2 Ssshh, the film *will/is about to* start!
3 Clare is *on the brink of having/is due to have* her baby in June.
4 Their new company is *sure to/bound to* make a profit this year.
5 The management is *unlikely to/probably not going to* offer a pay rise.
6 Prices *are falling/are set to fall* in the next month or so.
7 He's *on the point of applying/about to apply* for a place at university.

b) Work in pairs. Compare answers.

3 **a)** Use these prompts to write true or false sentences about yourself. `G4.2`

1 I'm due to …
2 I'm unlikely to …
3 I'm on the verge of …
4 I'm about to …
5 I'm likely to …
6 I'm bound to …

b) Work in pairs. Swap sentences. Guess which are true.

4 **a)** Match words/phrases 1–7 with near synonyms a)–g). `V4.2`

1 make someone   a)
2 infuriate
3 like
4 allow
5 urban
6 friend
7 huge

a) force someone
b) let
c) city
d) enjoy
e) exasperate
f) large
g) mate

b) Work in pairs. Compare answers.

5 **a)** Complete these sentences with the correct form of words/phrases 1–7 from **4a)**. `V4.2`

1 I really love ___urban___ life.
2 Dave's got a _____ problem with his boss.
3 Good afternoon, Madam. Someone left a message for you. She said she was a _____ of yours.
4 His behaviour _____ me at times. He's so selfish.
5 I _____ to listen to music when I'm driving.
6 They _____ me tell them everything I knew about what Jason had done.
7 I was _____ to leave work early.

b) Work in pairs. Can you complete sentences 1–7 in **5a)** with words/phrases a)–g) in **4a)**? If not, why? (Think about formality, grammatical agreement, etc.)

6 **a)** Read the story. Then fill in the gaps with the correct form of the phrases in brackets. `G4.3`

Last Saturday Brigit and I [1] ___were to meet up___ (meet up) in town and join the anti-war demonstration. She [2] _____ (supposed to call) from the station but she didn't. I waited an hour then I decided I [3] _____ (will not stay) any longer. However, just as I [4] _____ (about to leave) another friend shouted my name. I didn't know he [5] _____ (going to be) there. Anyway, we decided we [6] _____ (will join) the march. Then two minutes later I saw my brother and his girlfriend. I had no idea they [7] _____ (going to demonstrate) either. Ten minutes after that, I saw Brigit. Apparently, she [8] _____ (just going to call) me when I spotted her. There were two million people on that march. It's hard to believe that the five of us [9] _____ (will bump) into each other, but we did!

b) Work in pairs. Compare answers.

Progress Portfolio

a) Tick the things you can do in English.

☐ I can recognise and use phrases which refer to the future.

☐ I can keep up with an animated discussion.

☐ I can identify near synonyms in a complex text.

☐ I can talk about the future when seen from a point in the past.

☐ I can recognise and discuss different styles of newspapers.

b) What do you need to study again? ● **4A–C** .

Accurate Writing

CONNECTING WORDS: contrast (2)
PUNCTUATION: capital letters and full stops

 1 Choose the correct connecting word. Sometimes both answers are possible. **AW4.1** p128.

1 This coat is so old, *despite/but* it's still my favourite.
2 *In spite of/Although* it was freezing, they went for a bike ride.
3 *Nonetheless/In spite of* the fact that he was ill, he went into work.
4 I'm not hungry. *Nevertheless/However*, I will have one of those cakes.
5 He only got 50% in his exam, but *nevertheless/however* that's better than last year.
6 *Despite/Although* being late, they allowed us into the theatre.
7 *In spite of/Although* the weather, we had a great time.
8 *Despite/In spite of* all their hard work, they failed to make the deadline.
9 I told him not to phone. *Nevertheless/Even though*, he did.

2 Add capital letters and full stops to this postcard. Circle the full stops where their use depends on personal style. **AW4.2** p128.

dear sam,
i'll meet you on tues 11 dec at waterloo station at 8 30 am i've checked out films, music gigs, etc there's loads on. do you fancy a trip down the river thames? if you do, we could get a boat to the tower of london look forward to showing you the sights
all the best,
pete

mr sam baker
25 lime st
bradford
bd5 8lm
uk

 3 **a)** Read this extract from a student's written work. Then correct the <u>underlined</u> mistakes. Sometimes there is more than one possible answer.

b) Find and correct seven mistakes with capital letters.

c) Look at all the full stops. Which are a) essential? b) a matter of personal style? c) generally considered incorrect?

Have you ever been to New York. ? I went to New York, U.S.A. for the first time last december. The trip was a birthday present from my Parents. ¹<u>Although</u> only being there for a long weekend, thursday to sunday, I had an amazing time. I visited all the main sights, The Rockefeller Building, Central Park, etc. – they were great. In fact, ²<u>despite</u> it snowed, I went to the Park every day. I stayed with my father's friends – Prof. Anais Boyer and Dr. Pierre Boyer, who both teach at New York university. Their apartment is quite far from the city centre, but ³<u>however</u>, I walked into town every day.

Preview 5

1 REFLEXIVE PRONOUNS (1)

What is the difference in meaning between sentences a) and b)? How does the use of the reflexive pronoun affect the meaning? **G5.1** p130.

1 a) She's teaching her to swim.
   b) She's teaching herself to swim.

2 a) The children are allowed to read to themselves before they go to bed.
   b) The children are allowed to read to each other before they go to bed.

3 a) I'm having my house redecorated soon.
   b) I think I'll redecorate my house myself.

4 a) Geoff went to the cinema by himself.
   b) Geoff went to the cinema.

2 VERB + INFINITIVE WITH *TO* OR VERB+*ING* (1)

Complete the sentences with the correct form of the verb in brackets. **V5.2** p129.

On January 1st of this year my girlfriend persuaded me ¹_____ (cut down on) the amount of television I was watching. She said she would ²_____ (allow) me ³_____ (choose) one soap opera a week and obviously I would need ⁴_____ (keep on) ⁵_____ (watch) my football team on Saturday afternoons. I had expected ⁶_____ (find) this very difficult because I was a real telly addict, but surprisingly I managed ⁷_____ (break) the habit quite quickly. I admit I missed ⁸_____ (sit down) in front of my favourite programmes every evening, but having free evenings has encouraged me ⁹_____ (see) my friends more often and helped me ¹⁰_____ (organise) my time better. I have stopped ¹¹_____ (think) about the characters in my favourite programmes and I am trying ¹²_____ (take up) other interests such as learning ¹³_____(play) the saxophone.

5 It's just a job!

> **Vocabulary** word building (1): prefixes with multiple meanings
> **Grammar** reflexive pronouns (2)
> **Review** news collocations

QUICK REVIEW ●●●
Write as many news collocations as you can. Work in pairs. Take turns to say the noun in the collocation. Your partner says the verb. A *publicity*. B *seek publicity*.

Reading and Vocabulary

 1 Work in pairs. Discuss these questions.

1 Why do so many people want to know about celebrities?
2 What kind of lives do you think celebrities have? Do you work hard?

 2 **a)** Check the meaning of these words and phrases. Use them to talk about the possible advantages and disadvantages of being a celebrity personal assistant (CPA).

> flexible   demanding   drudgery   a perk
> a 'can-do' attitude   trivial   sacrifice
> rub shoulders with   proximity to   a limo

b) Read the article and check your ideas.

 3 **a)** Choose the correct answer. Find evidence in the article.

1 CPAs *originated in LA/have their own organisation*.
2 People become CPAs *as a route to stardom/to be near famous people*.
3 Dean Johnson says his job makes him *feel important/well-known*.
4 CPAs are required to *commit to regular hours/sacrifice their own domestic life*.
5 Annie Brentwell describes the relationship with her employer as *selfless/genuine*.
6 Annie enjoys the frequent *challenges/glamorous nights out*.
7 Annie regrets not *working for more people/having more time for herself*.

b) Work in pairs and discuss these questions.

1 Do you envy people who become CPAs, or are you surprised they would want this job?
2 If you could work for any celebrity, who would you choose? Give reasons.

THE *Cinderellas* OF HOLLYWOOD

The personal assistants to film stars are **over**worked, **under**paid and invisible. Why would anyone want the job? Jake Halpern went to investigate.

T HE ROMANS HAD PERSONAL ASSISTANTS, or 'courtiers' as they were known then, and Napoleon Bonaparte allegedly employed an assistant with the same size feet, whose primary job it was to break in the emperor's new shoes. It stands to reason that a city like Los Angeles, home to so many of the famous and the **semi**-famous, is also home to the Association of Celebrity Personal Assistants (CPAs).

Unlike lawyers and agents, who rub shoulders with Hollywood stars and often make millions of dollars, assistants are not paid particularly well, especially given their round-the-clock obligations. Proximity to the stars appears to be the only perk their profession offers. Most describe the bulk of their work as drudgery: doing laundry, fetching groceries, paying bills. What's more, the job is usually an end in itself, rather than a stepping stone to fame.

I spoke to a personal assistant, Dean Johnson, about why he does it. "I don't consider myself vain or superficial, but entertainment is what captivates the world today and these celebrities are known around the world. We assistants are the gatekeepers, and that's a powerful position to be in."

Dean invited me along to a seminar titled 'Becoming a CPA'. The organiser began the seminar by laying down some hard truths. "You must be in good health at all times. If you get recurrent colds or generally stressed, this job is not for you. You also need to be flexible, which means it's probably better if you don't have a spouse, or kids, or pets or even plants. And you have to have a 'can-do' attitude. If there's one word that celebrities don't want to hear, that word is 'no'."

A participant at the seminar, Annie Brentwell, agreed with that. "The most important thing is not to express or even think about your own needs. If my employer has to think about me, it detracts from what they are doing."

Brentwell felt she was constantly changing how she was, to become the perfect **counter**balance: she could play the humble servant, the trusted confidante, the admirer, or the supportive family member. And yet, even when she pretended she was a friend, it was only a **pseudo**-friendship, in which one person did all the talking. There was never any real **inter**action.

Before her present post, she had worked for the actress Sharon Stone, an even more demanding job. As hard as it was, however, she said she did manage to enjoy herself at times. The first and rarest occasion was when she could play 'dress up' and go to a premiere as she did once, wearing her employer's jewellery and shoes. "Best of all there's the limo ride and the whole experience of walking along the red carpet, seeing the flashing lights and having that very special feeling for one night."

Another, more common joy came on the days when she worked so hard she was almost in a stupor. "If you have worked from early morning until late at night and you've done all the things they throw at you – both important and trivial – you feel like **super**woman."

She felt proud of how many people wanted her to work for them but she was also serious about making more time for herself. "I wish I had travelled more. And I do wish that I had kids."

Adapted from *The Week* 27/01/07

Help with Vocabulary Word building (1): prefixes with multiple meanings

- If we don't know the meaning of a noun, adjective or verb, we can often make a guess from its prefix.

4 **a)** Match the prefixes in **bold** in the article to meanings a)–g).

a) between (two things, people, etc.) *inter*
b) in opposition to
c) better/more than usual
d) too much
e) partly
f) not enough
g) not real

b) The same prefix can sometimes have more than one meaning. Match the prefixes in **bold** in sentences 1–6 to meanings a)–f).

1 The wires were tightly **inter**locked.
2 There has just been a **counter**-attack by the rebels.
3 I've heard that man is **super**-rich.
4 Lightning flashed **over**head as we walked.
5 Next, you have to draw a **semi**circle.
6 The ground was very wet **under**foot.

a) from above/on top/across
b) joined together
c) as a reaction to
d) half
e) below
f) extremely

c) Check in V5.1 p129.

5 **a)** Fill in the gaps with a prefix from **4a)** and **4b)**. There is sometimes more than one possible answer.

1 What kind of landscape would you like your bedroom to ....look?
2 Have you ever been ....charged for anything?
3 What do you use the ....net for?
4 Have you ever done something which turned out to be ....productive?
5 Do you prefer full cream, skimmed or ....-skimmed milk?
6 Who would you say was the greatest ....star of all time?

b) Work in pairs. Take turns to ask and answer the questions. Ask follow-up questions.

Listening and Grammar

 6 **a)** Work in pairs and look at the photo of 'extras' on a film set. What do you think their job is like? Think about these things.

1 their working hours
2 their pay
3 the kind of roles they get

b) R5.1 Listen to an interview with two extras and make notes under headings 1–3 in **6a)**. Then work in pairs and compare notes.

c) R5.2 Listen again to Daniel. What does he say about these things?

1 why he became an extra
2 what he does while he's waiting
3 seeing himself act
4 getting a slightly better part
5 becoming an actor himself

7 **a)** R5.3 Listen again to Kate. What does she say about these things?

1 why she became an extra
2 the people who become extras
3 what the stars are like
4 the negative things about the job
5 the positive things about the job

b) Work in pairs. Give reasons why you would or wouldn't like to be an extra. If you would, which films or television series would you most like to appear in?

Help with Grammar Reflexive pronouns (2)

See Preview, p45.

8 **a)** Match examples a)–c) to uses of reflexives 1–3.

a) Daniel, what makes people like **yourself** want to be an extra?
b) She read the script to **herself**.
c) I like the job **itself**, but …

1 after *like*, *as well as*, *as (for)*, etc. instead of object pronouns, although these are possible. This use of the reflexive can show politeness.
2 to emphasise a noun, pronoun or noun phrase
3 to make it clear that the object (after a preposition) refers to the same person/thing as the subject of the verb.

b) Which of these verbs are not used with a reflexive pronoun? Choose the correct answer.

1 … unless I really *concentrate/concentrate myself*.
2 It's a great opportunity to *meet/meet ourselves* and have a chat.
3 I thought it would be a way of supplementing my income and *enjoying/enjoying myself* at the same time.
4 You let the crew and principals *help/help themselves* first.
5 There are times when you *feel/feel yourself* very tired.

c) Check in G5.2 p130.

9 Tick the correct sentences. Then correct the mistakes.

1 Concentrate yourselves on what I'm saying.
2 I myself am not very interested in ballet but my daughter loves it.
3 I'm feeling myself a bit tired today.
4 I've brought a friend with myself.
5 Help yourself to any books you need.
6 As well as yourselves, there are lots of other people coming.
7 They're going to meet themselves outside the cinema.
8 She's watching television by herself.

Get ready … Get it right!

 10 Work in pairs. Student A → p110. Student B → p113. Follow the instructions.

Vocabulary verb + infinitive with *to* or verb+*ing* (2); verb-noun collocations
Review prefixes with multiple meanings

Reading and Vocabulary

1

a) How many very successful young people do you know/have you heard of? What have they done?

b) Read the title and introduction to the article, and look at the photos and captions. What factors do you think make some young people very successful?

2

a) Work in groups. Read an extract from the article *The Young Ones.*
Group A → p110.
Group B → p113.
Group C → p115.
Group D → p116.
Make notes on the answers to these questions for your young person.

1 When did he/she take up his/her interest? Was there a reason for it?
2 What exceptional personal qualities do you think he/she has?

b) Discuss the questions in **2a)** in your groups.

3 Work in groups of four, with one student from each group, A, B, C, and D. Tell each other about the people you read about and discuss your answers to the questions in **2**.

The Young Ones

From musicians to horse riders to campaigners to footballers, they are all young people who made an impact at a very early age. *Emma Hardy* interviews them about their success.

A

Theo Walcott. *Footballer, who became the most expensive 16-year-old professional and the youngest full England international of his time.*

B

Dizzee Rascal. *The first rapper and youngest person to win the Mercury Music Prize for his debut album in 2003 while still a teenager. He went on to have his own recording label.*

C

Sophie Christiansen. *European Paralympics horse-riding champion for dressage at the age of 16. Born with cerebral palsy, she did not walk unaided until she was nearly four.*

D

Iris Andrews. *Campaigned for the organisation Peace One Day while still at school. She went on to work for the organisation full-time.*

4 **a)** Read these sentences. Which of the four young people do they apply to, and why?

1 Without this focus to my life, I probably wouldn't have a job.
2 I used to be quite difficult to live with at times.
3 Sometimes I feel like an impostor.
4 I have learned a lot from the people I work with.
5 This work has helped me to cope with my personal problems.
6 I have had to make personal sacrifices to do this.
7 I often feel isolated from other people.
8 I feel I have changed my personality because of what I do.

b) Work in pairs. Discuss these questions.

1 Which of the four young people do you think is the most impressive? Give reasons.
2 What are the pros and cons of becoming successful at a young age?

Will

Claire

Help with Vocabulary
Verb + infinitive with *to* or verb+*ing* (2)

See Preview, p45.

5 **a)** Look at these pairs of sentences from the article and complete the explanations with verb + infinitive with *to* or verb+*ing*.

1 a) I never **forget** to sit with my head down and visualise myself scoring a goal.
   b) I'll never **forget** getting picked for the World Cup squad at only 16.

   forget + ... = looks back to memories of the past;
   forget + ... = refers to now or the future

2 a) The biggest thing has been learning just to **go on** doing it.
   b) Making beats **went on** to become my life,

   go on + ... = continue an action;
   go on + ... = begin a new action

3 a) Riding was just **meant** to make physiotherapy fun.
   b) … it **means** coordinating really well.

   mean + ... = involve/necessitate;
   mean + ... = intend

4 a) I **regret** to say that at school I was trouble.
   b) I will always **regret** losing them.

   regret + ... = be sorry for what's already happened;
   regret + ... (formal) = be sorry for what you're about to say

TIP! ● Verbs of the senses (*see*, *notice*, etc.) can be followed by:
a) object + verb+*ing* when describing a repeated action or an action in progress: *He noticed me playing*.
b) object + infinitive when describing a single action or a completed action: *I saw him get into the car*.

b) Check in V5.3 p129.

6 Choose the correct verb form.

1 I regret *telling/to tell* you that on this occasion your application has not been successful.
2 If I take the job, it will mean *to leave/leaving* home before 6 a.m.
3 I'll never forget *to meet/meeting* Jo for the first time.
4 After her best-selling novel she went on *to write/writing* two others, which weren't successful.
5 Sorry, I meant *locking/to lock* the door but I forgot.
6 The audience began to get very restless, but the lecturer went on *to talk/talking* regardless.
7 Don't forget *emailing/to email* when you get home.
8 She really regrets *shouting/to shout* at him.

7 **a)** Complete these sentences about yourself.

1 I really regret …
2 I'll never forget …
3 After this course I'm going to go on …
4 Next year I really mean …
5 I must remember …

b) Work in pairs. Take turns to say your sentences from **7a)**. Ask follow-up questions.

Charlie

Listening

- In the UK, young people either leave school at 16 after their GCSE (General Certificate of Secondary Education) exams, or stay on for another two years to do their A (Advanced) level exams at school or at a sixth-form college.

 8 **a)** [R5.4] Listen to an interview with Claire, Will and Charlie, three 18-year-olds who have taken their A levels. Answer these questions.

1 Who has taken a year off to plan his/her future?
2 Who has decided to do research into a range of different jobs?
3 Who changed his/her mind about which subject to do at university?

b) Listen again. Tick the true sentences.

1 a) Claire has really enjoyed all the different jobs she has been doing.
  b) She feels there is so much choice these days that it's difficult to make a decision.
2 a) Will thinks that his time in the sixth form was quite stressful.
  b) He has not yet decided what to do after his year off.
3 a) Charlie is still not sure she has chosen the right subject.
  b) She felt that English was not the right choice for her to study at university.

c) Do you think life for Claire, Will and Charlie is easier or harder than it was for your parents and grandparents? Is it more enjoyable? Give reasons.

Vocabulary Verb-noun collocations

 9 **a)** Which of these words/phrases collocate with *do*? Which collocate with *get*? Sometimes there is more than one possible answer. Check in [V5.4] p129.

> a ~~degree~~   good results   English
> a good education   work experience
> a place at university   a course
> an exam   research

do *a degree*

get

b) Which of these verbs also collocate with the words/phrases in **9a)**? Sometimes there is more than one possible answer. Check in [V5.4] p129.

> ~~go on~~   carry out   sit   enrol on   take   gain
> obtain   have   be awarded   achieve

go on *a course*

c) Work in pairs. Ask and answer questions using the verb-noun collocations in **9a)** and **9b)**.

> Have you been on any courses, other than English, in the last few years?

Get ready ... Get it right!

 10 If you were the Minister of Education in your country, how would you improve schools? Write six suggestions. Use these ideas or your own.

- The range of subjects which are offered
- The curriculum
- How subjects are taught
- Whether certain subjects should be compulsory or optional
- The system of exams and assessment
- Careers advice
- The standard of teacher training

11 **a)** Work in groups. Discuss your ideas. Agree on the best three.

> I think it would be great if music were made compulsory.

b) Tell the class your ideas. Which is most popular?

Vocabulary work expressions
Real World conversational strategies
Review verb + infinitive with *to* or verb+*ing*

QUICK REVIEW ●●●
Write one sentence with verb + infinitive with *to* and one sentence with verb+*ing* for these verbs: *go on; regret; mean; forget*. Work in pairs. Say your pairs of sentences: *He went on to talk about the weather. He went on talking about the weather.* What is the difference in meaning between your partner's two sentences?

1 a) Tick the phrases in **bold** you know. Check in V5.5 p130.

1 Have you ever been **stuck in a rut** or in a **dead-end** job?
2 Have you ever **taken on too much work** and been **snowed under**?
3 Do you know anyone who always **talks shop**?
4 Are you a good **team player** or would you prefer to **be self-employed**?
5 Which jobs can you think of that either pay **a pittance** or **a fortune**?
6 Would you prefer a **high-powered** or **run-of-the-mill** job?
7 Have you ever done any kind of **work experience** or **shadowed** anyone at work?
8 Do you like **deadlines** and working **against the clock**?
9 Are you **up to your eyes** in work at the moment or are you **taking it easy**?
10 How important is it for you to **climb the career ladder**?

b) Work in pairs. Take turns to ask and answer the questions in **1a)**. Ask follow-up questions.

2 a) Look at cartoons A–D and their captions. What social issues are they addressing? Do you have similar issues in your country?

b) Work in groups of three. Discuss topics a)–d). Talk about each topic for one or two minutes and try to come to some conclusions.

a) Is it fair that a company director earns much more than a cleaner?
b) How important is work to you or the people you know? Do you/they work to live or live to work?
c) Is there or should there be a legal minimum wage in your country? If there is one, do all employers keep to it?
d) Should employers be forced to make it easier for mothers to return to work?

3 R5.5 Listen to Josh, Tracey and Liz discussing jobs. Match extracts 1–3 to three of the topics in **2b)**. Which topic do they <u>not</u> discuss?

I'm afraid we'll have to make you all redundant so we can afford the director's £300,000 bonus!

Hey everyone, it's official. We work the longest hours in Europe.

Less than minimum wage – less than minimum clean.

They said no to a crèche, then.

4 a) R5.6 **Listen again to Extract 1. Then answer these questions.**

1 What do the first two speakers agree on?
2 What counter-argument does Liz mention?

b) R5.7 **Listen again to Extract 2. Which of these arguments for and against 'living to work' are <u>not</u> mentioned?**

a) a good income
b) illness
c) divorce
d) enjoying your job
e) promotion
f) early retirement

c) R5.8 **Listen again to Extract 3. Then answer these questions.**

1 Liz says, "What I do feel strongly about is that employers make provision for working mothers." What provisions?
2 Josh says, "Well, perhaps they would if it were more accepted." Who are 'they'? What would they do?
3 Tracey says, "The problem is people with no kids …" What's the problem?

Real World Conversational strategies

 5 a) Match conversational strategies a)– j) with phrases 1–10.

a) including someone in the conversation
b) adding something to the argument
c) stressing an important point

1 Not to mention …
2 That's exactly what I was trying to get at.
3 You look dubious, (Liz).

d) encouraging someone to continue
e) justifying what you say
f) getting the conversation back on track
g) saying you agree with someone

4 I'm with (you) on that.
5 All I'm saying is …
6 Carry on, (Liz). You were saying?
7 Anyway, (assuming you do want promotion) …

h) conceding someone is right
i) disagreeing politely
j) asking someone to say more about a topic

8 By (provision) you mean …?
9 You've got me there!
10 Oh, I don't know about (that).

b) Look at these sentences/phrases and match them to conversational strategies a)–j).

1 You're very quiet, (Josh). *a)*
2 That's precisely what I mean.
3 What I'm trying to say is …
4 What were you about/going to say (Tracey)?
5 Well, I can't disagree with that.
6 To get back to what (I) was saying about (promotion) …
7 I'd go along with that.
8 What do you mean when you say (provision)?
9 Actually, I'm not sure you can say (that).
10 And of course there's always …

c) Check in RW5.1 **p131.**

 6 a) Work in pairs. Change the words in bold in these conversations using one phrase from 5. You may need to change other parts of the sentence.

1
A Smoking is very expensive.
B **And also** it's a disgusting habit. *Not to mention it's a disgusting habit.*
A But I thought you just said you smoked for most of your life.
B That's true. **I admit it!**

2
A I think parents should try and leave some inheritance to their kids.
B **I disagree!** What about enjoying your money yourself in your old age!

3
A Becca's invited a few friends round for a sleepover tonight.
B **A few friends?** Two or twenty?

4
A I think the Prime Minister's foreign policy is misguided because …
B I agree. And what he plans to do with education is misguided, too.
A Yes, well, but **to go back to** his foreign policy, I think it's dangerous.

5
A It's a waste of time and money buying CDs these days because …
B Well, I think it's easier and cheaper just to download them.
A **That's what I meant.**

b) Role-play your conversations.

 7 a) Work in groups of three. Look at R5.5, p153. Choose one of the extracts and add at least eight more lines to end the conversation.

b) Practise the lines you added. Then act them out to the class. The class decides which extract the lines complete.

c) The class votes for the best ending for each extract.

 8 Work in groups of three. Choose an issue that's in the news at the moment. Have a discussion using some of the strategies in **5**.

1 **a)** Cross out the word that <u>doesn't</u> match the prefix. V5.1

1 **super** *woman/-rich/locked*
2 **semi** *action/-circle/-famous*
3 **counter** *balance/foot/-attack*
4 **inter** *action/locked/worked*
5 **over** *worked/-famous/head*
6 **under** *foot/balance/paid*

b) Work in pairs. Compare answers.

2 **a)** Tick the correct sentences. Correct the mistakes. G5.2

1 It's really important to concentrate yourself when driving.
2 He can't come himself, but he'll send a representative.
3 Shall we meet ourselves outside the cinema?
4 The event is open to people such as yourself.
5 Are you feeling yourself ill today?
6 Please feel free to help yourselves to food.
7 I think I'd better take a jumper with myself.
8 He didn't shave himself this morning. He went to the barber's.

b) Work in pairs. Compare answers.

3 Fill in the gaps with the correct verb form. V5.3

1 *to go/going*
  a) I'll never forget .... abroad for the first time.
  b) I'm always forgetting .... to the bank.
2 *to tell/telling*
  a) I regret .... you that I'm leaving the company.
  b) I regret .... my boss what I thought of him.

3 *to do/doing*
  a) Taking up the guitar means .... lots of practice.
  b) I've been meaning .... a computer course for ages
4 *to study/studying*
  a) In the future I'll probably go on .... a new subject such as business.
  b) At school I found it hard to go on .... maths, because I was hopeless at it.

4 **a)** Choose the correct words/phrases. There is sometimes more than one possible answer. V5.4

I left school after [1]*doing/sitting* my A level exams in three subjects and [2]*taking/getting* good results in all of them. I then decided to [3]*gain/get* some work experience before going on to university, so I went to work in a solicitor's office. The following year I [4]*got/achieved* a place at Edinburgh University, where I [5]*did/carried out* a degree course in psychology. After two years I gave psychology up and [6]*did/took* English instead, which I much preferred. After [7]*obtaining/getting* my degree, I then went on to [8]*do/gain* research on 16th-century English literature.

b) Work in pairs. Compare answers.

c) Take turns to tell your partner about your education. Ask follow-up questions.

5 **a)** Match sentence beginnings 1–7 to sentence endings a)–g). V5.5

1 My job could be described as **run-of-the-mill**, because *d)*
2 There are lots of **perks** with my job, even if I don't **earn a fortune** –
3 I'm **snowed under** at the moment –
4 I'm prepared to **work against the clock**,
5 I don't want to **earn a pittance** even if it means I can **take it easy** –
6 I've worked here for 20 years and feel **stuck in a rut** –
7 I'm not a **team-player**, really,

a) I've taken on too much work.
b) I get a company car, free lunches and gym membership.
c) I need to retrain and do a different kind of job.
d) I sit behind a desk doing undemanding work.
e) I don't mind **deadlines** as long as the job is **flexible**.
f) I'd prefer a **high-powered**, **well-paid** job.
g) I'd prefer to be **self-employed**.

b) Work in pairs. Choose four of the words/phrases in **bold** and talk about jobs you have done or would like to do.

Progress Portfolio

a) Tick the things you can do in English.

☐ I can recognise and use prefixes which have multiple meanings.

☐ I can take part in a discussion on education and express my ideas clearly.

☐ I can summarise a complex written text concisely.

☐ I can follow an extended informal monologue even when it's not clearly structured.

☐ I can use a range of conversational strategies appropriately.

b) What do you need to study again? ⦿ 5A–C .

Accurate Writing

CONNECTING WORDS: time (2)
SPELLING: *ie* or *ei*

1 Choose the correct connecting word. **AW5.1** p131.

1 When I saw Kay at the party that summer I *instantly/at once* fell for her.
2 *Previously/Before* this I'd only ever seen her in photographs.
3 I *immediately/straightaway* went up to her and introduced myself.
4 *Subsequent/After* that day, we were inseparable all through the summer.
5 However, the year *after/later* we had to go back to college in different parts of the country.
6 *Eventually/At the end*, we decided we would have to split up.
7 *Lately/Finally*, in the last month or so, we have begun seeing each other again.
8 *Up until/Prior* a month ago, we hadn't seen each other for 20 years.

2 Complete these words with *ie* or *ei*. **AW5.2** p131.

1 Did you rec _ _ ve a card from Jim on your birthday?
2 Have you met my n _ _ ghbour, Elsa?
3 It takes great pat _ _ nce to do that kind of work.
4 She doesn't have enough exper _ _ nce for that job.
5 The house is surrounded by f _ _ lds.
6 You must be very rel _ _ ved that he is back safely.
7 To ach _ _ ve good grades, you'll have to work hard.
8 She s _ _ zed the money and ran.
9 I like Hal, but he's a bit conc _ _ ted.
10 I will never forgive her for dec _ _ ving me.

3 **a)** Read the extract from a student's written work. Then correct the underlined words/phrases using connecting words of time.

b) Look at the words in **bold**. Correct the words which are spelled incorrectly.

Once I'd finished my GCSEs my parents suggested I got a part-time job to earn some money. My first job was on the checkouts in a supermarket in our **nieghbourhood**. I ¹at once hated it because it was so boring and I'm not very **pateint**. I was so **relieved** when it was over. But at least I knew I would not be going into that **feild** of work!

A year ²subsequent I gave out tickets at a theme park, which gave me **experience** of meeting people, but was very tiring.

³Lately I found a job I really enjoyed, which was as a tour guide in my local town. ⁴Previously then I hadn't really done anything useful, but I felt this was a real **acheivement**.

---

1 WAYS OF COMPARING

a) Complete these sentences using the prompts in brackets. **G6.1** p133.

1 Street surveys are *a great deal more successful than* telephone surveys. (**a great deal** / successful)
2 Interviewing people in the street is .... as I imagined. (**nowhere near** / scary)
3 However, it's .... in the winter, when the weather is bad. (**twice** / hard)
4 I've noticed that women are usually .... to stop than men. (**slightly** / willing)
5 But men are .... if you do interview them. (**just** / helpful)
6 One tip is to make sure the interview takes .... than three minutes. (**no** / long)
7 Over the years I've got .... at getting the information I need. (**considerably** / good)
8 But dealing with the paperwork is .... as doing the interviewing. (**almost** / difficult)

b) Which of the words/phrases in bold in 1a) are used to talk about: a) a big difference? b) a small difference c) no difference?

2 ADVERBS

Choose the correct words. **G6.3** p134.

1 Have you travelled anywhere interesting ~~late~~/*lately*?
2 Nowadays, people have to work really *hard/hardly* to earn a good living.
3 That pony can jump very *highly/high*.
4 We arrived at the meeting really *late/lately*.
5 Unfortunately, the story ended *unhappy/unhappily*.
6 It's amazing how *easy/easily* she got that work done.
7 He has settled in here really *well/good*.
8 It's *surprising/surprisingly* cold for this time of year.
9 Fortunately, she's feeling *fine/finely* now.

Listening and Vocabulary

5 a) Check the meanings of these words/phrases.

> crawl   a hedge   chicken wire
> glamorously   patrol   a stuffed toy
> a pebble   wind up

b) **R6.1** Listen to four friends talking about strange behaviour. Which story does the picture illustrate?

c) Listen again. Complete these summaries using one word.

1 a) Martina had to protect her .... from the rabbits.
  b) When the speaker first met Martina, the rabbits came out of her ....

2 a) Natalie talked about the man who always gets on at the .... end of the train.
  b) He always walks up and down, looking for the perfect ....

3 a) The couple on the train used to line up their .... at the window.
  b) The other passengers always .... them.

4 a) Keith thinks his little girl collects .... so that she and her friends can .... them.
  b) She prefers to wear .... socks.

d) Which of this behaviour did you find the quirkiest?

- Sometimes one word can have completely different meanings: *I commute on the **train** to work every day. She wants to **train** to be a psychologist.*
- Sometimes one word can have different meanings but the meanings are related: *The weather's **fine** today. I'm feeling **fine** now.*

6 a) Look at the words in **bold** in A. Match them to the definitions in B.

	A	B
1	She wanted to put on **odd** socks every day.	a) strange or unexpected
2	It was **odd** that he didn't phone.	b) not matching
3	His daughter is really **sweet**.	c) sugary
4	Dark chocolate isn't **sweet** enough for me.	d) charming, attractive
5	They hopped out of the **top** of her sweater.	e) the highest part
6	He's always **top** of the class.	f) the most successful

b) Match these general meanings to the pairs of words in **6a)**.

> the highest point or part in distance or quality *top*   unusual or peculiar
> pleasant

c) Look at these phrases. All the words in **bold** are related in meaning. What do you think is the general meaning of each group?

1 a **branch** of a tree; a **branch** of a bank; a **branch** of science
2 feel **flat**; a **flat** piece of land; this lemonade is **flat**
3 have a **break** for coffee; **break** a window; **break** the law
4 **plain** paper; **plain** food; a **plain** face
5 **heavy** traffic; a **heavy** coat; a **heavy** sleeper

d) Check in **V6.1** p132.

7 a) Fill in the gaps with words from **6a)** or **6c)**.

1 We had .... snow here at the weekend.
2 I find .... shoes much more comfortable than heels.
3 I'd prefer a .... carpet to a patterned one.
4 Where are you going for your summer .... ?
5 She has been made .... manager of a big insurance company.
6 The kitten was so .... that we had to buy it.

b) Work in pairs. Think of five more sentences using words from **6a)** and **6c)**.

Get ready ... Get it right!

8 Make notes on the unusual habits of four people you know. Use these ideas or your own.

- food   ● routines   ● superstitions   ● clothing   ● pets   ● travelling

9 a) Work in groups. Talk about the people in **8**. Ask follow-up questions.

> My brother always eats cereal without any milk on it.

b) Tell the class about the unusual behaviour your group discussed.

Vocabulary word pairs
Grammar position of adverbials
Review words with different but related meanings

QUICK REVIEW ●●●
Write two phrases for these words: *sweet; odd; plain; heavy; flat.* Work in pairs and compare your phrases: A *sweet coffee* B *a sweet smile*

Vocabulary Word pairs

1 a) Tick the phrases in **bold** that you know. Check new phrases in V6.2 p132.

1 A Do you watch much TV?
  B Not really. I can **take it or leave it**.

2 A Do you ever buy things online?
  B Yes, **on and off**.

3 A Do you think ad campaigns around at the moment are effective?
  B Some are, but some are a bit **hit and miss**.

4 A When you go to the supermarket, do you always choose the same brands?
  B No, I tend to **pick and choose**.

5 A What do you think can **make or break** an ad campaign?
  B You can't generalise. **Each and every** one is different.

6 A Do you think TV advertising is **part and parcel** of everyday life?
  B Sadly, yes. But I do get **sick and tired** of seeing the same ones **over and over again**.

7 A Can you think of a product which took off **in leaps and bounds**?
  B Yes, the iPod.

b) Work in pairs. How would you reply to A's questions in **1a)**?.

Listening

2 a) Look at adverts A and B. Do you know them? Do you like the design? Why?/Why not?

b) R6.2 R6.3 Listen to Graham and Lindsay, who have a background in advertising, talking about the adverts. What are their opinions?

c) Work in pairs. Compare answers. Do you agree with Graham and Lindsay? Why?/Why not?

Real life calls for real taste.
For the taste of your life Coca-Cola

It's the real thing. Coke.

(A)

(B)

3 a) R6.2 Listen to Graham again and choose the correct answers.

1 Graham *still works/used to work* in advertising.
2 What he liked about the Coca-Cola advert was *the design of the bottle/the effectiveness of the slogan*.
3 He thought the advert *should have mentioned/didn't need to mention* the name of the product.
4 He associated the word 'real' with *being ordinary/well-being*.
5 He points out that the slogan 'it's the real thing' *is/isn't* a common expression.

b) R6.3 Listen to Lindsay again and choose the correct answers.

1 Lindsay was impressed by the iPod advert because of its *visual effect/appeal to young people*.
2 She thinks iPod adverts are *informative/memorable*.
3 She thinks iPods are popular because they *make people look trendy/offer a convenient way of listening*.
4 She *has/would like* an iPod of her own.
5 She believes that other advertisers *will/won't* be influenced by the iPod campaign.

c) Work in pairs. Discuss these questions.

1 Would you ever consider a career in marketing or advertising? Why?/Why not?
2 If you were to go into advertising, would you prefer to be a copywriter or a designer?
3 Are young people in your country very image-conscious? What are the 'must-have' products or brands at the moment?

Vocabulary dramatic verbs
Skills Reading: a short story extract;
Listening: someone talking about
writing and reading short stories; a
short story extract; Speaking and
Writing: telling a story
Real World telling a story
Review word pairs

QUICK REVIEW ● ● ●
Work in pairs. Take turns to say the last part of these word pairs
with *and/or*: *make*; *hit*; *leaps*; *off*; *take it*; *pick*; *each*; *part*; *over*.
A *make or*. B *make or break*.

1 **a)** Work in groups. Do you read or listen to short
stories? If so, what genres (crime, sci-fi, etc.) do you
like or dislike?

b) Read this blog extract. What kind of story do you
think will work well on the radio?

> ▍ **SHORT STORY RADIO** is seeking short stories to be
> professionally recorded and broadcast. Over 70,000
> visitors, including English-language students from
> around the world, have visited our website.
>
> > • Submissions must be in English.
> > • We don't pay for your stories, but we do arrange
> >   for them to be recorded by professional actors.
> > • Stories must be fictional and work well on radio.

2 **a)** R6.4 John McRae is a professor of literature, an
actor and a writer. Listen to him talking about what
makes a good story and answer these questions.

1 What are the three things a story
  has to have?
2 What examples does he give of
  what a story can be?
3 What does he say a radio story has
  to do at the very beginning?

b) Listen again to John talking about the components of
a short story. Fill in these gaps with one word.

1 The .... sets the story in its situation and context.
2 The .... is when another character is introduced.
3 The .... occurs when something else happens and
  the story gets more interesting.
4 The .... happens at the end, when the situation
  gets sorted out.

3 **a)** Read the first part of this story. What genre is it?
How is the story organised? What are the premise and
development so far?

b) Write a summary of the story in as few words as you
can. Compare your summary with another student.

c) Is the story told in a formal or informal style? Give
examples.

4 Work in groups. What do you think is going to
happen next (the complication)? What do you think
the resolution is going to be?

5 **a)** R6.5 Listen to the end of the story. What
happened? Did you have a similar ending?

b) Tick the true sentences. Correct the false ones.

1 James had been deceived by Kirsti.
2 James had to stay and listen to the presentation.
3 Kirsti threatened to expose James as a liar.
4 James didn't care about impressing his friends.
5 Kirsti got her own way in the end.
6 James's comment at the end implies he felt the
  experience wasn't worth it.

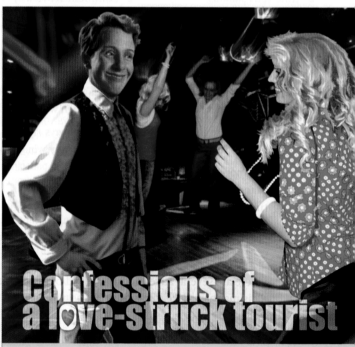

**Confessions of
a love-struck tourist**

**The prettiest girl in town only had eyes
for the luckless James Robbins. Why?**

It was 1982. Tight Fit had just spent three weeks at No. 1
with 'The Lion Sleeps Tonight', and me and my mates were 19
and on holiday. We sunbathed till we burnt, we danced till we
dropped, but there was a distinct lack of excitement.

Then my luck changed. We were in a club and I'd just left the
dance floor when an out-of-this-world beautiful girl smiled at

6 **a)** These verbs are used for dramatic effect. Check their meaning in p133. Then complete sentences 1–7 with the correct form of one of the verbs.

> ~~cajole~~ leap up grab storm out
> nudge hiss drag

1 Kirsti tried to _cajole_ James into staying for the presentation.
2 James .... of the room when he realised it was a time-share presentation.
3 James .... in alarm as Kirsti came up to their table.
4 Kirsti .... to James that they were going to the bank.
5 Kirsti .... James so that she could give him a kiss.
6 Kirsti .... James out of the club to get the money.
7 Mike .... James to warn him that Kirsti was coming.

b) Work in pairs. Put the sentences in the order they happened. Give more information about each sentence.

me. I thought she must be looking at someone behind me. Then she smiled again and beckoned to me. I cringe to recall how I literally pointed to myself and mouthed "Me?" She laughed and nodded. My stomach somersaulted.

"See you later, lads," I whispered to my mates. "Yours truly has other fish to fry."

I knew they'd look to see where I was going, but resisted the urge to turn round and gloat when I reached Kirsti. I led her over to a quiet corner of the club and we chatted. I kept talking too quickly and saying stupid things. Kirsti didn't seem to notice, though. She seemed to be hanging on my every word. After the most blissful 45 minutes, Kirsti had to go. I was just plucking up the courage to ask to see her again when she suggested meeting up for a bite to eat the following evening. A local restaurant at 8 p.m.? "Don't be a single minute late," she pouted. As if! I was outside the restaurant on the dot of eight. A big burly man eyed me.

Adapted from *The Times* 02/05/04

7 **a)** R6.6 Listen to John McRae's tips for involving a listener. Fill in the gaps in these notes.

- pauses, _rhythm_ and stress
- range of lively words (e.g. .... , adjectives, ...)
- vary the .... and the ....
- build up the .... (perhaps make it more scary or hold something back)
- .... of voice as you tell the story
- give it a flow to make sure the listener enjoys it

b) What do you think *a twist in the tail* means?

8 **a)** Think of a story that you would like to tell. Remember, a story can also be an anecdote or a joke. Use these ideas or your own.

- an embarrassing/amusing situation you've been in
- a meeting or relationship that changed your life
- a wonderful or disastrous holiday
- a party or celebration you've attended
- a memory from your childhood

b) Plan your story, using John McRae's tips from **7a)**. Make notes, but don't write the whole story.

Real World Telling a story

- We can use these techniques to add interest to a story.

Short, dramatic sentences	It was 1982. Then my luck changed.
A range of verb forms	It took me a full ten minutes to realise where I was. Me at a time share presentation? Do I really look the sort of person who would buy a share in a holiday home?
Descriptive language	My stomach somersaulted.
A mixture of direct and indirect speech	I protested, but she frowned, shooing me along. "There's no time."
Idiomatic language	A big burly man eyed me.
A personal comment at the end	Time-share scams are a thing of the past these days ... a bit of a shame, really.

c) Work in pairs. Take turns to practise telling your stories.

d) Work in groups and tell your stories. Is there one you all prefer?

Writing Extension

9 **a)** Write your story as if you were going to submit it to shortstoryradio.com.

b) Read other students' stories.

R6.7 Look at the song *Chasing Cars* on p107. Follow the instructions.

Help with Grammar Conditionals: non-basic forms

See **Preview**, p65.

● We can use a variety of verb forms in conditional sentences, not only those used in the four 'basic' conditionals.

5 a) Look at sentences 1–4. Find a variation of a zero conditional, a first conditional, a second conditional and a third conditional.

1 If you're going to commit a burglary, you'll have to be careful what you wear. *first conditional*
2 One burglar would have got away with it completely if he hadn't been sweating.
3 If I were committing a burglary, I'd be better off wearing gloves.
4 If a person doesn't want to leave forensic evidence, they should just slide through a window.

MIXED CONDITIONALS

b) Compare these pairs of sentences. Then answer questions i)–iv).

1 a) If the kidnapper **hadn't licked** that envelope, he **wouldn't be** in prison now.
  b) If the kidnapper **hadn't licked** that envelope, he **wouldn't have gone** to prison.
2 a) If they **weren't** such good actors, most of them **would have been found out** much earlier.
  b) If they **hadn't been** such good actors, most of them **would have been found out** much earlier.

i) Are all the sentences referring to real or imaginary situations?
ii) Is each clause referring to past or present time?
iii) Which sentences are 'mixed' conditionals? Why are they called that?
iv) What is the difference in meaning between the 'basic' and 'mixed' conditional sentences in each pair?

c) Check in G7.2 p137.

6 Choose the correct verb form in these conditional sentences. Sometimes both are possible.

1 They wouldn't have caught the burglar if he hadn't *dropped/been dropping* his wallet.
2 If the police *were hoping/hoped* to make an arrest they would need to do it now.
3 If you're *going to borrow/ borrowing* the car, can you remember to get insurance?
4 If you*'re making/'ll make* those cakes, you need a special kind of flour.
5 You must let me know if you*'ll/'re going to* need a lift.
6 If I'd known what *was going to/would* happen, I might have changed my plans.

7 a) Change these sentences, using mixed conditional forms.

1 I've only got this car because I took out a huge bank loan.
If I hadn't taken out a huge bank loan, I wouldn't have this car.
2 We missed a lesson, which is why we don't understand what the teacher's saying.
3 I only agreed to go to the club because Fred works there.
4 I twisted my ankle, so Tim is playing in the tennis tournament today instead of me.
5 My brother loves working with young people, which is why he became a teacher.
6 Jess is really lazy and so she has still not finished her coursework.
7 You didn't take my advice, which is why we're now so late!

b) Work in pairs. Discuss these questions. Ask follow-up questions.

1 If you could have the last few years of your life over again, what would you have done differently?
2 If you could choose, what special talent would you like to have been born with?
3 If you were able to go back in a time machine, which period of history would you have liked to live in?

Get ready ... Get it right!

8 Work in pairs. What are the advantages and disadvantages of open and closed prisons? Use these ideas or your own.

Open prisons try to educate people not to re-offend but they can be difficult and expensive to run.

Closed prisons are often popular with the general public because it's felt that prisoners should be severely punished for their crimes, but they don't help to change prisoners' behaviour.

9 Work in groups. Group A → p108. Group B → p111. Follow the instructions.

Vocabulary phrasal nouns
Grammar impersonal report
structures
Review mixed conditionals

Ⓐ **Tax exemptions to discourage marriage break-ups**

Ⓑ **PUBLIC OUTCRY OVER FURTHER SMOKING BANS**

Ⓒ **Setbacks** in plans to charge households for rubbish

Ⓓ **Onset** of obesity in childhood common, warn doctors

Listening and Vocabulary

1 **a)** Look at the newspaper headlines. Check the meaning of any new words. Have any of these topics been an issue in your country?

b) R7.3 Listen to Stefano from Italy, Hiltrud from Germany and Justyna from Poland giving their opinions about how much the state should intervene in people's lives. Which topic from the headlines is <u>not</u> discussed?

c) Listen again. In which areas do the speakers feel that state intervention is/isn't justified? Why?

2 Work in pairs. Discuss whether the government should get involved in matters such as these:

1 smoking in public places
2 environmental issues
3 relationships and marriage
4 the food people eat

Help with Vocabulary Phrasal nouns

● Phrasal nouns are compound nouns formed from verbs and a particle (a preposition or adverb).

3 **a)** Look at the phrasal nouns in **red** in headlines A–D. What verbs and particles are they made up of?

TIPS! ● When phrasal nouns begin with a particle, they have no hyphen (*outlook, downpour, input*). When phrasal nouns begin with a verb, they may or may not have a hyphen (*kick-off, breakdown, get-together*).

● Not all phrasal verbs can be made into phrasal nouns: *They pulled down two houses.* not ~~There was a pulldown of two houses~~.

● Some phrasal nouns are made up of the same words as phrasal verbs, but have different meanings: *The **intake** (enrolment) on that course was over 100. He spoke so fast I couldn't **take** it **in** (understand and remember)*

b) Look again at the phrasal nouns in headlines A–D. Which phrasal nouns reverse the order of the verb and the particle? Which ones can't be made into a phrasal verb with the same meaning?

c) Which phrasal nouns in headlines A–D are countable?

d) Check in V7.2 p136.

4 Match the phrasal nouns in **bold** to these words/phrases.

> heavy rain   beginning of the football match
> contribution   number of people who are accepted
> forecast   informal gathering   delay caused by a problem

1 **Kick-off** at Wembley will be at 3 p.m.
2 There has been a **setback** in plans to ban junk food from schools.
3 The **outlook** for the weekend is for yet more rain.
4 Your **input** to that meeting was much appreciated.
5 We sheltered under trees during the **downpours**.
6 My parents are having a **get-together** with friends.
7 The university has restricted its **intake** to those with good grades.

7C Not guilty!

Vocabulary metaphors
Real World functions and intonation of questions
Review phrasal nouns

QUICK REVIEW ●●●

Write sentences using phrasal nouns made from these phrasal verbs: *pour down; break down; set back; get together*. Work in pairs. Take turns to say your sentences: *The match was cancelled after a heavy downpour.*

1 a) Look at these pairs of sentences. Which words/phrases in bold have a literal meaning (L)? Which have a non-literal meaning (NL)? What are the non-literal meanings? Check in V7.3 p136.

1 a) I **grilled** the meat for five minutes. *L*
   b) The police **grilled** him for hours about what he'd done that night. *NL questioned*

2 a) We got a **warm** welcome from my cousin.
   b) The pizza wasn't **warm** enough so I put it in the microwave.

3 a) The forecast warns a severe **storm** is on its way.
   b) The police **stormed** the building and rescued the hostages.

4 a) The market is **flooded** with cheap, plastic goods.
   b) If it rains any more, the roads will soon be **flooded**.

5 a) It was such a **bright** day I needed my sunglasses.
   b) He's a really **bright** lad – I can't believe he'd turn to crime.

6 a) I have to get up at **dawn** to drive to work.
   b) It suddenly **dawned** on the inspector who the suspect might be.

7 a) When I saw the burglar, I **froze** and couldn't move.
   b) It was so cold that the lake **froze**.

8 a) My parents **flew** to Brazil last week.
   b) The crime novel was so exciting, the time **flew**.

9 a) Vicky is a good choice for the job because she doesn't **crack** under pressure.
   b) I suddenly noticed the large **crack** in the ceiling.

b) Write five sentences about your life. Use metaphors from **1a)**.

c) Work in pairs. Take turns to say your sentences. Ask follow-up questions.

2 a) Look at the picture. What is happening?

b) R7.4 Listen to this extract from a play. Why is Mike a suspect? What crime is he alleged to have committed?

c) Listen again. Fill in the gaps with one or two words.

1 Emma is Mike's _____ .
2 The police think that Mike is using Emma as an _____ .
3 George usually goes out at about _____ past _____ on Friday evenings.
4 George had hidden _____ pounds in the flat.
5 George works as a _____ .
6 George hid the money under the _____ .
7 Mike left Emma's house to get a _____ .
8 He was seen by his _____ at about 8.20.
9 Mike told the police he watched a _____ on TV when he got back.
10 Mike hasn't got much money because he's _____ .

d) Do you think Mike is guilty? Why?/Why not?

3 What do these phrases from the extract mean?

1 it all **strikes me as** very odd
2 living right **on your doorstep**
3 we're not **joined at the hip**
4 we **weren't born yesterday**
5 **I lost track of** what was happening
6 must have **hit you hard,** losing your job

Real World Functions and intonation of questions

● Intonation patterns in English are varied and complicated. However, the following guidelines may be helpful.

4 a) R7.5 Listen to questions 1–5. Which questions are asking for new information (N)? Which are checking information (C)?

1 What does?

2 Isn't this about the time George usually goes out?

3 How much?

4 So, you went on your own, did you?

5 How come?

b) Listen to the questions again and choose the correct answers.

We often use:
1 a *rising/falling* tone when asking questions to find out new information.
2 a *rising/falling* tone when checking information we think is right.
3 a *rising/falling* tone in question tags when we expect the listener to confirm that we are right.

TIP! ● We sometimes have different reasons for asking questions, other than requesting new or checking old information. Sometimes no reply is expected and a falling intonation is used.

c) R7.6 Listen to questions 1–4 and match them to functions a)–d).

1 Could we just go over this one more time?
2 How should I know? / So what?
3 Isn't that a coincidence?
4 He never stays in on a Friday evening, does he?

a) giving instructions
b) a rhetorical question (expecting agreement)
c) aggressive/defensive response to a question
d) making a sarcastic comment

d) Check in RW7.1 p139.

---

5 a) R7.7 Listen to these questions. Which one is requesting new information?

1 A I haven't got any money on me!
  B Isn't that a surprise!?
2 A So we're meeting at 9, are we?
  B Yes. Sorry, I've forgotten already. Where are we meeting?
3 A Could you put everything in the dishwasher, please?
  B Why should I always do it?
4 A Thank goodness it's arrived at last!
  B What has?
5 A I heard from Terri last night.
  B Oh, so she finally decided to phone, did she?
6 A I believe 200 people are coming to the wedding.
  B Are you sure?
7 A I need some money.
  B Oh you do, do you?

b) Look at R7.7, p156. Listen again and notice the sentence stress and intonation.

c) Work in pairs. Listen again and practise reading the exchanges.

6 Work in pairs. Student A, follow the instructions below. Student B → p115.

1 **Student A** Work on your own. You are a police officer. You are going to interview Emma to see if her story contradicts Mike's. Think of questions using a variety of question types, including question tags. Find out:

● if Emma had been expecting Mike to go round that evening
● whether his behaviour seemed normal
● why she didn't go out with him to have a pizza
● how long he took to get back with his pizza
● what they did when he got back
● when he left to go home
● where he got his phone from.

2 Work with your partner. Ask Emma the questions above and any of your own. Make notes. Does anything Emma says contradict Mike's story?

3 Work in groups of four. Have you changed your mind about whether Mike is guilty or not? Discuss the evidence.

8 What's stopping you?

8A Finding time

Vocabulary phrases with *time*
Grammar past verb forms with present or future meaning
Review metaphors

QUICK REVIEW ●●●
Choose four of these words: *bright; flood; fly; freeze; storm; warm*. Write one sentence for each word with its literal meaning and one sentence with its metaphorical meaning. Work in pairs and compare sentences.

Vocabulary Phrases with *time*

a) Tick the phrases in **bold** that you know. Check new phrases in V8.1 p140.

1 If I **have time to kill** at an airport, I usually read a book.
2 I like to get to class **in plenty of time**.
3 I always **take my time** when I do homework.
4 I usually **have** very little **time to spare** in the morning.
5 **For the time being**, I'm happy doing what I'm doing.
6 **It's only a matter of time** before I change my job/course.
7 I believe in the saying '**there's no time like the present**'.
8 **I've got no time for** people who don't care about climate change.
9 It's difficult for me to **find time** to get involved in environmental issues.
10 I **give people a hard time** when they don't recycle things.

b) Tick the sentences that are true for you. Change the other sentences so that they are true for you.

c) Work in pairs. Take turns to say your sentences.

Reading and Grammar

a) Make a list of people who have had a profound effect on the world, either for good or for bad.

b) Work in pairs. Compare lists and choose two people who you think have had the greatest effect.

c) Tell the class who you chose and why.

d) Read an interview with Eddy Canfor-Dumas, an author, TV scriptwriter, peace activist and candidate for the Green Party. Match the interviewer's questions, a)–c) to sections 1–3 of the article.

a) Do you believe that one person can really make a difference?
b) What have you done on a personal level to address the issue of climate change?
c) You have recently become seriously involved in green issues. How did this come about?

One person can make a difference ...

Eddy Canfor-Dumas, television's favourite 'disaster' drama scriptwriter, has recently added politics to his 'to do' list. Irene Core asks why.

1 _____ ?

In 2003 I was working on a BBC 'disaster' drama, *Supervolcano*, about the fictional eruption of Yellowstone National Park in the USA. To help my research I spoke to a scientist who had just written a book about all the ways the world might end. Top of the list was global warming, created by man-made CO_2 emissions. But, he said, one of the worst offenders, the USA, would not start to change until a series of devastating hurricanes hit its Gulf and east coasts.

Two years later I was working on another disaster project, *Superstorm*, about the effect of global warming on hurricanes in the Atlantic, and visited the National Center for Atmospheric Research in Boulder, Colorado. At the time, a number of violent hurricanes were hitting the Gulf and east coasts of the USA, notably Katrina, that wrecked New Orleans, so I asked the head of NCAR two questions: is global warming a reality, and is it man-made? He looked at me as if I was mad. How could anyone still be asking such basic questions? He gave me a short tutorial on climate science, and after further discussions with other scientists I came home convinced that this was a real and very serious problem.

It's time we all accepted the fact that everyone can make a difference.

2 _____ ?

Well, I realised I had to be more than just a 'direct-debit environmentalist', paying a small sum of money each month to Friends of the Earth to ease my conscience. So I employed someone to do an eco*-audit on my house to see how my

3 Read the interview again. Find answers to these questions.

1 Why did Eddy go to America in 2003? *work on a BBC dist*
2 Why do you think the head of NCAR was surprised by Eddy's questions?
3 Why was Eddy's conversation with the scientist so significant?
4 In what ways did Eddy become more than just a 'direct-debit environmentalist'?
5 Why does Eddy mention people like Gandhi and Nelson Mandela?

4 Work in pairs. Discuss these questions.

1 Look at this saying: *If not you, who? If not now, when?* What do you think it means?
2 What do you think is involved in having an eco-audit done on your home?
3 How 'green' do you think your lifestyle is? How could you and your home be 'greener'?
4 What could every person immediately do to fight climate change?

> **Help with Grammar** Past verb forms with present or future meaning
>
> See **Preview**, p75. *invironmentally = friendly*
>
> ● Past verb forms do not always refer to past time.

5 a) Compare these pairs of sentences. Then answer the questions.

1 a) **It's** time to accept the fact that everyone can make a difference.
 b) It's time **we** (all) accepted the fact that everyone can make a difference. *would*
2 a) **I'd** sooner do one of the jobs.
 b) I'd sooner **someone** else was doing one of the jobs. *informal Perter*
3 a) **I'd** prefer to get directly involved.
 b) I'd prefer it if a lot more **people** got directly involved.
4 a) **I'd** rather look at the small things I could do.
 b) I'd rather **people** looked at the small things they could do.

i) Do any of the sentences refer to past time?
ii) Do all the sentences tell us what the speaker would like to happen?

b) Look again at the sentences in **5a)**. Which verbs (**pink** or **blue**) are infinitive verb forms? Which are either Past Simple or Past Continuous?

c) Look at the subjects in **bold** in the sentences in **5a)**. Then choose the correct words in the rule.

● When *it's time, would sooner, would rather,* and *would prefer it if* are followed by a subject + verb, we use *an infinitive/a past* verb form.

TIP! ● We can also say *it's about time ...* or *it's high time ...* to suggest something is urgent: *It's high time we realised we can't keep using up the earth's resources like this.*

d) Check in G8.2 p141.

environmentally friendly

family could become greener, and went along to a meeting of my local Green Party. I left the meeting as the candidate for my area in the upcoming local government elections and the election organiser for a much bigger area!

For the time being I'm OK about doing both jobs but I admit it's hard trying to fit everything in, so obviously I'd sooner someone else was doing one of the jobs. In fact, I would prefer it if a lot more people got directly involved. But I'm confident that this will happen as people see that we cannot continue to live as though the planet had unlimited resources and an unlimited capacity to absorb the effects of ever-greater consumption.

3 _____ *a* _____ ?

There is an ancient Japanese saying, 'One is the mother of ten thousand.' Everything begins with the individual. One person changes and sets off a change in another person, and so it goes on, even if it takes a great deal of time. If the change in the individual is profound and focused on relieving or preventing suffering, the change he or she sets off in others will be all the greater and far-reaching. Look at the great religious teachers in history or people from more modern times such as Gandhi and Nelson Mandela.

Of course, we don't need to think in such grand terms. In fact, I'd rather people looked at the small things they could do, bit by bit, right on their doorstep. Otherwise they get put off by thinking they have to change the world. And that will happen anyway, if we all do our bit and perhaps just a little more.

just inside the door.

*eco = connected to the environment

6 Make sentences with these words. Sometimes more than one answer is possible.

1 I / prefer it if / we / meet / at the cinema.
2 I / sooner / David / do / the clearing up.
3 It / time / have / a break.
4 We / prefer / go / on Tuesday.
5 I / rather / you / not smoke / in here.
6 It / about time / Pete / admit / he was wrong.

7 **a)** Tick the correct sentences. Then correct the mistakes. Sometimes there is more than one possible answer.

1 I'd rather people don't drop litter in the streets.
2 I'd sooner travel by train than by bus.
3 I'd prefer more people were environmentally conscious.
4 It's high time people stop using cars in cities.
5 I'd rather my family spend more time together.
6 I'd prefer it if people don't use their mobiles on public transport.
7 It's time I had a holiday.
8 I'd prefer I live nearer to the coast.

b) Work in pairs. Compare answers.

c) Take turns to say which sentences are true for you. Ask follow-up questions.

Listening and Speaking

8 **a)** Check the meaning of these words.

| soot   scrub   an incinerator   federal law |

b) **R8.1** Listen to Eddy talking about Hazel Henderson, an ordinary woman who has made a significant difference to the world. Choose the correct answer in these sentences.

1 All the children who played in the local park in New York were *dirty/ill*.
2 Hazel succeeded in getting *better playgrounds in parks/levels of air pollution made public*.
3 Hazel is now an advisor to *the President of the USA/governments all round the world*.

c) Work in groups of three. You are each going to summarise part of Hazel Henderson's story. Student A, look at list 1. Student B, look at list 2. Student C, look at list 3. Which of the items from your list could you already talk about?

1 Bristol, school, qualifications, jobs, New York, an American man, child
2 local playground, soot, pollution, other mothers and children
3 in New York, the quality of the air, ABC news network, weather forecasts

d) Listen again. Make notes on your section of the story.

e) Think about how to summarise your part of the story using the prompts from **8c)** and your notes.

f) In the same groups of three, take turns to read out your summary. Do you think you have covered all the main points?

Get ready ... Get it right!

9 **a)** Imagine you could spend an evening with three famous people that you think have made a difference to the world, positively or negatively. They can be from the present or the past. Which three people would you choose and why?

b) Write one question you would like to ask each of your guests.

10 **a)** Work in pairs. Say who you chose and what questions you would ask. What topics of conversation might your questions inspire?

b) Agree on the three most interesting guests.

I'd like to invite Jimi Hendrix.

Oh, I'd rather we invited John Lennon. His music had a great influence on the world.

c) Tell the class who your three guests are and the topics of conversation that are likely to come up.

d) Which group would you like to join for the evening? Why?

8B Fear!

Vocabulary *wherever, whoever, whatever*, etc. ;
word building (2): suffixes
Review past verb forms with present or future meaning

QUICK REVIEW ●●●

Use four of these prompts to write true and false sentences about yourself: *Most of my friends prefer* … ; *I'd prefer it if my friends* … ; *I'd sooner* … ; *I'd rather I didn't have to* … ; *I think it's time to* … ; *It's about time I* … . Work in pairs. Take turns to say your sentences. Guess if your partner's sentences are true or false.

Listening and Vocabulary

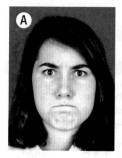  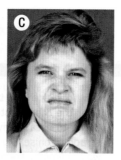 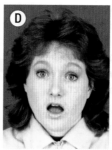 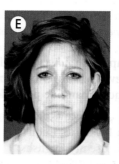 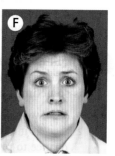

1 **a)** Work in pairs. Discuss these questions.

1 Do you agree on which photos, A–F, illustrate each of these emotions: anger; disgust; fear; joy; sadness; surprise?
2 Do you think all cultures experience the same basic emotions?
3 How do you think basic emotions helped our ancestors to stay alive?
4 What other emotions are there besides the basic ones?

b) **R8.2** Listen to a radio programme about emotions. Check your answers to questions 2–4 in 1a).

c) Listen again. Read these quotes from the radio programme and answer the questions.

1 "**Whoever** said that is wrong." Said what?
2 "**Wherever** this experiment was carried out, the results were the same." What experiment?
3 "**Whoever** saw the photos identified the same emotions." Which emotions?
4 "**Whenever** you do this in private … it's unlikely to cause embarrassment." Do what?
5 "That's the difference between higher and basic emotions." What is the difference?

d) Work in groups. Discuss whether this statement is true or not. Consider things such as sports, food, dress, attitude to relationships, attitude to animals, privacy, etc.

Things that might make people from one culture proud, embarrassed, guilty, angry, sad, disgusted, happy, etc. might not trigger the same emotion in people from another culture.

Help with Vocabulary *wherever, whoever, whatever*, etc.

2 **a)** Read the rule. Then match the words in **bold** in sentences 1–4 in 1c) to meanings a) or b).

- When we add *ever* to question words (*wherever, whoever, whenever, whatever, whichever, however*) it usually has one of these meanings:

  a) It doesn't matter where, who, when, etc. It can be any place, anyone, any time.
  Start the experiment whenever you want to.
  (it doesn't matter when you start)
  Give the results to whoever wants them.
  (anyone who wants them)
  b) An unknown place, person, time, etc.
  Whoever wrote this report did a fantastic job.
  (I don't know who the person was)

TIPS! ● *Whenever* can also mean 'every time':
***Whenever** she calls, I'm out.* (= every time she calls, I'm out.)

● *Whoever, whichever* and *whatever* can be the subject or the object of the verb: ***Whoever** saw you* … (subject) ***Whoever** you saw* … (object)

b) Check in **V8.2** p140.

8C The pros and cons

Vocabulary idiomatic phrases
Skills Reading: a modern poem;
Listening: people discussing whether
it's better to be a man or a woman;
Speaking: class survey about gender;
Writing: summarising a class survey
Real World explaining choices
Review *wherever, whoever,
whatever,* etc.

QUICK REVIEW ● ● ●

Complete these sentences about yourself: *Whenever I go to …* ;
Whenever I see … ; *Whenever I try to …* ; *Whatever I do to …* ; *Whoever says …* ;
It seems that however … . Work in pairs. Take turns to tell each other your
sentences. Ask follow-up questions.

a) Work in groups (of the same sex if
possible). Make a list of reasons why
you think it's easier and reasons why
you think it's harder to be a member
of the opposite sex in your country.
Use these ideas or your own.

● jobs
● relationships
● physical strength
● emotions
● appearance
● society's expectations of and attitude
  towards men and women

b) Tell the class your group's
conclusions. Do you agree with what
the other groups said?

c) Are there any points that the whole
class agrees on?

a) R8.3 Read and listen to Sophie
Hannah's poem about a problem she's
experiencing. Then answer the
questions.

1 What is her indecision about?
2 Why is the poem called *The Pros and
  Cons*? .
3 How many pros and how many cons
  does she mention? There may be
  different interpretations.

b) Read the poem again. Match
meanings a)–g) to verses 1–7.

Phoning him means:
a) I'll embarrass myself because I'll seem
   overkeen. *7*
b) he might think I'm too enthusiastic
   and I might put him off.
c) he'll think I'm a nice person.
d) he'll know that I'm keen to see him
   again.
e) I won't be wasting time wondering if
   he's going to phone me or not.
f) it's OK because it shouldn't matter
   who approaches who.
g) it'll be less embarrassing for him in
   front of his colleagues.

The Pros and Cons

1   He'll be pleased if I phone to ask him how he is.
    It will make me look considerate and he likes considerate people.

2   He'll be reassured to see that I haven't lost interest,
    Which might make him happy and then I'll have done him a favour.

3   If I phone him right now I'll get to speak to him sooner
    than I will if I sit around waiting for him to phone me.

4   He might not want to phone me from work in case someone hears
    him and begins (or continues) to suspect that there's something
    between us.

5   If I want to and don't, aren't I being a bit immature?
    We're both adults. Does it matter, with adults, who makes the
    first move?

6   But there's always the chance he'll back off if I come on too strong
    The less keen I appear, the more keen he's likely to be,

7   and I phoned him twice on Thursday and once on Friday.
    He must therefore be fully aware that it's his turn, not mine.

8   If I make it too easy for him he'll assume I'm too easy,
    while if I make no effort, that leaves him with more of a challenge.

9   I should demonstrate that I have a sense of proportion.
    His work must come first for a while and I shouldn't mind waiting

10 For all I know he could have gone off me already
    and if I don't phone I can always say, later, that I went off him first.

c) Match meanings h)–j) to verses 8–10.

Not phoning him means:
h) I can pretend I rejected him first if it turns out he doesn't want to see me.
i) it's probably better because men are hunters; they like the chase.
j) he'll know I understand that I can't be the most important thing in
   his life.

To phone or not to phone, that is the question.

 a) Listen again. Work in groups A and B. Group A make notes on the answers Em, Mick and Joey give. Group B make notes on the answers Bob, Kay and Dan give.

b) Work in pairs with a student from the other group. Compare notes.

 a) You are going to interview students in the class using the questions in **4a)**. Do you think the results of the class survey will be similar to **4b)**?

b) Interview as many students as you can in five minutes. Make notes on the answers.

Real World Explaining choices

- There's no way I'd want to be a … .
- I can't imagine what it would be like to be a … .
- I'd choose to be a … because I think they have more opportunities to … .
- Even though I think … have an easier time of it, I'd still choose to be … .
- I'd be quite curious to find out what it's like to be a … but I don't think I'd enjoy it.
- Whatever you think about women/men, they definitely … .
- Whereas/while women … , men … .

---

c) Work in pairs. Compare notes and then answer these questions.

1 Did anyone feel their gender had stopped them doing what they wanted to do? If so, how?
2 What reasons did students give for wanting to be a man or a woman?
3 Did any answers surprise you?
4 Were your survey results similar to those in **4b)**?

Writing Extension

 Write a report on the results of your survey. Use these guidelines.

a) Explain what the survey is about.
b) Give details about the people you interviewed, number of male and female, age range, etc.
c) Give the results of your survey.
d) Give your conclusions.

 R8.5 Look at the song *You Gotta Be* on p107. Follow the instructions.

---

3 **a)** Match these phrases from the poem to meanings a)–e).

> make no effort   make the first move   back off
> come on strong   go off

a) not try *make no effort*
b) stop liking or being interested in someone or something
c) stop being involved in a situation
d) be the person to take action
e) say someone is very attractive, but say it too forcefully

b) Work in pairs. Answer these questions.

1 What cultural issue does this poem raise? Did you mention it in your discussions in **1**? If not, does a similar issue exist in your country?
2 Do you think the writer's predictions about how the man might react are correct?
3 What would a) a man or b) a woman advise her to do?
4 Do you think a man would have a similar dilemma? If so, would it be for the same reasons?

4 **a)** How do you think most people would answer these questions?

1 Do you think that being a man/a woman has ever stopped you from doing something you wanted to do?
2 If you could live your life again as a man or a woman, which would you choose and why?

b) R8.4 Listen to six people answering the questions in **4a)**. How many answered 'yes' to question 1? How many would choose to be the same sex?

Match sentence beginnings 1–8 with sentence endings a)–h). `V8.1`

1 The flight is at ten, so if we leave at seven,
2 Take your time,
3 My parents used to give me such a hard time
4 We're very different. I usually put things off,
5 I'm so busy these days,
6 We can't move into the new flat yet,
7 I've got no time for Suzy –
8 It's only a matter of time

a) before there's another oil crisis.
b) but for Joe, there's no time like the present.
c) we'll get there in plenty of time.
d) that I can't even find time to see my friends.
e) there's no need to hurry.
f) for not studying enough.
g) so for the time being we're staying with my brother.
h) as far as I'm concerned she's lazy and selfish.

2 a) Fill in the gaps with the correct form of the verbs in brackets. `G8.2`

1 A Is it OK if I call by this evening, or would you prefer me _to come round_ earlier? (come round)
  B I'd rather you .... this afternoon. (come)
2 A What would you prefer .... this evening, go out for a meal or stay in? (do)
  B I'd sooner .... a film, actually. (see)
3 A Look, isn't it about time you .... to your sister? (apologise)
  B What for? I know she'd rather I .... the first move, but she started the argument. (make)

4 A You look exhausted. It's high time you .... a break from work. (have)
  B I'd prefer .... this, then I can forget about it. (finish)
5 A It's time the kids and I .... home. Thanks for looking after them. (go)
  B A pleasure. Shall I get you a taxi, or would you prefer it if I .... you a lift to the station? (give)
6 A Vince says it's time for him .... on. So, he's leaving this Friday. (move)
  B Yes, I know. I'd prefer it if he .... , though. (stay)

b) Work in pairs. Choose three of the conversations in 2a) and add three more lines to each one. Then role-play your conversations for another pair.

 Rewrite these sentences. Begin the sentences with the words in brackets. `V8.2`

1 I don't know who made this cake, but they must have a great recipe. (Whoever)
  Whoever made this cake must have a great recipe.
2 You can rely on me for anything that needs doing. (Whatever)
3 No matter how many times I wash my hair, it always looks greasy. (However)
4 It doesn't matter what you do, don't tell my mum I've lost her camera. (Whatever)
5 It doesn't matter which road you take to get to the station, it'll take the same amount of time. (Whichever)
6 I don't know who wrote this, but they certainly can't spell. (Whoever)
7 It doesn't matter when I ring Mick, he's always out. (Whenever)

4 a) Follow these instructions. `V8.3`

1 Make adjectives from these nouns: *courage*; *mood*; *culture*; *talent*; *sympathy*; *friend*.
2 Make adverbs from these adjectives: *confident*; *final*; *recent*.
3 Make verbs from these adjectives: *national*; *wide*; *clear*.
4 Make adjectives from these verbs: *create*; *depend*; *remark*.
5 Make nouns from these verbs: *disturb*; *recover*; *divide*; *excite*; *fail*; *plan*; *change*.

b) Complete these sentences with the correct form of the words in brackets.

1 I'm quite a _moody_ person, especially in the mornings. (mood)
2 He .... left at 11 p.m. (final)
3 There are plans to .... the motorway in order to cut traffic jams. (wide)
4 There's a strong .... she will be promoted. (possible)
5 She's an extremely .... person. (create)

c) Work in pairs. Compare answers.

Progress Portfolio

a) Tick the things you can do in English.

☐ I can recognise and use past verb forms which refer to present or future time.

☐ I can use suffixes to change a word from one form to another.

☐ I can describe people's feelings and emotions.

☐ I can understand a modern poem.

☐ I can summarise the results of a survey.

b) What do you need to study again? **8A–C** .

Accurate Writing

CONNECTING WORDS: comment adverbials
SPELLING: commonly misspelled words

1 **a)** Choose the correct word. `AW8.1` p141.

1 Zac broke his leg so *obviously/personally*, he can't play. But *frankly/fortunately*, Joe can.

2 *Quite honestly/Surely*, I hate my job. *In fact/Surprisingly*, I think I'll resign.

3 A *Unfortunately/Fortunately*, I can't give you a lift.
  B *To be honest/Clearly*, I don't think I'll go.

4 I overslept. *Amazingly/Frankly*, I wasn't late.

b) Replace the phrases in brackets with one of these words/phrases.

> apparently   actually   personally   frankly   according to

1 (to be honest), I never got on well with him.

2 (from what I have heard), the director is going to leave.

3 (something Dawn told me) Dawn, we owe you €50.

4 (in my opinion), I think this computer is hopeless.

5 You say that her work's OK, but (as a matter of fact) I've seen better!

2 Choose the correct spelling. `AW8.2` p141.

1 necesary/necessary
2 aquaint/acquaint
3 receit/receipt
4 government/goverment
5 suceed/succeed
6 address/adress

7 buisness/business
8 accomodate/accommodate
9 medecine/medicine
10 exagerate/exaggerate
11 admitted/admited
12 colleage/colleague

3 **a)** Read this extract from a student's work. Fill in the gaps with a commenting word/phrase from 1 to make the story more interesting.

b) Find and correct seven spelling mistakes.

> 1_____, we got lost so it was late when we arrived; 2_____, it was gone midnight. From the adress we hadn't guessed the cottage was in the middle of a dark wood and 3_____ my buisness colleage's description of the accomodation as luxurious was a gross exageration. 4_____, I wanted to leave but I wouldn't have admitted it. I told Ann that it wasn't necesary for us to stay but 5_____, she wanted to. 6_____, I could have insisted we left and 7_____ that is what I should have done because by 4 a.m. there was no guarantee that we would leave that place alive!

1 SIMPLE V CONTINUOUS

a) Look at these sentences. Which uses of the continuous are correct (C), incorrect (I) or unlikely (U)? `G9.1` p143.

1 I'**m not** often **meeting up** with old school friends.

2 I'**ve been reading** six of his books recently.

3 He **was dying** on 20 March 1997.

4 I'**ve been living** here for a long time.

5 I **was living** there for six years.

6 I think I'**m becoming** less materialistic.

7 A What are you doing?
  B I'**m looking for** my contact lens.

8 I **was** just **leaving** when Jim **was turning up**.

9 I'**m living** in rented accommodation at the moment.

b) Read these rules. Are the verbs in the box state verbs (S) or activity verbs (A)?

- Verbs that describe states are not normally used in the continuous form: *I believe you.* not *I'm believing you.*

- Verbs that describe activities can be used in both the simple or continuous form: *I live in Cornwall. I'm living in Cornwall.*

> hate (S)   work (A)   prefer   understand   plan
> play   know   recognise   want   do   walk
> suppose   agree   mean   seem   contain   listen
> consist   study   belong   talk   take   give   own

2 A/AN, *THE* OR NO ARTICLE (–)

Choose the correct answer, *a/an*, *the* or no article (–). `G9.3` p144.

Some of [1]*a/the* hottest nightclubs have [2]*–/a* method for checking the identity of [3]*a/–* VIP guest. They send [4]*an/–* entry pass in the form of a barcode to [5]*–/the* VIP's mobile phone. This is scanned by [6]*a/–* doorman. Even those who must pay to get in may need their handset. At a recent night at [7]*A/The* Ministry of Sound in [8]*–/the* London, students were offered discounts if they used [9]*the/–* mobile phones to buy electronic tickets.

9 Cash

9A Where does it all go?

Vocabulary *price* and *cost*
Grammar simple v continuous: verbs with different meanings
Review suffixes

QUICK REVIEW ● ● ●
Change these words into nouns: *recover, excite, disturb, happy, fail*. Change these words into adjectives: *coward, courage, culture, sympathy*. Change these words into verbs: *rational, wide, intense*. Work in pairs. Take turns to say your words. Are they the same?

Vocabulary
price and *cost*

 1 a) Fill in the gaps with the correct form of *price* or *cost*. Check in **V9.1** p142.

In your country

1 What's the most .... **-effective** way of travelling around cities?
2 Do you think basic products are **reasonably** .... ?
3 Has the .... **of living** risen much over the last year?
4 Do shops often have **half-** .... sales?
5 Is the .... of dental treatment high?

About you

6 Do you have anything that you think is .... **less**?
7 Have you ever bought something that .... **a fortune** and regretted it?
8 Do you always check the .... **tag** before you buy clothes?
9 Have you bought anything recently that you thought was **over** .... ?

b) Work in pairs. Take turns to ask and answer the questions in **1a)**. If you're from the same country, do you agree?

Reading and Grammar

 2 Read options **a)** and **b)**. Which would you choose and why?

1 a) have friends round for coffee
    b) meet them in a coffee shop

2 a) buy a new pair of designer trainers
    b) spend money on entertainment, e.g. a theatre ticket

3 a) spend money on state-of-the-art equipment, e.g. the latest hand-held computer
    b) spend money on travel

 3 a) Read the article. According to the writer, which type of things are becoming more popular and which are becoming less popular? Why?

b) Read the article again. Tick the true sentences. Correct the false ones.

1 The writer is likely to get fewer suits from Joe.
2 The Porsche's brakes weren't very expensive.
3 Extremely rich people still prefer possessions over experiences.
4 People go to cafés because there's a greater selection of things to eat.
5 All societies are moving away from materialism.

c) Look at the last paragraph. What do the phrases in **bold** mean?

d) Work in groups. Discuss these questions.

1 Do the issues raised in the article reflect current trends in your country? Why?/Why not?
2 Would you say that most people you know value experiences over possessions? Why?/Why not?

Have you got experience?

SPENDING PATTERNS ARE CHANGING. IT SEEMS PEOPLE WOULD RATHER PAY TO DO THINGS THAN TO OWN THINGS. BEN MAYNARD CHECKS OUT THE 'EXPERIENCE ECONOMY'.

I'm seeing my friend Joe tonight. He is the kind of person who buys a new suit every six months, which is great for me because we're the same size and his cast-offs fit me perfectly. I think he's someone you would describe as Mr Consumer, or at least he was, but there's been a change in him recently. Why? Well, they're fitting new brakes on his Porsche and according to Joe, the price he's been quoted is the same as the cost of flying lessons or a no-expense-spared weekend in Rome, both of which he'd prefer to spend his money on. So I now see why he's thinking of selling his flash sports car. In fact, he's expecting someone to come and look at it today. If he gets a good enough offer, I expect he'll sell it. And if he does, then it appears my friend is part of a growing trend. Apparently, people are choosing to spend their disposable income on experiences. They are prizing memories over materialism and becoming more particular about what they spend their money on.

Of course, it's all relative. For the super-rich, instead of asking for a Maserati as a birthday present they now want their favourite band to play at their party (I'm told a top band could cost over £1 million). But for more normal folk, like me, who couldn't even dream of such extravagance, there's the 'third space' – a term used by sociologists to describe places other than our home, work or place of study. People spend more time than ever before in coffee shops, restaurants or bars. Clearly, it would be much cheaper to have coffee or eat at home, but people are willing to pay that bit extra to enjoy the experience of eating or drinking in a social setting, with friends or even by themselves. And they'll keep that old car they've been driving for 20 years and watch a less than state-of-the-art TV set, if that allows them to have a season ticket to watch their local football team, a massage, a ride in a hot-air balloon or membership of a sports centre. There are many more leisure activities and opportunities for travel today than ever before. And now people are living longer, they have more time to try different things.

Research done by The Future Foundation showed that 'personal fulfilment' was the top priority for 50% of those interviewed, as opposed to 25% in 1983. So it seems that once a society reaches a certain point of affluence there follows a realisation that **a fat bank account** and a lot of possessions do not **tick all the boxes** – and we end up thinking, "There must be more to life than this."

Adapted from The Times 17/02/06

Help with Grammar
Simple v continuous: verbs with different meanings

See Preview, p85.

● Some verbs can describe states and activities but their meanings change.

 a) Look at the simple and continuous verb forms in pink in the article. Match the verbs to these meanings.

a) be the correct size *fit*
b) put in place
c) believe will happen
d) wait for
e) understand
f) meet
g) have an opinion
h) consider

b) Compare these pairs of sentences. What is the difference in meaning between the verb forms in bold in each sentence?

1 a) He **has** his own business.
  b) He's **having** second thoughts about the flying lessons.
2 a) He **appears** to be fast asleep.
  b) She's **appearing** on a TV show.
3 a) It **looks** expensive.
  b) He's **looking** at a new car today.
4 a) This material **feels** very nice.
  b) She's **feeling** better.
5 a) She **comes** from London.
  b) She's **coming** from London.
6 a) He's difficult.
  b) He's **being** difficult.
7 a) I **imagine** she really likes Canada.
  b) There's nobody there. You're **imagining** things!
8 a) My case **weighs** 15 kilos.
  b) They're **weighing** all the hand luggage.

c) Check in G9.2 **p143.**

4 What do you think the words in **bold** mean?

1 an **ovenproof** dish
2 **reddish** hair
3 a **pollution-free** environment
4 a **newsworthy** story
5 an **unforgettable** moment
6 a **government-led** initiative
7 a **politically-minded** person
8 **fashion-conscious** teenagers

5 **a)** Answer these questions about yourself.

1 Are you very safety-conscious? If so, in what ways?
2 Is there any electronic equipment that you think is idiot-proof?
3 What human characteristics do you think are the most praiseworthy?
4 Is it easy to find additive-free food in your country?
5 Do you think people should use disposable coffee cups?
6 Are any of your friends very strong-minded?
7 Have you ever lived in a smallish town?

b) Work in pairs. Take turns to ask and answer the questions in 5a). Ask follow-up questions.

Reading and Grammar

6 **a)** Work in pairs. Answer these questions.

1 How do you usually pay for things: by cheque, by credit/debit card, in cash, etc.?
2 Do you always have cash on you when you go out? If so, what do you mainly use it for?
3 Do you have smart cards for public transport where you live? Do you use them? Why?/Why not?
4 What do you think 'e-cash' means?

b) Read the article. Does the writer think we will become a cash-free society?

c) Read the article again. Underline sentences in the article which disprove these statements.

1 The use of mobile phones as a means of paying for things will become less popular.
2 It takes slightly longer to pay by mobile phone than by credit card, etc.
3 The only advantage of using e-cash is to increase the speed of transactions.
4 Banks don't have to fear e-cash.
5 Internet banking caused many banks in the USA to close down.

d) Work in pairs. Compare answers. In your country, have there been changes in how people pay for things since this article was written?

e) Work in groups of three. Discuss these questions.

1 What are the pros and cons of a cash-free society?
2 Do you welcome the idea of a world without cash? Why?/Why not?

MOBILE PHONES, the new cash?

When purchasing goods or paying for services, many of us move from one means of payment to another within the space of one day. We might use cheques to pay household bills, credit cards to pay for food and cash for bus or train fares. However, few financial experts would dispute the fact that some of these methods of payment will soon become a thing of the past. Some experts even believe that one day we could be living in a totally cash-free society.

Smart cards and mobile phones are becoming an increasingly popular way to make all sorts of payments. Even now, in Japan thousands of transactions, from buying rail tickets to picking up the groceries, take place every day with customers passing their handsets across a small flat-screen device. And predictions in the world of finance reckon that payments using mobile phones will have risen to more than $50 billion in the very near future.

What's the appeal of e-cash? Compared to cheques or credit cards, it offers the speed of cash, but more so. It takes just one tenth of a second to complete most transactions and as no change is required, errors in counting are eliminated. Fraud and theft are also reduced and for the retailer it reduces the cost of handling money. Sony's vision of having a chip embedded in computers, TVs and games consoles means that films, music and games can be paid for easily and without having to input credit card details.

And what about the future of the banks? With their grip on the market, banks and credit-card firms want to be in a position to collect most of the fees from the users of mobile and contactless-payment systems. But the new system could prove to be a 'disruptive technology' as far as the banks are concerned. If payments for a few coffees, a train ticket and a newspaper are made every day by a commuter with a mobile, this will not appear on their monthly credit card statements but on their mobile phone statements. And having spent fortunes on branding, credit card companies and banks do not want to see other payment systems gaining popularity. It's too early to say whether banks will miss out and if so, by how much. However, quite a few American bankers are optimistic. They feel there is reason to be suspicious of those who predict that high street banks may be a thing of the past. They point out that Internet banking did not result in the closure of their high-street branches as was predicted. On the contrary, more Americans than ever are using local branches. So, as to whether we'll become a totally cash-free society or not, we'll have to wait and see.

Adapted from the *Economist* 17/02/07

 8 a) Choose the correct words in these sentences. Sometimes both answers are possible.

1 He's so fortunate. He has *a few/ few* problems compared to me.
2 I've got *a/one* friend who really doesn't care about money.
3 I first met Max *one/a* day last summer.
4 I'm so busy I only have *one/a* free day a week.
5 She's working late, so sadly there's *little/a little* chance she'll be home before eight.
6 I never know what I'm going to be doing from *a/one* day to the next.
7 I have to have *a/one* snack in the afternoon.
8 Quite *few/a few* people I know upload their photos to the Internet.

b) Work in pairs. Compare and explain your answers. Then tell your partner which sentences in 8a) are true for you. Ask follow-up questions.

 9 a) Replace the words in **bold** with *one* where appropriate or necessary.

I phoned two insurance companies because I needed insurance for ¹**an** adventure holiday. ²**A** company refused to insure me, and ³**a** company said they would if I got ⁴**a** medical certificate. So ⁵**a** day last week I went to see ⁶**a** doctor and I had ⁷**a** checkup. I passed the examination and got ⁸**a** certificate. Once I had it, I decided to check out other insurers. I went from ⁹**a** company to another looking for the best price, but I didn't find ¹⁰**a** quote under €300!

b) Work in pairs. Compare answers.

Get ready ... Get it right!

 10 a) Work in pairs. You've agreed to take part in an experiment in which a group of people is left in a remote area of your country, with no money and no contact with the outside world. Make a list of the problems you'll face and the skills you'll need to overcome them.

b) Work with your partner and tick the things on your list that you could do.

11 a) Work in groups. Discuss these questions.

1 What skills can each person contribute?
2 Are there any essential skills your group is missing?

b) Tell the class how well and how long you think your group would survive. Which group has the best chance of survival?

> We are missing quite a few essential skills. We've got one person who can cook well but we haven't got anyone who can actually grow things to eat.

Help with Grammar *a/an* v *one*; *few*, *a few*, *quite a few*

See Preview, p85.

A/AN V ONE

- *A/an* and *one* both refer to one thing and can be used with singular countable nouns. However, we usually use *one* if we want to emphasise the number: *It takes just **a** tenth of a second to complete most transactions. It takes just **one** tenth of a second to complete most transactions.* (i.e. not two or three tenths).

- We also use *one*:
  a) when we are thinking of <u>one</u> particular day (in the future or the past), but we don't say exactly which day: *We paid that bill **one** day last month.* not ~~... **a** day last month~~. *We can see the bank manager **one** day next week.* not ~~... **a** day next week~~.
  b) in phrases with *one ... other/another/the next*: *Many of us move from one means of payment to another.* not ~~Many of us move from a means of payment to another.~~

 7 a) Read the question and choose the correct answer in the two replies.

> Have you got a five-pound note I could borrow?

> Sorry, I've only got ¹*a/one* ten-pound note.

> Sorry, I've only got ²*a/one* five-pound note and I need it.

b) Work in pairs. Compare and explain your answers.

FEW, A FEW, QUITE A FEW

c) Look at the words in pink in the article. Match *few*, *a few* and *quite a few* to 1–3.

1 a considerable number
2 some, but a small number
3 not many, or not enough

d) Check in G9.4 p144.

TIPS! • *few* is often used in more formal situations

• *little/a little* is used with uncountable nouns in the same way *few/a few* is used with countable nouns: *He spends **very little time** with his children* (not much time at all). *Every evening he spends **a little time** with his children* (not a lot of time, but some).

Vocabulary news and economics
Real World presenting information
Review productive suffixes

QUICK REVIEW ● ● ●

Write one word for each of these suffixes: *-free*; *-led*; *-conscious*; *-ish*; *-able*; *-minded*; *-worthy*; *-proof*. Work in pairs and swap papers. Take turns to say a sentence using the words from your partner's list. A *sugar-free*. B *Sugar-free drinks are much better for you.*

 1 **a)** Tick the words/phrases in **bold** you know. Check new words/phrases in V9.3 p143.

1 Can you name one thing that is **mass-produced** in your country and sold overseas?
2 Does your government send **overseas aid** to **developing countries**?
3 Is your government developing **renewable energy** technology such as wind farms?
4 How strong is the **housing market** at the moment?
5 Has your country ever been an **economic superpower**?
6 In what years were there **record levels** of unemployment?
7 In the last few years has there been **economic growth** or **economic decline** in your country?
8 What steps is your government taking to try and save the **earth's resources**?
9 Does your country have **nuclear power**?
10 Are there laws against **gender discrimination** in the workplace?

b) Work on your own. How much do you know about the economics of your country? Answer the questions in **1a)**.

c) Work in pairs. Compare answers. If you are from the same country, do you agree? If you are from different countries, how similar are your answers?

 2 **a)** Work in pairs. Make a list of school or university subjects that you think are interesting or fun. Then list ones you think are dry or dull.

b) Read out your lists to the class. Do you agree with other students' lists? Was economics mentioned? If so, was it considered to be an interesting subject? Why?/Why not?

The Tokyo Stock Exchange

 3 R9.5 Listen to a teacher addressing a group of students choosing which subjects to take at A level. Find answers to these questions.

1 Why did two students raise their hands?
2 What are the three sections of his talk about?

4 **a)** R9.6 Listen to the next part of the lecture. Tick the true sentence. Correct the false sentences about economics.

1 It can provide all the answers to world problems.
2 Without it you can't understand world issues properly.
3 You don't need any particular skills to study economics.
4 It is only useful if you want to go into the world of business and finance.

b) Listen again. Answer these questions.

1 What does the teacher say about current world food prices and what effect they will have on the world?
2 What does he mean when he talks about "the real cost of a plastic bag"?
3 What type of people does he say are suited to economics?
4 Does he think the study of economics is difficult?
5 Why does he mention careers such as architecture, politics and journalism?
6 At the end of the talk, which four adjectives does he use to describe economics?

c) Work in pairs. Compare answers.

 5 Work in pairs and discuss these questions.

1 Which of the teacher's arguments do you think would influence a young audience the most and why?
2 Do you know anyone whose job requires a knowledge of economics? If so, why?
3 If you have studied economics, did you enjoy it? If you have never studied economics, do you think you'd enjoy it? Why?/Why not?

Real World Presenting information

 a) Look at these quotes. Why does the teacher use these sentences in the introduction to his talk?

I'm going to divide the talk into (three sections).

First of all, (how economics is related to real life).

Then I'll go on to (the intellectual challenge).

And finally I'll (discuss future careers).

b) Match phrases 1–13 to headings a)–e).

a) to make the first point ......2...... ....

b) to refer to a point made earlier ....

c) to signal a new point ....

d) to summarise what's been said so far ....

e) to signal the last point/bring the talk to an end ....

1	In conclusion …	9	To go back to …
2	First of all …	10	Just to recap …
3	Now I'll talk about …	11	Leaving that aside for a
4	Let's move on to …		moment …
5	So, to sum up …	12	To return to something
6	As I said before …		I mentioned earlier …
7	Last but not least …	13	And finally …
8	Let's start with/by …		

c) Look at R9.5 and R9.6, p158. Look at the phrases in **bold** and notice how the talk is structured.

d) Check in `RW9.1` p145.

 7 **a)** Complete these sentences with the correct words.

a) First .... all, let's start .... looking at the problems that occur when young people can't find work.

b) Leaving that aside .... a moment, let's move .... the advantages for society in having apprenticeship schemes.

c) Now I'll talk .... how a transfer of skills will benefit individuals both young and old.

d) As I said .... , the benefits will be considerable.

e) And to go .... a point I made earlier, the elderly have skills they can pass on to the young, and vice versa.

f) To sum .... , what we need is to find a way to encourage more apprenticeship schemes.

g) .... conclusion, unless we do something soon, the outcome looks bleak.

b) Work in pairs. Answer these questions.

1 What is the talk in **7a)** about?
2 Do you think it's a good idea? Why?/Why not?
3 Would it be relevant to your country? Why?/Why not?

 8 **a)** Work in pairs. You are each going to give a two-minute talk on the same topic to a different partner. Choose one of these topics or your own and then follow instructions 1–3.

● Junk mail should be made illegal.
● Public transport should be free.
● Everyone should have a three-day weekend.
● People should have to retire at 50.

1 Make a list of things you could include in your talk.
2 Put your list in a logical order and make notes on what you are going to say about each one.
3 Think about how to open and close your talk.

b) Work on your own. Think about what you are going to say. Make notes.

c) Work with your partner from **8a)**. Take turns to practise giving your talk. Give each other advice on how to improve it.

Give clearer signals to show how the talk is structured.

Vary your voice more.

Give more eye contact.

 9 Work with a new partner who has prepared a different talk. Take turns to give your talk. Was your partner convinced by your arguments?

10A Be creative!

QUICK REVIEW ● ● ●

Choose four of these verbs and make sentences about yourself using both the simple and continuous forms: *have*; *come*; *be*; *think*; *see*; *expect*. Work in pairs. Tell each other your sentences: *I have three brothers. I'm having a party on Friday*. Ask follow-up questions.

Reading and Grammar

a) Work in pairs. Think of different ways in which animals used to help humans in the past.

b) Check the meaning of these words.

a cyclone	a conflict	a siege
ingenious	epitomise	
pioneering	swift	an orphan
wilderness	a sled	

c) Read the article. Which animals are mentioned, and how were they used in the postal service?

Fill in gaps 1–6 in the article with sentences a)–f). Which words/phrases in the article helped you?

a) Further north, mail was being delivered to the icy corners of the world by huskies.

b) Cats, meanwhile, were first employed by the Post Office in 1868.

c) There was clearly a gap in the market for a swifter service.

d) However, homing birds weren't only used in ancient times.

e) Airborne messengers are most useful in time of conflict, however.

f) There was no shortage of applicants.

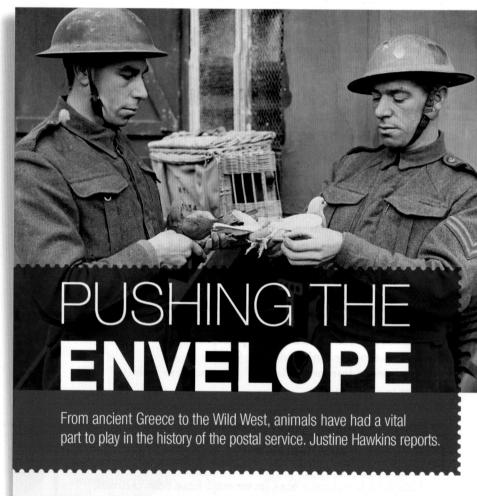

PUSHING THE ENVELOPE

From ancient Greece to the Wild West, animals have had a vital part to play in the history of the postal service. Justine Hawkins reports.

Postal workers these days tend to be human, but it hasn't always been so.

Pigeon post was used first by the Sumerians in 776 BC and it is known that the ancient civilisations of Egypt, Persia, Mesopotamia, Greece and Rome relied on pigeons to carry messages to **far-flung** corners of their kingdoms and empires. ¹_____ In 1850, Paul Julius van Reuter began his news agency by sending information between Aachen and Brussels by pigeon. And until the beginning of the 21ˢᵗ century, the police in the Indian state of Orissa were using a pigeon service during floods and cyclones. News comes via email these days, so the birds were **pensioned off** long ago.

2_____ When Paris was surrounded during the war in 1870, pigeons provided a **vital link** to the outside world. The birds were **smuggled out** in balloons, returning later with the information that everyone was so anxiously waiting for. During the four-month siege, more than a million letters were delivered to the citizens of Paris by this ingenious method. During the First and Second World Wars, the British army was also dependent on hundreds of thousands of pigeons. With great sadness, these prized flocks were handed over to support the war effort. Many lives were saved by the timely arrival of a pigeon and 32 of these winged heroes each received a medal for bravery in the Second World War.

Horses, too, have powered the information superhighway for thousands of years. No equine postal service is more iconic than the Pony Express. Although it lasted less than two years, the Pony Express came to epitomise the pioneering spirit of the United States. When the gold rush generation arrived in California in 1848, it took 24 days for letters to arrive from loved ones in New York. 3_____ So, in 1860, adverts were placed for "Young, skinny, wiry fellows, not over 18. Must be expert riders, willing to face death daily. Orphans preferred." 4_____ Pony Express riders had names like Charlie P Cyclone and Pony Bob and there were around 400 horses and 100 men. During its short romantic existence, it was the fastest means of delivering messages across the US; 2,000 miles is a long way to travel on horseback, but the riders would manage to get from the railroad station in Missouri across wilderness to California in only nine to ten days. The public were fascinated by the Pony Express but even so, the team was a financial failure and was put out of business by transcontinental telegraph.

5_____ Commercial dog teams in Alaska and Canada saw their source of income **ebb away** when mail delivery contracts were lost to the aeroplane in the 1920s. The dogs are still going, though, and many of today's dogsled races follow the historic mail routes.

6_____ . Initially, only a couple were **recruited** and an allowance was paid to a Post Office porter for their upkeep. In the decades that followed, dozens of cats were employed at UK sorting offices, ensuring that money orders were not eaten by rats and mice.

Alas, having cats as part of the Post Office workforce is now a thing of the past. Animals have been retired from the communications business and are now found only in the pages of stamp collections.

Adapted from the *Guardian* 14/02/02

3 **a)** Work in pairs. Look at the words/phrases in pink in the article. What ideas do they refer back to?

b) Match the words/phrases in **bold** in the article to these meanings.

1 taken out secretly	4 very important connection
2 employed	5 disappear slowly
3 remote	6 made to retire

c) In what ways do animals help humans today?

Help with Grammar Subject/verb agreement

4 **a)** Read the basic rule for subject/verb agreement and choose the correct words in sentences 1 and 2.

- A verb usually 'agrees' with its subject (i.e. a singular subject has a singular verb and a plural subject a plural verb.)

1 Horses, too, *has/have* powered the information superhighway for thousands of years.
2 Further north, mail *was/were* being delivered to the icy corners of the world by huskies.

b) Choose the correct word in these examples in groups A and B.

GROUP A
1 if the subject of the verb is a clause: *Having cats is/are now a thing of the past.*
2 with nouns which end in -*s* but are not plural: *News come/comes via email these days.*
3 with expressions of quantity, measurement, etc.: *2,000 miles is/are a long way to travel.*
4 after words such as *everyone, anything*, etc.: *The information that everyone was/were so anxiously waiting for.*

GROUP B
5 for nouns which don't end in an -*s* but are not singular: *The police was/were using a pigeon service.*
6 after words such as *both of, all of, plenty of, a number of, a couple: Only a couple was/were recruited.*

c) Choose the correct word in these rules.

- In group A, we use a *singular/plural* verb.
- In group B, we use a *singular/plural* verb.

d) Fill in the gaps in the rules with *singular* or *plural*.

- Some collective nouns and names can take either a singular or a plural form.

1 When focusing on countries which are a group of states, or an institution or organisation as a whole, the verb is usually _____ : *The USA **has** fifty states. The British army **was** also dependent on pigeons. The team **was** a financial failure.*
2 When focusing on a collection of individuals, the verb is usually _____ : *The public **were** fascinated by the Pony Express.*

e) Check in G10.1 p146.

5 Fill in the gaps with the present form of the verbs in brackets.

1 Both of my parents .... dogs to cats. (prefer)
2 Everyone .... that economics .... a really interesting subject. (say; be)
3 Five litres of water .... too much to drink in one day. (be)
4 Mathematics .... not a subject I enjoy at all. (be)
5 The army in my country .... people from the age of 16. (recruit)
6 The staff .... really friendly. (seem)

 6 a) Choose the correct words. Then complete the sentences so that they are true for you.

1 The news at the moment *is/are* …
2 Keeping pets *is/are* …
3 The United States *is/are* …
4 The general public *is/are* fascinated by …
5 Everyone I meet these days *talk/talks* about …
6 Lots of my friends *like/likes* …

b) Work in pairs. Compare sentences. Ask follow-up questions.

Listening

 7 a) Work in pairs. Do the quiz.

b) R10.1 Listen to part of a radio programme. Check your guesses.

8 a) Check the meaning of the noun collocations in **bold**.

1 What does the presenter say about many things we accept as **a matter of course**?
2 How did Marco Polo become **a mine of information** about ice-cream making?
3 Is it generally acccepted there is **an element of truth** in the way tea was first created?
4 Are the claims for how people began to eat coffee beans **a matter of opinion**?
5 What was **the centre of attention** in Chicago in 1885?
6 How did it set off **a train of events** which revolutionised city life?
7 What is described as **a stroke of genius**?

b) Listen again and answer questions 1–7.

c) Work in pairs. Compare your answers.

d) Which of the things discussed in the programme do you think had the most interesting beginnings? Do you know any others?

QUICK QUIZ

1 **Who invented ice cream?**
   A the Italians
   B the Chinese

2 **Who first started drinking tea?**
   A the English
   B the Chinese

3 **Where did coffee first come from?**
   A Ethiopia
   B Colombia

4 **How high was the first skyscraper?**
   A 10 storeys
   B 20 storeys

5 **Where was the first escalator invented?**
   A Japan
   B the US

Get ready … Get it right!

9 Work on your own. Look at these photos of useful inventions. Which ones couldn't you live without in your daily life?

10 a) Work in pairs. Choose the five most useful inventions from the pictures.

b) Work with another pair. Take turns to say which items are on your list and why you chose them. Then agree on the five most useful inventions.

c) Work with the whole class. Decide on the top three most useful inventions.

Vocabulary antonyms
Grammar modal verbs (2):
levels of certainty about
the past, the present and
future
Review subject/verb
agreement

QUICK REVIEW ● ● ●
Complete these sentences with your opinions and information about yourself: *I think
having pets ... ; Everyone I know ... ; I think the police ... ; My family ... ; My favourite
(football) team ... ; Only a couple of my friends ...* . Work in pairs. Take turns to say
your sentences. Ask follow-up questions.

Listening and Grammar

1 **a)** Make a list of people you know who have been
successful in what they do. Is their success due to
luck, talent or the fact that they were very dedicated?

b) Work in pairs. Take turns to tell each other about
the people on your list.

2 **a)** **R10.2** Listen to Adela and Louie. Who are the people in
photos A and B?

b) Listen again. Work in Groups A and B. Use the prompts
to make notes.

Group A What does Adela say about: Latin; Martin's talent;
Saturday night; his girlfriend; being positive?

Group B What does Louie say about: luck: Tang Yun's childhood;
Louie's school; gifted children; being a soloist?

c) Work with a student from the same group and compare
answers.

d) Work with a student from the other group and use your
notes from **2b)** to summarise what Adela or Louie said.

e) Fill in the gaps with one of the modal verbs in the boxes.

| ~~'ll~~   'll   might   can't   must   shouldn't |

1 Here it is Saturday night and I'm sure he _'ll_ **be working**.
2 He .... **be creating** a new animation character or he
could be working on his next short film.
3 Clearly, he .... **enjoy** what he does, why else would he
work so hard?
4 But I feel sorry for his girlfriend. It .... **be** easy having
Martin as your partner.
5 People are just starting to notice his work, so it .... **be**
long before he gets the recognition he deserves.
6 He's certain he .... **find** a buyer for his next animation film.

| ~~won't~~   may   must   wouldn't   can't |

7 Tang Yun, for example, you just know it _won't_ **have been**
easy for him as a kid.
8 He .... **have devoted** most of his childhood to practising.
9 I .... **have had** some natural talent, who knows.
10 My father says that I .... **have wanted** it badly enough or
I .... **have given** up.

f) Listen again. Check your answers.

Help with Grammar **Modal verbs (2):
levels of certainty about the past,
present and future**

See Preview, p95.

● Modal verbs are auxiliaries which express our
attitude to, or assessment of, an event or
situation and roughly divide into two groups:

a) functions such as obligation, advice,
permission, prohibition, etc.
b) levels of certainty.

3 **LEVELS OF CERTAINTY**

a) Look at sentences 1–10 in **2e)**. Complete
the rules with *possible, definite,* or *probable*.

● We use *will, won't, can't, must, would(n't)*
when we think something is ....
● We use *should* to express when we think
something is ....
● We use *may, might, could* when we think
something is ....

b) Look again at sentences 1–10 in **2e)**. Then
fill in the gaps with *past, present,* or *future*.

a) Sentences 1–4 refer to the ....
b) Sentences 5 and 6 refer to the ....
c) Sentences 7–10 refer to the ....

c) What verb form follows the modal verb
when it refers to: the present? the future?
the past?

d) Check in **G10.3** p147.

Vocabulary colloquial language
Skills Reading: a book review;
Listening and Speaking: language-learning
strategies; Writing: an action plan
Real World Giving advice
Review modal verbs

QUICK REVIEW ●●●

Make sentences about people you know: *It shouldn't be long before ...* ;
Tomorrow night ... will ... ; *Next month ... might ...* ; *Next weekend ...
won't ...* ; *Last week ... wouldn't have had time to ...* . Work in pairs.
Take turns to say your sentences. Ask follow-up questions.

1
a) Imagine you are giving advice to a
beginner in English or another
language. Make notes on things that
helped you to progress. What would
you have done differently?

b) Work in groups. Agree on a list of
'dos' and 'don'ts'.

c) Present your views to the class. Is
there any advice that the whole class
agrees on?

2
a) It is claimed that *Language
Revolution*, a language-learning
course for beginners, will teach you
how to learn a language in just eight
weeks. Look at the photo. What
technique do you think the series
uses?

b) Read the review. In what way is this
method of learning a 'revolution'?

Is this the fastest track to → fluency?

Tony Buzan's *Language Revolution* is about learning a language
the way a baby would, by absorption and association.

Simon Compton investigates

According to his publicity, Tony
Buzan, whose name is invariably
associated with the words 'mind
guru', has "revolutionised the way
people think and remember, in the
workplace, classroom and at
home." At the heart of all his
work are mind maps, a way of
graphically organising and
developing thoughts.

Mind maps help you to
remember by linking words and
images in an intuitive way. For
example, in his *Language
Revolution* Italian course Buzan
encourages learners to draw a
mind map of words they can
remember associated with a trip
to the bar. They are remembered
not as a list but as one suggests
the other, with colours and
pictures as prompts.

Buzan says this reflects the
organic and free-flowing way the
brain works naturally, meaning we
remember better by association.
Lists have no associations, so are
much harder work. He developed
the idea of 'mind maps' as a tool
for note-taking when he was a
student and has since written 95
books and taught his principles to
everyone from government
departments to the British
Olympic rowing team.

Remembering by association,
as a child does, permeates
Buzan's learning technique.
"Babies are the best language
learners in the world, but they
don't learn grammar," Buzan tells
me. "For example, a child will build
on the word 'Daddy' with 'Daddy
work' and 'Daddy go work' and
'Daddy go car'. And that's a mind
map in a baby's head."

Buzan claims that his
techniques reflect the workings of
the brain, but the science is
vague. In the past he has
explained it in terms of engaging
the parts of the brain that make
us creative in memory tasks, as
well as the systematic parts of the
brain that traditionally dominate.
But he prefers to talk to me about
natural learning styles. And what
he says certainly tunes in with
what child development experts
know about the importance of
learning by association.

Buzan's lack of linguistic
expertise is what makes his
approach so different. There is
nothing miraculous or complex
about his techniques; his great
knack is to take things that we
suspect are true from experience
and incorporate them into
learning programmes.

Adapted from The Times 01/03/08

3 a) Choose the correct words.

1 Buzan is in favour of *making lists/connecting ideas*.
2 He is inspired by the way *sports people/children* learn.
3 Buzan's claims about mind maps are *convincing/unclear*.
4 Children are believed to learn best by *making links/using mind maps*.
5 Buzan's approach is based on *linguistic theory/what he believes is self-evident*.

b) Work in groups. Discuss these questions.

1 What methods do you use to record vocabulary?
2 Have you ever used mind maps? Do you think they are useful?
3 Would you consider using this method if you were learning a new language? Why?/Why not?

 4 a) Work in pairs. What do you think makes learning English at an advanced level different from other levels? What do you need to do in order to be successful?

Maria Pia

Bruce

b) R10.3 Listen to Maria Pia, an advanced Italian learner of English. Does she agree with what you said in 4a)? Answer these questions.

1 What did Maria Pia do first at elementary level, before learning grammar?
2 What does she say are the advantages of reading newspapers at a more advanced level?
3 What disadvantage does reading the classics have?
4 What helps her to keep up-to-date with new language?
5 What has she found useful in order to understand different types of pronunciation?
6 What two tips does she have for remembering vocabulary?
7 What, for her, is the best way to put into practice the language you've learned?

c) R10.4 Listen to Bruce talking about his experience of learning languages. According to Bruce, are the following statements true or false?

1 He has learned four languages, all very successfully.
2 He has never liked learning languages in a classroom.
3 When you are advanced in a language, you need to be independent.
4 Learning a foreign language shouldn't take too long.
5 You shouldn't worry about making mistakes when speaking.

 5 a) Listen again to Bruce and answer these questions.

1 What does Bruce read in a foreign language?
2 In what ways does he think reading helps?
3 What does he listen to?
4 What does he say about grammar?
5 What technique does he have for learning vocabulary?

b) Work in pairs. What do the words/phrases in **bold** mean?

1 I would just **jot it down** in my little booklet.
2 I'm a very **gregarious** learner … you know, just try and interact with other people.
3 … anything from **trashy** magazines to crime novels.
4 … I'm still a bit **woolly** about the grammar.
5 He used to write in English and then he **switched** to French.

c) Work in groups. Discuss these questions.

1 What do both Maria and Bruce agree on?
2 Do you strongly agree/disagree with anything either of them said?
3 Do you think, like Beckett, that some people have more freedom to express themselves in a foreign language? Do you feel like a different person when you are speaking English?

 6 a) Make a list of the areas in which you still need to improve your English. Put them in order of importance for you.

b) Work in groups and talk about how you are going to continue to improve your English outside the classroom. Give advice to other people.

Real World Giving advice

- Take every opportunity to …
- Make sure you don't …
- Try to avoid …
- If you can, don't …
- Thinking back, I wouldn't have …

- It's a good idea to …
- The main thing …
- It's absolutely essential to …
- What I'd do is …
- Whatever you do, avoid …

Writing Extension

7 a) Write an action plan for the next few months, giving examples of how you are going to continue to improve your English.

b) Compare your action plan with other students' plans. Add any useful ideas to your plan.

Little Wonders 2C p23

1 **a)** Match verbs 1–5 to definitions a)–e).

1	roll	a)	gradually disappear
2	twist	b)	when liquid moves and carries things with it
3	slide	c)	turn over and over
4	fall away	d)	bend and turn (something)
5	wash away	e)	move smoothly over a surface

b) Work in pairs. Compare answers.

2 **a)** Read the song. Then fill in the gaps with one of these words/phrases.

> ~~roll~~ falls away feel heart remember
> shoulder twists shine turns remain slide
> turn wash away

Let it go
Let it ¹ ......*roll*...... right off your ² ....
Don't you know the hardest part is over?
Let it in
Let your clarity define you
In the end
We will only just ³ .... how it feels

CHORUS
Our lives are made in these small hours
These little wonders
These ⁴ .... and ⁵ .... of fate
Time ⁶ .... , but these small hours
These small hours still ⁷ ....

Let it ⁸ ....
Let your troubles fall behind you
Let it ⁹ ....
Until you feel it all around you
And I don't mind
If it's me you need to ¹⁰ .... to
We'll get by
It's the ¹¹ .... that really matters in the end

CHORUS
All of my regret will ¹² .... somehow
But I cannot forget the way I ¹³ .... right now

CHORUS (x 2)

b) Work in pairs. Compare answers.

c) R2.7 Listen to the song. Check your answers.

3 Which of these ideas do you think best summarises the mood of the song?

It's one person telling another that:

1 their relationship is in difficulty and has to end.
2 all their troubles are over/coming to an end.
3 it's OK now but problems are about to happen.

Summer in the City 4C p43

1 Work in groups. Discuss these questions.

1 What do you like/dislike about the summer?
2 Do you like spending summer in the city? Why?/Why not?
3 Where do you most like to spend the summer?
4 Which is the best summer you've ever had?

2 **a)** R4.7 Listen to the song. Choose the correct words/phrases.

Hot ¹*town/~~down~~*, summer in the city
Back of my ²*neck/head* getting dirty and gritty
³*Seen/Been* down, isn't it a pity?
Doesn't seem to be ⁴*any shade/a shadow* in the city
All around, people looking ⁵*half dead/stressed out*
⁶*Talking/Walking* on the sidewalk, hotter than a match head

CHORUS
But at night it's a different ⁷*world/place*
Go out and find ⁸*some fun/a girl*
Come on, come on, we'll ⁹*dance/talk* all night
Despite the ¹⁰*noise/heat* it'll be all right
And babe, don't you know it's a ¹¹*pity/shame*
That the days ¹²*won't/can't* be like the nights
In the summer, in the city
In the summer, in the city

¹³*Great/Cool* town, evening in the city
Dressing so fine and looking so ¹⁴*pretty/lovely*
Cool ¹⁵*guy/cat* looking for a kitty
Gonna ¹⁶*look/wait* in every corner of the city
Till I'm ¹⁷*standing/wheezing* like a bus stop
Running up the stairs, gonna ¹⁸*see/meet* you on the rooftop

CHORUS
REPEAT FIRST VERSE AND CHORUS

b) Work in pairs. Compare answers.

3 **a)** Read the song again. Find a word that:

a) is American English for 'pavement'.
b) can mean fashionable, excellent or slightly cold.
c) means to have difficulty breathing.

b) Work in pairs. Answer the questions.

1 What does the singer think are the pros and cons of being in a city in the summer?
2 Which words/phrases in the song support your ideas?

Chasing Cars 6C p63

 Work in groups. Discuss these questions.

1 What are your favourite love songs?
2 Which is more important in a good love song, the words or the music?

 a) Look at verses 1–8 in which lines are mixed up. Put the lines in order.

1 a) Everything
  b) We'll do it all 1
  c) On our own

2 d) Anything
  e) We don't need
  f) Or anyone

CHORUS (1)
If I lay here, if I just lay here
Would you lie with me and just forget the world?

3 g) How to say
  h) I don't quite know
  i) How I feel

4 j) They're not enough
  k) Are said too much
  l) Those three words

CHORUS (2)
If I lay here, if I just lay here
Would you lie with me and just forget the world?
Forget what we're told before we get too old
Show me a garden that's bursting into life

5 m) Around our heads
  n) Let's waste time
  o) Chasing cars

6 p) I need your grace
  q) To remind me
  r) To find my own

CHORUS (2)

7 s) All that I ever was
  t) Is here in your perfect eyes, they're all I can see
  u) All that I am

8 v) Just know these things will never change for us at all
  w) Confused about how as well
  x) I don't know where

CHORUS (1)

b) Work in pairs. Compare answers.

c) R6.7 Listen and check your answers.

 Work in pairs. What do you think ...

1 is the relationship between the people?
2 is the singer's attitude to other people?
3 he means by 'a garden bursting into life'?
4 the title means?

You Gotta Be 8C p85

 a) Match the words that rhyme.

you	holds
tears	read
said	face
you	fears
pace	to
unfolds	view

b) Read the song. Try to fill in the gaps with words from **1a)**.

Listen as your day [1] _unfolds_
Challenge what the future [2] _____
Try and keep your head up to the sky
Lovers, they may cause you [3] _____
Go ahead release your [4] _____
Stand up and be counted, don't be ashamed to cry
You gotta be

CHORUS
You gotta be bad, you gotta be bold
You gotta be wiser, you gotta be hard
You gotta be tough, you gotta be stronger
You gotta be cool, you gotta be calm
You gotta stay together
All I know, all I know, **love will save the day**

Herald what your mother [5] _____
Readin' the books your father [6] _____
Try to solve the puzzles in your own sweet time
Some may have more cash than [7] _____
Others take a different [8] _____ , my oh my heh, hey

CHORUS

Time asks no questions, it goes on without [9] _____
Leaving you behind if you can't stand the [10] _____
The world keeps on spinning
Can't stop it, if you try [11] _____
That's what is danger staring you in the [12] _____
Remember

REPEAT LINES 1–5 OF VERSE 1
CHORUS (X 2)
Got to be bold, got to be bad
Got to be wise, no never sad
Got to be hard, not too too hard
All I know, love will save the day

CHORUS

c) R8.5 Listen and check your answers.

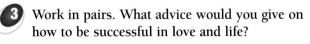 Read the song again. What do you think the phrases in **bold** mean?

Work in pairs. What advice would you give on how to be successful in love and life?

Pair and Group Work: Student/Group A

1C 7 p13

a) Read definitions 1–3. Make sure you understand them and can say them fluently.

1
> **rave** /reɪv/ **about something** to talk very enthusiastically about something: *Jan raved about Tarantino's new film. Apparently it's great.*

2
> **hit the roof** to get very angry about something: *When June saw how much Pete had spent on his new car she hit the roof.*

3
> **lose your bottle** when you no longer have the courage to do something: *I went to the bungee-jumping place but I lost my bottle at the last minute.*

b) Work in groups of three. You are going to give three definitions of each idiom to Group B: the correct definition and two false definitions. Work together to invent two false definitions and three example sentences for each idiom.

c) Decide who is going to give the true definition and the false definitions for each idiom. Then rehearse exactly what you are going to say. Remember you are all trying to convince Group B that your definition is correct.

d) Work with three students from Group B and follow these instructions. Your group starts.

1 Give your definitions for idiom 1. Group B discusses which definition is correct. Repeat your definitions if necessary.
2 Group B says which definition they think is correct, which are false and why. The student in your group with the correct definition then reads it out.
3 Group B then gives their definitions for idiom a). Continue with the game until both groups have guessed three definitions.

e) Which group guessed the most correct definitions?

4B 4 p40

a) Work with another student from Group A. Look at this list of cities. Which country is each city in?

> Berlin   Istanbul   London   Mumbai   Warsaw

b) These figures show the population growth per hour in the cities in **a)**. Try to match the figures to the cities.

> +0   +1   + 6   +17   +42

c) Work with a student from Group B. Give your answers to **a)** and **b)**. Your partner will check your answers. How many did you get right?

d) Listen to your partner's answers and check the information. Say how many your partner got right.

> **Student B's answers**
>
> Los Angeles (USA) +9
> Madrid (Spain) +8
> São Paulo (Brazil) +25
> Shanghai (China) +31
> Tokyo (Japan) +3

e) Did any of the figures surprise you?

7A 9 p68

a) Work with another student from Group A. You are in favour of closed prisons. You are concerned about the increase in crime and feel that the courts should give tougher sentences to deter criminals. Make a list of reasons why closed prisons are the best way forward.

b) You are at a meeting to discuss how best to deal with crime. Work in groups of four with a pair from Group B. Take turns to give your points of view. Decide on the best way to deal with crime.

There wouldn't be as much crime on the streets if we hadn't been so soft with criminals in the first place.

c) Decide which is the best way to deal with crime: open or closed prisons.

d) Tell the class what your group decided.

3B 3 p29

a) Read extracts 1–3 from the article 'Great ways to well-being'. Then answer these questions.

a) What is the advice? Did it match any of your predictions?
b) According to the research, how can the advice contribute to a person's well-being?
c) What facts or figures, if any, support the research?

1

Eat more curry. Only recently have experts come to appreciate the health benefits of eating curries. Not only do curries protect against Alzheimer's, stress and depression, but they can also help you lose weight. Apparently, meals containing chillies burn up more calories* than other meals.

2

Get a hobby. Having a hobby can ease depression, lower levels of stress, improve mood and immune systems* and may reduce the risk of high blood pressure. According to research at Maastricht University, men who have hobbies are less likely to be sick and absent from work than men who don't.

3

Drink more coffee. Not until recently has the world's most widely used stimulant been considered good for you. It can lower the risk of diabetes*, relax muscles and improve speed of thought. According to research done at Harvard University, women who drink coffee may reduce the risk of having a heart attack by up to 30%. The research was carried out on 32,000 women over six years. Drinking six or more cups a day also reduces the risk of diabetes by 54% for men and 30% for women.

calorie = a unit for measuring the amount of energy that food will produce
immune system = system by which your body protects itself against diseases
diabetes /daɪəˈbiːtiːz/ = a serious disease in which there is too much sugar in your blood

b) Work with the other people in your group. Take turns to tell each other your answers to the questions.

4B 14 p41

a) Work with another student from Group A. Look at inventions 1 and 2. Then discuss these questions.

1 What were these inventions supposed to do?
2 Why did the inventors think they would be popular?
3 What do you think were the good and bad aspects of the inventions?
4 Do you think they would be popular in your country? Why?/Why not?

b) Work with a student from Group B and a student from Group C. Take turns to describe your inventions, explaining what they were supposed to do. The other students should try and draw what you have described.

The person who invented this obviously thought it was going to help people in rainy climates. It was supposed to …

c) Compare your drawings with the original pictures on p112 and p114. Decide which you think is the best and the weirdest invention.

109

4C **4** p43

a) Work in pairs with a student from Group A. You are news editors from a tabloid newspaper. Look at these notes for two possible lead stories. Think of photos and a dramatic headline for each story. What extra details could the stories include to have maximum impact?

1

200 drivers trapped in cars and coaches on A66 in north of England last night because of heavy snow and gales. Snow came in very fast, no warning. Some occupants waited for several hours before being rescued by police. Many rescued from A66 were taken to nearby villages. 45 pensioners taken to hotel to wait for a bus. Many motorists arrived on foot, cold and wet. Villagers helped with refreshments, etc. but village hall had no sleeping facilities. Roads now closed.

2

A two-year-old boy has been hailed as a hero after he found his mother collapsed on the floor and calmly dialled 999. He was too frightened to give his name but Joshua Brookes explained to the operator that his mummy wouldn't wake up. Police traced their address and paramedics went to the house but couldn't get in, so Joshua stood on a box and let them in. His mother, Isobel, who suffers from a rare heart condition, was taken to hospital, where she made a full recovery.

b) Work in a group of three with students from groups B and C. Listen to the two reporters' presentations of their stories. Decide which should be the main story that day, and give reasons.

7B **9** p71

a) Work with a student from Group A. Read these newspaper headlines. Choose two and add extra information, e.g. why you think the measures have been introduced and what will happen as a result.

1
WARNINGS TO BE PUT ON COMPUTER GAMES

2
Football boots outlawed as being 'too dangerous'

3
Cameras on beaches to monitor safe sunbathing levels

b) Work in pairs with a student from Group B and tell your stories. What do you think about these issues?

c) Work in the same pairs. Think of any other similar stories that have happened or could happen in the future.

5A **10** p48

a) You are a personal assistant to a famous person. You are paid well, but these are some things you would like to change about your job. Think of any other ideas.

- You are expected to be 'on duty' from 6 a.m. until midnight six days a week.
- Your employer phones you on your day off.
- You have only one week's holiday every year.
- You have not done any of the overseas travelling you were promised.
- The job advert asked for an educated person to organise your employer's diary. However, your job includes clearing up after the dog, washing clothes and babysitting the children.

b) Work with your partner. Complain about your hours and the kind of work you have to do and discuss how your situation could be improved.

It's humiliating for someone with my qualifications to clear up after a dog!

5B **2** p49

Theo Walcott

Before a game, once I've put my kit on, I never forget to sit with my head down and visualise myself scoring a goal. When you score goals, it puts an absolute smile on your face.

You have to have the right attitude – calm, relaxed and dedicated – and work really hard. You want to be better every day, try to learn something from every training session. In the early days Dad used to ask me, "How do you think you did?" on days I hadn't done so well, putting the ball in my court. In the next training session I'd prove him wrong.

I discovered football purely by chance, at the age of 10, when a coach came to do skills sessions at my school and noticed me on the pitch. When I joined Arsenal, my dad and I lived in a rented flat during the week. I found it really tough, as I've always been very close to my family. The hardest bit was living away from my mum. But my parents have always been there for me.

I'll never forget getting picked for the World Cup squad at only 16. I learned so much about how players cope with all the pressure and about being part of the team. I did realise that my life was very different to that of other young teens. But even if I'd still been at school I probably wouldn't have been out partying, as I'm not one to do that at the best of times.

Pair and Group Work: Student/Group B

1C ⑦ p13

a) Read definitions a)–c). Make sure you understand them and can say them fluently.

> **ⓐ**
> **be up for something** to want to do or try something: *We're going clubbing this weekend. Are you up for it?*

> **ⓑ**
> **talk shop** when colleagues talk about work when they could be relaxing and having fun: *Even though it was a New Year's party, Chris and Ben spent all night talking shop.*

> **ⓒ**
> **call it a day** to decide to stop working or doing an activity usually because you are tired or you have done enough: *I'm really tired. Let's call it a day. We can finish the cleaning tomorrow.*

b) Work in groups of three. You are going to give three definitions of each idiom to Group A, the correct definition and two false definitions. Work together to invent two false definitions for each idiom.

c) Decide who is going to give the true definition and the false definitions for each idiom. Then rehearse exactly what you are going to say. Remember you are all trying to convince Group A that your definition is correct.

d) Work with three students from Group A and follow these instructions. Group A starts.

1 Listen to Group A's definitions for idiom 1. Discuss which definition you think is correct. Ask Group A to repeat their definitions if necessary.
2 Tell Group A which definition you think is correct. Say why you think the other two definitions are false. Group A then reads out the correct definition. Were you correct?
3 Give your definitions for idiom a). Continue with the game until both groups have guessed three definitions.

e) Which group guessed the most correct definitions?

4B ④ p40

a) Work with another student from Group B. Look at this list of cities. Which country is each city in?

> Los Angeles Madrid São Paulo Shanghai Tokyo

b) These figures show the population growth per hour in the cities in a). Try to match the figures to the cities.

> +3 +8 +9 +25 +31

c) Work with a student from Group A. Listen to your partner's answers and check the information. Say how many your partner got right.

> **Student A's answers**
>
> Berlin (Germany) +0
> Istanbul (Turkey) +17
> London (UK) +6
> Mumbai (India) +42
> Warsaw (Poland) +1

d) Give your answers to a) and b). Your partner will check your answers. How many did you get right?

e) Did any of the figures surprise you?

7A ⑨ p68

a) Work with another student from Group B. You are in favour of open prisons. Because of recent advances in forensic science, more arrests are being made and there is a danger of overcrowding in prisons. Make a list of reasons why there should be more open prisons for all categories of offenders.

b) You are at a meeting to discuss how best to deal with crime. Work in groups of four with a pair from Group A. Take turns to give your point of view. Decide on the best way to deal with crime.

If prisoners acquired skills in prison they would be less likely to re-offend when they come out.

c) Decide which is the best way to deal with crime: open or closed prisons.

d) Tell the class what your group decided.

3B ❸ p29

a) Read extracts 4–6 from the article, 'Great ways to well-being'. Then answer these questions.

a) What is the advice? Did it match any of your predictions?
b) According to the research, how can the advice contribute to a person's well-being?
c) What facts or figures, if any, support the research?

④

Eat dark chocolate. Although dark chocolate was once thought to be unhealthy, with its high levels of cocoa beans it is now believed to be good for you in moderation, with research showing it can reduce blood pressure* and bad cholesterol. According to research at Harvard University, flavonoids in dark chocolate reduce the risk of dying from heart disease by 20%.

⑤

Brush your teeth. Not only does good dental hygiene save painful and expensive visits to the dentist, it may also prevent strokes* or heart attacks. Columbia University research based on around 700 people found that those with gum disease were more likely to suffer from narrowing of blood vessels that can lead to heart attacks.

⑥

Laugh a lot. Laughing reduces pain and diabetes* symptoms and also improves the immune system*. Researchers have calculated that laughter burns up calories* at the rate of 2.31 a minute. An average day's laughter gets rid of all the calories in a pepperoni pizza.

blood pressure = the force with which blood travels round the body
a stroke = when a blood vessel in the brain becomes blocked or bursts
immune system = system by which your body protects itself against diseases
diabetes /daɪəˈbiːtiːz/ = a serious disease in which there is too much sugar in your blood
calorie = a unit for measuring the amount of energy that food will produce

b) Work with the other people in your group. Take turns to tell each other your answers to the questions.

4B ⓮ p41

③

④

a) Work with another student from Group B. Look at inventions 3 and 4. Then discuss these questions.

1 What were these inventions supposed to do?
2 Why did the inventors think they would be popular?
3 What do you think were the good and bad aspects of the inventions?
4 Do you think they would be popular in your country? Why?/Why not?

b) Work with a student from Group A and a student from Group C. Take turns to describe your inventions, explaining what they were supposed to do. The other students should try and draw what you have described.

> The person who invented this obviously thought it would help office workers. It was supposed to ...

c) Compare your drawings with the original pictures on p109 and p114. Decide which you think is the best and the weirdest invention.

7B 9 p71

a) Work with a student from Group B. Read these newspaper headlines. Choose two and add extra information, e.g. why you think the measures have been introduced and what will happen as a result.

① **RFID tags soon to check how much food we have in our fridge**

② *Cameras in streets to monitor responsible pet ownership*

③ **LOCAL FIREWORK DISPLAY CANCELLED 'IN CASE OF POTENTIAL INJURY'**

b) Work in pairs with a student from Group A and tell each other your stories. What do you think about these issues?

c) Work in the same pairs. Think of any other similar stories that have happened or could happen in the future.

4C 4 p43

a) Work in pairs with a student from Group B. You are reporters on a tabloid newspaper. Read this outline of a possible lead story.

> 200 drivers trapped in cars and coaches on A66 in north of England last night because of heavy snow and gales. Snow came in very fast, no warning. Some occupants waited for several hours before being rescued by police. Many rescued from A66 were taken to nearby villages. 45 pensioners taken to hotel to wait for a bus. Many motorists arrived on foot, cold and wet. Villagers helped with refreshments, etc. but village hall had no sleeping facilities. Roads now closed.

b) Write a short first paragraph and think of a dramatic photo. Make a note of what else you intend to include. Think of reasons why your story should make the 'splash' tomorrow.

c) Work in a group of three with students from groups A and C. Take turns to present your story to the news editor and say why your story is the best.

d) Listen to the news editor's reasons for choosing one of the stories.

5B 2 p49

Dizzee Rascal

I started writing lyrics when I was 14. The biggest thing has been learning just to go on doing it – to keep pressing on. I feel alone a lot. All you've got is yourself, so if you're not trying hard enough or working your best, it's you who has to live with that.

I've always had an interest in music. As a person, you hope to get wherever you can, but for me all of this is almost an accident. I regret to say that at school I was trouble – four times I was kicked out of places. At my last school I was walking a tightrope, but the music teacher let me stay there and encouraged me to experiment. Making beats went on to become my life, without me knowing it. If I hadn't had music, I would have been on the streets.

Often, I'll be working myself until I'm ill. I'm always trying to find the next song, the next move, the next whatever, and worrying about it. A lot of the time I feel separated from other people my age. I didn't try to be a role model. When I do the right thing, I hope I can help. I always try to reach out.

5A 10 p48

a) You are a famous person. You know that your employee is not entirely happy with his/her working conditions. You don't want to lose him/her because otherwise you would have to pay for a housekeeper, babysitter and dog walker as well. Look at the list of some things you know he/she would like to change. Think of ways in which you are prepared to compromise.

- He/She is annoyed about having to work long hours in a six-day week.
- He/She has little holiday time.
- He/She was expecting more administrative work and travel, and less domestic work.

b) Work with your partner. Tell him/her about the ways in which you are prepared to compromise.

> OK, I'll make sure you have time to get yourself some lunch from now on.

Pair and Group Work: Other activities

⑤

⑥

a) Work with another student from Group C. Look at inventions 5 and 6. Then discuss these questions.

1 What were these inventions supposed to do?
2 Why did the inventors think they would be popular?
3 What do you think were the good and bad aspects of the inventions?
4 Do you think they would be popular in your country? Why?/Why not?

b) Work with a student from Group A and a student from Group B. Take turns to describe your inventions, explaining what they were supposed to do. The other students should try and draw what you have described.

> The person who invented this obviously thought it was going to help commuters. It was supposed to ...

c) Compare your drawings with the pictures on p109 and p112. Decide which you think is the best and the weirdest invention.

a) Work in pairs with a student from Group C. You are reporters on a tabloid newspaper. Read this outline of a possible lead story.

> A two-year-old boy has been hailed as a hero after he found his mother collapsed on the floor and calmly dialled 999. He was too frightened to give his name but Joshua Brookes explained to the operator that his mummy wouldn't wake up. Police traced their address and paramedics went to the house but couldn't get in, so Joshua stood on a box and let them in. His mother, Isobel, who suffers from a rare heart condition, was taken to hospital, where she made a full recovery.

b) Write a short first paragraph and think of a dramatic photo. Make a note of what else you intend to include in the story. Think of reasons why your story should make the 'splash' that day.

c) Work in a group of three with students from groups A and B. Take turns to present your story to the news editor and say why your story is the best.

d) Listen to the news editor's reasons for choosing one of the stories.

3B ③ p29

a) Read extracts 7–9 from the article, 'Great ways to well-being'. Then answer these questions.

a) What is the advice? Did it match any of your predictions?
b) According to the research, how can the advice contribute to a person's well-being?
c) What facts or figures, if any, support the research?

(7)

Drink tea. Tea, both black and green, has been associated with a wide range of health benefits, from helping to prevent heart disease and flu, to hair growth and weight loss. A King's College study says that three or more cups a day reduce the risk of heart attack, and there is some evidence that it can improve mental performance.

(8)

Get a pet. Laughter is linked to good health and research shows that dog owners have the most giggles during the day. Pet dogs can lower heart rate and reduce stress, but having a cat reduces the risk of a child developing eczema* and hay fever. Researchers at Rakuno Gakuen University in Japan calculate that 30-minute walks with a dog are 87% more effective for heart health than going for walks on your own.

(9)

Chew gum. Not only is chewing gum good for oral health, especially sugar-free gum, but research at Glasgow Caledonian University shows that people who chew gum eat fewer snacks and 10% fewer calories*. It's also good for face muscles and high blood pressure* and diabetes*. And according to a report published by the University of Michigan, chewing gum may prevent tooth decay.

*eczema = a skin condition when the skin becomes red and sore
*calorie = a unit for measuring the amount of energy that food will produce
*blood pressure = the force with which blood travels round the body
*diabetes /daɪəˈbiːtiːz/ = a serious disease in which there is too much sugar in your blood

b) Work with the other people in your group. Take turns to tell each other your answers to the questions.

5B ② p49

Sophie Christiansen

When I first took up riding at the age of six, it was just meant to make physiotherapy fun. I would have to do ten different exercises just to loosen up my muscles, because they get really tight. Riding really helps.

Cerebral palsy has affected all my limbs, so I find coordination difficult. Dressage is about many things – beauty, grace, movement – but above all it means coordinating really well in order to control the horse. It makes you feel amazing.

It has been hard on my family. When I compete, I get really intense and argue with Mum. She's done very well to put up with that, especially as she's allergic to horses! But competing has turned my life around. I used to be quite shy and self-conscious.

I've always been quite determined not to let anything get in the way. Unless you have the mindset it's no use having the ability to do a sport. I don't let anything stop me. I still go out clubbing with my mates. I'm a normal young person. My anthem is *Don't Stop Me Now* by Queen.

7C ⑥ p73

a) Work on your own. You are Emma. You are going to be interviewed by a police officer. Read this information and add your own ideas.

- You were surprised when Mike turned up, and he seemed strange. (In what way?)
- You hadn't seen him for a long time before that day. (How long?)
- Mike seemed to be doing well at work – he was wearing new clothes and had a new phone. (What did you think?)
- You offered to make you both some pasta but he seemed very eager to go out and get pizza. (What did you say to him?)
- He was a long time getting back – he said there'd been a queue for pizzas.
- He insisted on staying at your house until late. You couldn't understand why, especially as he obviously didn't want to watch TV. (Why? What do you think he wanted?)

b) Work with your partner. Answer the police officer's questions.

c) Work in groups of four. Have you changed your mind about whether Mike is guilty or not? Discuss the evidence.

3B ③ p29

a) Read extracts 10–12 from the article, 'Great ways to well-being'. Then answer these questions.

a) What is the advice? Did it match any of your predictions?

b) According to the research, how can the advice contribute to a person's well-being?

c) What facts or figures, if any, support the research?

⑩

Eat fish. Very rarely do you hear anything negative about eating fish. That's because according to more than 10,000 pieces of research, fish and its oils can protect you from or treat just about everything, from bad backs to asthma*. It can also contribute to healthy brain cells and good eyesight. A study from Harvard University shows that women who eat plenty of sardines, tuna and salmon during pregnancy may have cleverer children.

⑪

Take up singing. Choral singing increases immunity, reduces depression, improves cognitive function* and mood, and increases feelings of well-being. Work carried out at Sydney University and the University of Frankfurt shows singing helps people cope better with chronic pain, lowers stress levels and boosts the immune system*.

⑫

Get married. Seldom do people associate being married with being healthy. However, having a good marriage can extend your life, reduce the risk of heart disease, and catching colds, and can lower blood pressure. A study by the University of Tampere, Finland, shows that married men are 70% more likely to live longer than single men.

asthma = illness that causes breathing difficulties
cognitive function = ability to think
immune system = system by which your body protects itself against diseases

b) Work with the other people in your group. Take turns to tell each other your answers to the questions.

5B ② p49

Iris Andrews

What I do is nothing to do with talent. It's a passion. I have been passionate and aware and asked questions about the world for as long as I can remember but I only began to focus my energy on this stuff when I was 15. I managed to get support from some of my peers by campaigning and holding assemblies and discussions.

Far from being voiceless and insignificant, young people have enormous power. If my generation could screw up just a tiny bit less than previous generations and be slightly more conscious of the impact we have on our planet and our people, I'd be very happy.

Doing this helps me to get a broader perspective on my own life. For me, the biggest struggle has been losing both parents when I was still at school. Although I will obviously always regret losing them, having opened my eyes to the bigger picture I now see that this is nowhere near the end of the world. I often feel like I'm a complete fraud – that I'm going to get found out soon – and that what I do isn't that special or impressive. I try to make my little difference. A lot of people think I can.

Vocabulary

V1.1 Communicating (1A **2** p6)

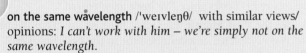

make eye contact when two people look into each other's eyes at the same time

come into contact with be in communication with people or ideas

gossip talk about other people's private lives

butt in interrupt someone who is talking

overhear accidentally hear what other people are saying without their knowledge

have a row /raʊ/ argue, especially loudly

witter /ˈwɪtə/ **on** talk about unimportant things for a long time

grumble /ˈgrʌmbl/ complain about somebody or something

chat talk to somebody in a friendly informal way

bicker /ˈbɪkə/ argue about unimportant matters

chat (sb) up talk to somebody in a way that shows them that you are sexually attracted to them

TIPS! • In the Language Summaries we only show the main stress (·) in words and phrases.

• We can sometimes combine a verb and a noun to describe an action: *They had a gossip over coffee.* instead of *They gossiped over coffee.*

• We do not use *butt in* in formal contexts, e.g. in a meeting.

V1.2 Prepositions and phrases (1B **7** p11)

on the same wavelength /ˈweɪvleŋθ/ with similar views/opinions: *I can't work with him – we're simply not on the same wavelength.*

on purpose intentionally, not by accident: *We can't prove it but we're sure he broke it on purpose.*

on good terms have a good relationship with one another: *Jerry always tries to stay on good terms with ex-girlfriends.* (opposite: **on bad terms**)

on a regular basis /beɪsɪs/ happening or doing something often: *She sees her ex-husband on a regular basis, so they must still get on.*

on average typically: *On average, I go to the cinema twice a month.*

in phases /ˈfeɪzɪz/ for short, irregular periods of time: *I'm a member of a gym but I only go in phases.*

in the long run after a very lengthy period of time: *Although taxes have risen twice recently, in the long run the government believes we will all benefit.*

in touch in communication (with): *I'm still in touch with my old school friends.* (opposite: **out of touch**)

in common sharing interests, experience, or other characteristics with someone or something: *I've never had much in common with my sister, but we still get on.*

in contact communicating with someone: *I stay in contact with my friends abroad by email.*

out of habit something you do often, without thinking about it: *Many people smoke out of habit rather than because they want a cigarette.*

out of your depth /depθ/ without the knowledge or skills to deal with something: *Within half an hour of the start of the meeting, it was clear he was out of his depth.*

out of control not under the authority or power of someone: *The economic situation is out of control at the moment.* (opposite: **in control**)

out of fashion being unpopular at a particular time, especially clothes, hair, etc.: *Fur coats have gone out of fashion in recent years.* (opposite: **in fashion**)

out of necessity /nesesɪti/ because of a need: *He doesn't work out of necessity, but because he wants to.*

TIP! • Make a note of nouns together with their prepositions and try to learn them as 'chunks' of meaning.

V1.3 Sayings (1C **1** p12)

Rome wasn't built in a day. said to emphasise that you can't expect to do a lot of things in a short period of time

Don't make a mountain out of a molehill. don't make a slight difficulty seem like a serious problem

Once bitten, twice shy. said when you are frightened to do something again because you had an unpleasant experience doing it the first time

Actions speak louder than words. said to emphasise that what you do is more important and shows your intentions and feelings more clearly than what you say

One man's meat is another man's poison. said to emphasise that people like different things

Engage brain before mouth. think about something before saying anything about it

Nothing ventured, nothing gained. said to emphasise that you have to take a risk in order to obtain a benefit

Better late than never. said when you think that it is better for somebody or something to be late than never to arrive or to happen

Rome wasn't built in a day

Language Summary 1

Grammar

G1.1 Past Simple and Present Perfect

Preview 1 1A **1** p6

Past Simple

- We use the **Past Simple**:
  a) for a single completed action in the past: *How old **were** you when you **had** your first English lesson? When **was** the last time you **spoke** English outside class?*
  b) for a repeated action or habit in the past: *My son **had** some lessons at that school.*
  c) for a state in the past: *I **was** always good at languages.*

- We also use the **Past Simple** with expressions such as *the first/last time: The last time I **bought** a dictionary was when I was at school.*

- We use the **Present Perfect** to talk about things that connect the past and the present.

- We often use the **Present Perfect Simple**:
  a) for experiences: ***Have** you ever **read** a novel that was written in English?*
  b) for states or activities that started in the past and continue in the present: *I**'ve had** this dictionary for years.*
  c) for completed actions that happened recently, but we don't say exactly when: ***Have** you **seen** any films in English recently?*
  d) with superlatives: *It's the easiest language I**'ve learned**.*
  e) to talk about change: *My English **has improved** since this course started.*

- We often use the **Present Perfect Continuous**:
  a) for longer actions that started in the past and continue in the present: *I**'ve been working** on this for two hours.*
  b) for longer actions that have recently finished, but have a result in the present: *I'm tired because I**'ve been revising** for an exam.*
  c) for actions that happened repeatedly in the past and still happen in the present: *How long **have you been coming** to this school?*

SIMPLE OR CONTINUOUS?

- We often use the **Present Perfect Continuous** to emphasise the action we've been doing rather than the result: *I**'ve been reading** this book.* (we don't know if the book is finished or not)

- We often use the **Present Perfect Simple** to say that something is completed: *I**'ve read** that book.* (the book is finished now)

G1.2 Time expressions with Past Simple and Present Perfect

1A **5** p7

- We can use the **Present Perfect** with time expressions which mean up to and including now: *I**'ve bought** quite a few self-help books <u>over the past few months</u>. I**'ve read** about 150 pages <u>so far</u>. <u>During the last couple of weeks</u> I**'ve** actually **been trying** out some of Carnegie's suggestions. <u>Up until now</u>, I**'ve** never really **had** any contact with the guy in the ticket office.*

- We use the **Past Simple** with definite time expressions in the past (*yesterday, a few weeks ago, last year*, etc.): *... in 1937 the book's runaway success **meant** the publishers **had** difficulty keeping up with demand.*

- Some time expressions can be used with both the **Present Perfect Simple** and **Past Simple**. Compare these sentences:

  A *I **told** at least ten people about it at work <u>this week</u>.*
  B *I**'ve told** at least ten people about it at work <u>this week</u>.*

  Speaker A uses the **Past Simple** because he/she considers the period of time (this week) as finished. Speaker B uses the **Present Perfect** because he/she considers the period of time (this week) as still continuing.

  A *I **read** it <u>during</u> the summer holidays.*
  B *I**'ve read** a lot of books <u>during</u> the last month.*

  Speaker A uses the **Past Simple** because the event (reading the book) was completed at a definite time in the past (during the summer holidays). Speaker B uses the **Present Perfect** because the time period (during the last month) is still continuing.

  A *<u>Since</u> Ann **suggested** this one I've read a couple of his other books.*
  B *I**'ve read** lots of his books <u>since</u> I**'ve been** unemployed.*

  Speaker A uses the **Past Simple** after *since* because the event (Ann's suggestion) was completed at a definite time in the past. Speaker B uses the **Present Perfect** because the event (being unemployed) is continuing to happen.

  A <u>*As soon as* I **finished**</u> reading it, I gave it to my brother.
  B <u>*As soon as* I**'ve finished**</u> reading it, I'm going to give it to my brother.

  Speaker A uses the **Past Simple** because the event (reading the book/magazine, etc.) was completed at a definite time in the past. Speaker B uses the **Present Perfect** because the event (reading the book) started in the past but is continuing to happen. After *as soon as* the Present Perfect refers to future events.

TIPS! • We can replace *as soon as* with *once/when/after: I'll lend it to you once I've finished it.*

• We use *during* or *in + the last few days/weeks/months/years*, etc.: *During/In the last couple of months I've read three of her books.*

• We use *up until / until / till / up to + now: I've written four pages up to now.*

• We use *It's (not) the first time* with the Present Perfect to talk about the first instance of something happening: *It's the first time I've read a book like this, really.*

• We can also say *This is (not) / That's (not) the first (second, third, fourth, etc.) time ... : This is the fourth time I've written a review of a book.*

Grammar

G1.3 Cleft sentences: *what* and *it* clauses (1B ❸ p9)

- Cleft sentences divide a message into two parts, using *what* or *it* clauses. They can focus attention on new, more important or contradictory information.
  (*I can get a bit stressed by work.*) **What** *I do if I get stressed* **is** *talk to my friends.* (new information)
  (*I get on well with my parents.*) *However,* **it's** *my friends* **that** *I talk to if I have a problem.* (contradiction).

WHAT CLAUSES

- Cleft sentences with *what* are very common in spoken English.
  (*We'll have a drink and talk afterwards.*) **What** *we talk about* **isn't** <u>deep and meaningful, though</u>.

- The *what* clause is immediately followed by known information. We know that they talk because of the speaker's previous sentence.

- The new information, that their conversation isn't deep and meaningful, is in the <u>underlined</u> part of the sentence.

- We join the two clauses in this type of cleft sentence with *be*.

- To focus on an action we can use *what* + subject + *do* + *be* (+ subject) + infinitive clause:
  (What Simon does) is (pretend he hasn't heard me.)

- To focus on a whole sentence, we can use *what happens* + *be* + subject + clause:
  (What happens) is (we always end up having a row.)

TIPS! • When we use *who, why, whose, when, where*, etc. instead of *what*, we usually use an expression such as *a person, the reason*, etc. with or without the *wh-* word: *A person* (**who**) *I tend to confide in* **is** *my hairdresser.* *The reason* (**why**) *we meet there* **is** *because they put up with all our noise.*

• We can reverse the order of the clauses in *wh-*cleft sentences without changing the meaning: *The person* (*who*) *I used to sound off to most was my hairdresser* = *My hairdresser was the person* (*who*) *I used to sound off to most.*

• We can use *the thing/something/all/anything/one thing*, etc. in place of *what/whatever* in cleft sentences. These phrases are especially common in informal spoken language: *The thing I hate is men chatting me up.* *Anything I do is wrong, it seems.*

IT CLAUSES

- In cleft sentences with an *it* clause, the speaker emphasises the information in the clause with *it*.
  It'd probably **be** <u>my parents</u> **who** *I'd talk to first.*
  It wasn't *until he* <u>broke up with his girlfriend</u> **that** *my hairdresser started to confide in me.*

- The verb that follows *it* is *be*.

TIPS! • In cleft sentences with an *it* clause, *who* can be used instead of *that* when referring to a person/people.

• When there is a plural noun in the *it* clause we still use a singular form of verb *be*: *It's his friends that I can't stand.* not *It are his friends* … .

• We use an object pronoun after *it* + *be*: *He's always gossiping.*
  → *It's* **him** *that's always gossiping.*

Real World

RW1.1 Explaining and paraphrasing (1C ❸ p13)

- When we need to clarify, simplify or explain something we have already said, we often use phrases which signal to the listener that we are going to say the same thing again in a different way.
  Which simply/just/basically means …
  And what it/this/that means is …
  What I mean by that is …
  By which I mean …
  What I'm trying to say is …
  Which is to say …
  To put it simply, …
  That is to say, …
  Or to put it another way, …
  In other words, …

TIP! • We can also say *i.e.* /ˈaɪjiː/ (= *that is*) or *meaning* to paraphrase: *We'll meet there, i.e. at the station. He said he was a bit busy, meaning he wasn't going to come.*

Accurate Writing

AW1.1 Connecting words: addition (❶ p15)

- We sometimes use connecting words to join clauses and sentences that add information.

- We usually use **as well** and **too** at the end of a clause: *She's been running the company since November. She's got three children to look after,* **as well/too**. *Chinese food is very tasty. It's quite cheap* **as well/too**.

- We can use **also** at the beginning or in the middle of a clause: *The traffic is really heavy at this time of day. The roads are* **also** *extremely icy, so be careful/***Also** *the roads are extremely icy so be careful.*

- We usually use **not only** with **but**: *The village is* **not only** *remote* **but** *totally inaccessible by road.*

- We use **what's more** and **besides** at the beginning of a sentence: *I haven't got any change on me.* **What's more/Besides**, *you already owe me money from last time.*

TIPS! • We do not usually use **also**, **too**, or **as well** in negative clauses. Instead we use phrases such as *either*: *I haven't read the Harry Potter books or seen the films either.* not ~~I haven't read the Harry Potter books or seen the films too~~.

AW1.2 Spelling: homophones (❷ p15)

- Homophones are words that sound the same, but have different spellings and different meanings.

- Some common homophones are: *whose/who's, there/they're/their, of/'ve, you're/your*

119

Language Summary 2

G2.3 Verb + *ing* and past participles

Preview 2 **3** p15

We use verb+*ing*:

- as an adjective: *We found the prospect of giving a talk rather **frightening**.*

- in reduced relative clauses: *People who are leaving early should do so very quietly.* → *People **leaving** early should do so very quietly.*

- after certain verbs: *However much I ask her not to, she can't **resist spoiling** her grandchildren.*

- after prepositions: *According to the manual, that switch is **for opening** the boot.*

We use past participles:

- in reduced relative clauses where the original clause contains a passive verb: *The castle, which was built in the tenth century, is just round the corner from where we're staying.* → *The castle, **built** in the tenth century, ...*

- as an adjective: *Karen was soon **bored** out of her mind by the guided tour.*

G2.4 Participle clauses (2B **3** p20)

- Some participle clauses give more information about a verb or idea in a sentence. They are often used to make a piece of writing more varied and sophisticated.
  Because we arrived late, we couldn't find a room. → *Arriving late, we couldn't find a room.*

- There are three types of participle clauses:

PRESENT PARTICIPLE CLAUSE

*... **acting as a vital means of communication** between remote villages and crowded towns.*

Gliding silently along in a canoe you get to see a rural Kerala... .

PAST PARTICIPLE CLAUSE

Caught locally every day, it's always wonderfully fresh.

Poured very slowly across your forehead, the oil feels like a cow is licking you.

PERFECT PARTICIPLE CLAUSE

... having had an indulgent lunch, I'd lie in a hammock ...

- Participle clauses can replace connecting words such as *so, while, because, if, after,* etc. When we use participles instead of connecting words, we usually leave out the subject and sometimes the auxiliary. We also change the verb to the present, past or perfect forms of the participle. Compare the following sentences:

While you → glide silently along in a canoe, you get to see a rural Kerala.
Gliding silently along in a canoe, you get to see a rural Kerala.

- Participle clauses often give information about the causes, results, conditions or time of the events described.

... acting as a vital means of communication between remote villages and crowded towns. (result)
Gliding silently along in a canoe you get to see a rural Kerala. (time)
Caught locally everyday it's always wonderfully fresh. (cause)
Poured very slowly across your forehead, the oil feels like a cow licking you. (condition)
Having had an indulgent lunch, I'd lie in a hammock. (time)

TIPS! • The subject of a participle clause is usually the same as the subject of the main clause: *Looking out of the window, Verity noticed the sun had almost set.* (the subject of both clauses is Verity) not ~~Looking out of the window, the sun had almost set~~. (This suggests that the sun is looking out of the window.)

• When we use *not* in a participle clause, it usually comes before the participle: *Not wanting to wait any longer, he left.* ('not' refers to 'wanting to wait any longer' which means that he didn't want to wait any longer.) However, *not* can also follow the participle: *Pretending not to notice him, she walked straight past.* ('not' refers to noticing him, which means that she pretended that she hadn't noticed him)

• We use a perfect participle (*having* + past participle) instead of a present participle if the action in the main clause is the result of the events in the participle clause: *Having lost our credit cards, we had to get some money sent to us.* (We had to get some money sent to us because we had lost our credit cards). not ~~Losing our credit cards~~ ... .

• We can use prepositions such as *after, by, in, while, with, since,* etc. with a present or perfect participle clause to make the meaning clearer: *After visiting / having visited several temples, we returned to the hotel for a rest. By not eating between meals, she managed to reach her target weight.*

Pretending not to notice him, she walked straight past

Accurate Writing

AW2.1 Connecting words: time (1) p25

We can use:

- *the moment/as soon as* at the beginning of a clause to say something will happen immediately after something else has happened. When we refer to a point in the future we usually use the **Present Simple** after *the moment/as soon as* rather than a future form: *The moment I get home, I'm going straight to bed.* not ~~The moment I will get home~~ ... .

- **Past Simple** after *the moment/as soon as* when talking about the past: *The moment I met him I decided he was the man I was going to marry.*

- *ever since* at the beginning of a clause to mean 'continually since that time': *Ever since he came to the school he's been nothing but trouble.*

- *first/originally* at the beginning of a clause, in front of the main verb or after the verb *be* to talk about something as it was in the past: *The cottage was originally a post office but it was converted a hundred years ago.*

- *from then on* at the beginning of a sentence to mean 'continually since that time'. However, *from then on* refers to information in a previous sentence or clause. Note that we can also use *ever since then* instead of 'from then on': *I bought a new computer last month. From then on/Ever since (then) I've had nothing but trouble with it.*

- *while/as* at the beginning of clauses to say that something happens during the same time that something else happens: *I caught a glimpse of Steve while I was hurrying down the street.*

- *afterwards/then* at the beginning of sentences to talk about an event that happens after the time mentioned or later: *I accepted their invitation to supper. Afterwards, I regretted it. He began asking the boss about his plans. Then he realised the mistake he'd made and changed the subject quickly.*

- *meanwhile* at the beginning of a sentence to talk about an event that happens while something else is happening: *I sat anxiously waiting for the call. Meanwhile, I tried to get on with some work but kept looking at the clock.*

AW2.2 Punctuation: apostrophes p25

We use an apostrophe ('):

- in contracted forms of *be*, *have* and modal verbs and between 'n' and 't' in contracted forms with *not*: *I'm, I've, I'd* (= I had or I would), *don't, didn't, shouldn't, there's.*

- in front of an 's' added to a noun, or after a plural noun ending in 's' to show a relationship of possession: *Sally's friend, the friends' relationship.*

- in front of an 's' added to an irregular plural to show a relationship of possession: *the children's father.*

We do not use an apostrophe:

- in possessive pronouns such as *his, hers, ours* or *theirs.*

- in the possessive adjective *its*: *The house has its own swimming pool.* not ~~The house has it's own swimming pool.~~

The moment I get home, I'm going straight to bed

I sat anxiously waiting for the call. **Meanwhile**, I tried to get on with some work but kept looking at the clock.

Language Summary 3

Vocabulary

V3.1 Positive character adjectives 3A ❶ p26

Courageous /kəˈreɪdʒəs/ people have the ability to control their fear in a dangerous or difficult situation: *It was very courageous of her to resign without finding another job first.*

Determined people want to do something very much and don't let anyone or any difficulties stop them: *If you're determined to lose weight, you will.*

Meticulous /meˈtɪkjʊləs/ people are very careful and pay great attention to every detail: *I can't believe this was written by Paul – it's so inaccurate! He's normally meticulous in everything he does.*

Generous /ˈdʒenərəs/ people are willing to give money, help, etc., especially more than is usual or expected: *It was very generous of you to pay for dinner.*

Trusting people always believe that other people are good or honest and will not harm or deceive them: *This is the second time she hasn't paid me back. I shouldn't be so trusting.*

Thrifty /ˈθrɪfti/ people are careful with the use of money, especially by avoiding waste: *He earns a lot of money these days but he's still quite thrifty.*

Confident people are certain of their abilities or have trust in people, plans or the future: *I think your idea is brilliant. You should be a bit more confident.*

Spontaneous /spɒnˈteɪnəs/ people do things in a natural, often sudden, way, without any planning or without being forced: *She's always been a spontaneous sort – flying off all over the place at a moment's notice.*

Cautious /ˈkɔːʃəs/ people act with great care and attention, especially to avoid taking risks: *I wouldn't exactly describe Sam as a cautious driver! He's had three accidents in the last year.*

V3.2 Connotation: positive and negative character adjectives 3A ⓫ p28

- *Connotation* means a feeling or idea that is suggested by a particular word. Sometimes two character adjectives can describe similar traits, but one may have a positive connotation and one may have a negative connotation.

- Both *arrogant* and *confident* refer to someone who is very sure of themselves, but arrogant means the person also thinks they are better than other people. *Confident* has a positive connotation. *Arrogant* has a negative connotation.

negative connotation	positive connotation
arrogant	confident
reckless*	courageous
tight-fisted*	thrifty
finicky*	meticulous
extravagant*	generous
gullible*	trusting
obstinate*	determined
impetuous*	spontaneous
timid*	cautious

Reckless people do dangerous things and do not care about the risks and the possible results.

Tight-fisted people are unwilling to spend money.

Finicky /ˈfɪnɪki/ people are difficult to please.

Extravagant people spend money in an uncontrolled way.

Gullible people are easily deceived and believe everything that other people say.

Obstinate /ˈɒbstɪnət/ people are unreasonably determined to act in a certain way despite persuasion.

Impetuous /ɪmˈpetjʊəs/ people act on a sudden idea without considering the results of their actions.

Timid people are shy or are easily frightened.

V3.3 Phrasal verbs: health 3B ❶ p29

get over sb/sth get better after an illness, or feel better after something or somebody has made you unhappy

swell up when a part of your body becomes larger and rounder than usual, often because of an illness or injury

pick up catch an illness from somebody or something

be blocked /blɒkt/ **up** when a part of your body, e.g. your nose, is filled with something that prevents anything getting past

go down with sth become ill, usually with a disease that is not very serious

go around when a lot of people get an illness in the same time period because the illness passes from person to person

put sb on sth give somebody a particular type of medical treatment or food

come out in sth when spots or a rash appear on your skin

V3.4 Euphemisms 3C ❶ p32

- A euphemism is a word or phrase used to avoid saying something unpleasant or offensive.

economical /iːkəˈnɒmɪkl/ **with the truth** not tell the truth; lie

a senior citizen an old person

behind the times be old-fashioned

see better days be old and in bad condition

get on a bit get old

hard of hearing not able to hear well

be/feel under the weather be or feel ill

a bit of a handful difficult to look after, especially children and animals

challenging very difficult

a bit on the chilly side cold

Grammar

G3.1 Introductory *it* (3A **6** p27)

INTRODUCTORY *IT* AS SUBJECT

- If the subject of the verb is a long and grammatically complex structure, we often put it at the end of the clause/sentence and use *it* as the subject of the verb at the beginning of the clause/sentence. Compare these sentences. The subject of the verb is underlined:

  That no one was hurt is incredible.
  It's incredible that no one was hurt.

- We can use several structures with introductory *it* as subject:

  it + verb:

  a) + adjective + (*that*): **It's clear that** …

  b) + (*not*) + noun + (*that*): **It's not an aspect** …

  c) + adjective + infinitive with *to*: **it's difficult to know** …

  d) + *that* clause: **it follows that not winning** is stressful. Other verbs we use with this structure include *appear*, *transpire*. The *that* clause cannot go in initial position in these sentences, e.g. not ~~That not winning is stressful it follows~~.

  e) + object + infinitive with *to* + *that*: **it surprised him to discover** that … . Other verbs we can use with this structure are connected with feelings, e.g. *amaze, annoy, astonish, concern, frighten, hurt, scare, shock, upset, worry.*

INTRODUCTORY *IT* AS OBJECT

- We often use *it* as the object of a verb where *it* refers to a clause later in the sentence:

  I love it that my parents are always supportive. not ~~I love that my parents are always supportive.~~

- We can use these structures with introductory *it* as object:

  verb + it:

  a) + *when*: … *we all* **hate it when** *we lose!* Other verbs we use this structure with include: *can't bear, can't stand, dislike, enjoy, like, love, prefer, resent, understand.*

  b) + adjective + infinitive with *to*: … **find it difficult to cope** with losing.

TIPS! • We don't use introductory *it* if the subject of the verb is a noun. *Their fears were completely unfounded.* not ~~It was completely unfounded their fears~~.

• Common expressions with introductory it: **It's no good** getting all upset about it. **It's no use** asking her, she's busy. **It's no wonder** that he got ill. **It's no coincidence** that they arrived together.

G3.2 Subject and verb inversion (Preview 3 **1** p25)

- In statements the verb usually follows the subject: *I don't know him.*
- Sometimes we invert the subject and verb so that the verb comes before the subject.
- We use inversion:

  a) after *so, neither/nor*: *I need an eye test. So* **do I**. *I didn't know there was sugar in this. No, neither/nor* **did I**.

  b) in the phrases *Here comes/come* + noun and *There goes/go* + noun: **Here comes** *the doctor.*

  c) in question tags: *She's a doctor,* **isn't she**?

- We **do not** put the verb before the subject:

  a) when we include a question in another question. Instead, we use a normal word order of subject + verb: *Where* **are my glasses**? → *Have you any idea where* **my glasses are**?

  b) when we include a question in another sentence: *What's his* **diet** *like?* → *I wonder what his* **diet's** *like.*

  c) when we are using a question word to introduce a relative clause in phrases such as *I don't know what/when* etc. or *I wonder what/ why* etc.: *I don't know* **what his problem is**. not ~~I don't know what is his problem~~.

  d) in indirect speech. We use *if* when we report a *yes/no* question. We usually (but not always) change the verb form in reported speech: **Are you** *taking any vitamins?* → *He asked me if* **I was** *taking any vitamins.*

TIP! • We can't use inversion when we use pronouns with *Here come(s)* or *There go(es)*: *Here they come,* not ~~Here come they~~.

G3.3 Inversion (3B **5** p30)

- Inversion is a way of adding emphasis or dramatic effect.
- An adverbial is any word or phrase which functions as an adverb. When we begin a sentence with a limiting adverbial (e.g. *seldom*) or a negative adverbial (e.g. *under no circumstances*), the subject and the auxiliary verb are inverted: **I am rarely** *able to get out before seven.* **Rarely am I** *able to get out before seven.*
- Look at the underlined examples of inversion structures in these sentences:

  a) *People seldom associate being married with being healthy.* → **Seldom** <u>do people associate</u> being married with being healthy.

  b) *Dental hygiene saves painful and expensive visits to the dentist …* → **Not only** <u>does dental hygiene save</u> painful …

  c) *He didn't agree to stop smoking until last week.* → **Not until** last week <u>did he agree</u> to stop smoking.

  d) *You very rarely hear anything negative about eating fish.* → **Very rarely** <u>do you hear</u> anything negative about eating fish.

  e) *Experts have only recently come to appreciate the health benefits of eating curry.* → **Only recently** <u>have experts come</u> to appreciate …

  f) *You should not, under any circumstances, exercise immediately after eating a heavy meal.* → **Under no circumstances** <u>should you exercise</u> immediately after eating a heavy meal.

- When using inversion with Present Simple and Past Simple, the subject must agree with the auxiliary not the main verb: *Not only* **does he** enjoy… . not ~~Not only do/does he enjoys …~~ .

Language Summary 3

Grammar

- With modal verbs, e.g. *will, should, would*, etc., we invert the subject with the modal: *Under no circumstances* **would I** *ask him to do this.*

- Inversion can occur after another complete clause beginning with *not until, only when, only if, only after*: **Not until** *she learns to relax* **will things get** *any better.* **Only when** *we got the dog* **did we start** *going for long walks.*

- We use inversion after *neither* or *nor* when it introduces a negative clause that is related to one mentioned previously: *Unfortunately, Colin didn't listen to me, and* **neither did he take** *the doctor's advice.*

TIPS! • Although inversion is usually found in literary and formal texts, we also use it in less formal spoken and written English when we want to add emphasis or dramatic effect: **No way** *should people drive to work if they can possibly walk.*
• We don't use inversion when we use *not … either*; *I don't like fish and I don't like curry either.* not *… either do I not like curry*.
• We can find inversion in literature after adverbials of place: **Into the room** *walked Johan.*

Real World

RW3.1 **Being tactful** 3C p33

- We sometimes soften a message by using particular words/phrases.

Using past forms

We **were planning** to go the cinema tomorrow.

Using modals

They **could** do with being (a bit looser).
It **could** have been a bit hotter.
I**'d** go for black instead if I were you.

Using vague language

We must all get together **some time**.
(They could do with being) **a bit** looser.
It was **sort of** interesting in parts.
The steak was **on the tough side**.

Not sounding negative

I think darker colours **suit you better**.
I've **seen better** performances.

Using adverbs of attitude

Quite honestly, I've seen better performances.
Unfortunately, the steak was …

Accurate Writing

AW3.1 **Connecting words: contrast (1)** p35

We use:

- *although* to contrast two clauses in the same sentence: *Mo still smokes,* **although** *she knows she shouldn't.* (Mo still smokes contrasts with Mo knowing that she shouldn't smoke). **Even though** is similar in meaning to *although* but it is more emphatic: *I never bother to lock my car,* **even though** *I know I should.* We can also put *although* and *even though* at the beginning of sentences: **Although/Even though** *I never bother to lock my car, I know I should.*

- *whereas* to introduce a subordinate clause which you are comparing with what you are saying in the main clause: *They fell asleep* **whereas** *I was awake for hours.* We can also put *whereas* at the beginning of sentences: **Whereas** *I was awake for hours, they fell asleep.*

- *however* to contrast two sentences. We usually put *however* at the beginning of a sentence and we put a comma (,) after the word *however*: *I like cats.* **However**, *I prefer dogs.*

- *but* to contrast two clauses in the same sentences. In formal written language, we do not usually use *but* at the beginning of sentences: *Frank is very athletic,* **but** *his brother isn't.* not ~~Frank is very athletic. But his brother isn't.~~

AW3.2 **Spelling: one word, two words or hyphenated** p35

- *Everyday* is an adjective which we use to describe something which is normal and not exciting in any way: *This isn't an* **everyday** *occurrence.*

- *Every day* is an adverbial. If something happens every day, it happens regularly each day: *Carla's mother makes pasta* **every day**.

- We use *everyone* to refer to all the people in particular group: **Everyone** *is coming.*

- We use *every one* to emphasise that something is true about each of the things or people you are talking about: **Every one** *of his jackets is handmade.*

- When we make an adjective from a number and unit of measurement, we hyphenate the number and its unit of measurement and we use the singular form of the unit of measurement: *The fence was two metres high.* → *It was a* **two-metre high** *fence.* With ages we hyphenate the complete phrase: *The house was a hundred years old.* → *It's a* **hundred-year-old house**.

- We use *anyone* to talk about people in general, or about each person of a particular kind: *Does* **anyone** *know Pete's mobile number?*

- We use *any one* to emphasise that you are referring to only one of something: **Any one** *of you can do this. There isn't* **any one** *person here who opposes the proposal.*

- We use *anyway* when you are adding a remark you have just thought of to something you have just said. Usually the remark makes the previous statement seem less important than it did: *I can't ask him out.* **Anyway**, *I think he's seeing that friend of Jackie's now.*

- We use *any way*, usually in the phrase *in any way*, to mean 'in any respect' or 'by any method': *Is there* **any way** *I can help?*

- We use *maybe* to indicate that something is possible: **Maybe** *we should offer to pick them up.*

- We use *may* to talk about possibility. It is a modal and is used with the infinitive form of the verb, e.g. *may be*: *She* **may be** *coming tonight.* (= *Maybe she's coming.*)

Vocabulary

V4.1 News collocations 4A ① p36

read the tabloids* / glossy magazines
seek publicity*
hold a press conference*
receive a lot of coverage*

sue for libel*
hit the headlines
make the front page
issue a press release*
run a story

*tabloid /'tæblɔɪd/ a type of popular newspaper with small pages, which has many pictures and short simple reports

*seek publicity the activity of making certain that somebody or something attracts a lot of publicity

*press conference a meeting at which a person or organization makes a public statement and reporters can ask questions

*coverage /'kʌvrɪdʒ/ the reporting of a particular important event or subject

*libel /'laɪbəl/ a piece of writing or speech which contains bad and false things about a person

*press release a public statement given to the press to publish if they wish

V4.2 Near synonyms 4B ⑤ p40

- We often avoid repeating the same words (particularly nouns, adjectives, verbs and adverbs) so that what we say or write sounds less repetitive and more interesting: *The Industrial Revolution brought important change to the entire country. The whole of Britain was forced to address fundamental questions.*

- Examples of synonyms from page 39 are:

humans	man	people
a village	a settlement	
country folk	rural inhabitants	villagers
improvements	developments	
the land	the countryside	
disease	pestilences	

TIPS! • Not all near synonyms are interchangeable in all contexts. These are some reasons why:

a) **formality:** *kid* and *child* have the same meaning but *kid* is more informal than *child*. To a friend we could say either: *How are the children/kids?* However, in more formal, written English, we would not find the word *kid*: *There are 14.8 million children in the UK.*

b) **words that go together (collocation)** e.g. We can say *A huge/large number.* However, *large* does not collocate with *problem*: *A huge/large problem.*

c) **grammatical agreement** e.g. We can say either *I like / enjoy travelling.* However, we also use *like* + infinitive: *I like/enjoy to travel.*

d) **connotation** e.g. if we describe someone's personality as *determined/obstinate*, they have different connotations: *determined* (positive connotation) *obstinate* (negative connotation).

Grammar

G4.1 Future verb forms Preview 4 ① p35

- We use the **Present Simple** for a fixed event on a timetable or a calendar: *The new airport tax **comes** into effect on Monday.*

- We use the **Present Continuous** for future arrangements: *Who**'s meeting** you at the station?*

- We use **be going to** for a personal plan or intention: *I**'m going to** stop reading this paper, it's so right-wing.*

- We use **be going to** for a prediction that is based on present evidence: *Look at the time. We**'re going to** be late.*

- We use **will** for a prediction based on opinion rather than evidence: *I think they**'ll** have an early election.*

- We use the **Future Continuous** for something that will be in progress at a certain time in the future: *This time next week we**'ll be having** talks with the Prime Minister.*

- We use the **Future Continuous** for something that will happen in the normal course of events – not because you planned it: *I**'ll be passing** the post office, so I can post that for you.*

- We use the **Future Perfect** for something that will be completed before a certain time in the future: *By the end of the year we**'ll have built** 10,000 new homes.*

TIP! • We also use the **Present Simple** in clauses beginning with *by the time, before, as soon as, after, until* and *when*: *As soon as he **arrives**, I'll tell you.*

G4.2 Phrases referring to the future 4A ④ p37

- Newspaper journalists often use phrases such as *due to/set to/about to/on the verge of* to refer to the future in headlines: *Shocking environmental data **set to** be released.*

- To make a headline into a sentence we might need to add other words such as articles or missing auxiliary verbs, e.g. *be*:
  *New airport 'green' tax due to be introduced → A new airport 'green' tax **is** due to be introduced.*
  *Driving age set to rise → **The** driving age **is** set to rise.*
  *Sale of bugging devices about to go through roof → **The** sale of bugging devices **is** about to go through **the** roof.*
  *New TV boss on the verge of axing reality TV shows → A/**The** new TV boss **is** on the verge of axing reality TV shows.*
  *Dry cleaner's to face lawsuit over pair of trousers → **A** dry cleaner's **is** to face a lawsuit over **a** pair of trousers.*

- We use *(be) due to / set to / about to / on the verge of (+ing)* or *am/is/are to* to talk about something that is ready to happen, probably in the near future.

- We use *(be) likely to, unlikely to, sure to, certain to, bound to* to say how certain we are that something will happen.

- We use a verb+*ing* (or noun) after *on the verge of*: *She's **on the verge of leaving** her job.*

- We use an infinitive after *(be) due to / set to / about to / likely to / sure to / unlikely to / certain to / bound to / is to.*

Language Summary 4

Grammar

TIPS! • *due to* is often used when we state a particular time. *Building work is due to start in March.*

• We sometimes use *not about to* when we mean 'not willing to': *I'm not about to drop everything just to go and pick her up from the station.*

• We can say *on the point/brink of* + verb+ing (or noun) to refer to things in the near future. *On the brink of* usually refers to something that is bad, exciting or very important and is usually used in formal English. *A large bank is on the brink of collapse.*

• We can't refer to specific time after *on the verge of/on the brink of*: *He's on the verge of/on the brink of resigning ~~next week~~.*

G4.3 Future in the past 4B 11 p41

● Compare these two sentences:
We didn't know our ideas were going to be successful.
We believe our ideas are going to be successful.

● In the first sentence we know the result (our ideas were successful). In the second sentence we are predicting the result (our ideas are going to be successful).

● Look at the diagram. In the first sentence we are talking about the future seen from a point in the past. In the second sentence we are talking about the future seen from now.

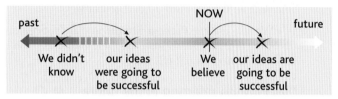

● To talk about the future seen from the past, we use the past tenses of the verb forms we would usually use to talk about the future. Compare these sentences:

The future seen from now	The future seen from the past
am/is/are going to + infinitive *... our ideas are going to be successful ...*	*was/were going to* + infinitive *... our ideas were going to be successful ...*
will + infinitive *... these young fans will go on to spend...*	*would* + infinitive *... these young fans would go on to spend...*
is/are supposed to + infinitive *... Star Trek is just supposed to offer....*	*was / were supposed to* + infinitive *... Star Trek was just supposed to offer....*
am/is/are about to + infinitive *... these bits of cardboard and plastic being used on set are about to be...*	*was / were about to* + infinitive *... these bits of cardboard and plastic being used on set were about to be...*
is/are to + infinitive *... they are to find out ...*	*was / were to* + infinitive *... they were to find out ...*

TIPS! • We often use these forms when we are reporting. *She said she was going to come early.*

• We often need to change time expressions when we talk about the future seen from the past: *There is to be a meeting about it* **tomorrow**. → *There was to be a meeting about it the* **following day**.

Accurate Writing

AW4.1 Connecting words: contrast (2) 1 p45

We use:

● **but** to introduce something which contrasts with what you have just said: *This coat is so old,* **but** *it's still my favourite.*

● **although/though** to introduce a subordinate clause which mentions something that contrasts with what you are saying in the main clause: **Although** *it was freezing, they went for a bike ride.*

● **despite / in spite of** to contrast two clauses in the same sentence when we are talking about circumstances which surprisingly, do not prevent something from happening or being true: **Despite / In spite of** *the fact that he was ill, he went into work.* **Despite / In spite of** *all their hard work, they failed to make the deadline.*

● **nevertheless/nonetheless/however** to add a comment which contrasts with what has just been said to mean 'despite what has just been said or referred to'. You can use *nevertheless/however* to introduce a simple clause and we put a comma (,) after the word *nevertheless/however: I'm not particularly hungry.* **Nevertheless/However**, *I will have one of those cakes.*

● We can also use **nevertheless/nonetheless** after *but* to emphasise the contrast: *He only got 50% in his exam, but* **nevertheless**, *that's better than last year.*

TIPS! • We do not use *in spite of/despite* as a conjunction. We use *although/though: Although he was late, he stopped to buy some flowers.* not *~~In spite of/Despite he was late~~ ... .*

• After *in spite of/despite* we usually use a noun or verb+ing: **In spite of/Despite** *the weather, we had a great time.* **In spite of/Despite** *being late, they allowed us into the theatre.*

AW4.2 Punctuation: capital letters and full stops 2 p45

We use capital letters for:
● names: *Sam Baker*
● streets and roads: *25 Lime St*
● town and cities: *Bradford*
● postcodes: *BD5 8LM*
● countries/nationalities/language: *UK*
● titles: *Mr, Mrs, Ms, Dr, Sir, Madam,* etc.
● days of the week: *Sunday, Monday,* etc.
● months of the year: *January, February,* etc.
● places: *Waterloo Station, River Thames,* etc.
● the pronoun 'I': *I'm sorry I'm late.*

TIPS! • We sometimes use full stops after abbreviated words such as *Dr., etc., U.S.A.* This is a personal style and is not necessary in most contexts.

• We do not use a full stop at the end of abbreviated words before a question mark: *Have you been to the U.S.A?* not *... ~~to the U.S.A.?~~*

Vocabulary

V5.1 Word building (1): prefixes with multiple meanings (5A ❹ p47)

- If we don't know the meaning of a noun, adjective or verb, we can often make a guess from their prefixes.

prefix	meaning	example
inter-	between (two things, people, etc.)	interaction
	joined together	interlocked
counter-	in opposition to	counterbalance
	as a reaction to	counter-attack
super-	more than usual	superwoman
	extremely	super-rich
over-	too much	overworked
	from above/on top/across	overhead
semi-	partly	semi-famous
	half	semicircle
under-	not enough	underpaid
	below	underfoot
pseudo-	not real	pseudo-friendship

V5.2 Verb + infinitive with to or verb+ing (1) (Preview 5 ❷ p45)

- When we use two verbs together, the form of the second verb usually depends on the first verb.

- The verbs in **bold** in the table have more than one verb pattern. Both verb patterns have the same meaning.
I began to watch soaps while I was ill at home. =
I began watching soaps while I was ill at home.

- The verbs in **red** in the table have a different meaning when they are followed by verb+ing or infinitive with *to*.
I remember telling him about tomorrow's training session. (= I told him and now I can remember that I did that.)
I remembered to tell him about tomorrow's training session. (= I remembered and then I told him.)

- The underlined verbs are those tested in exercise 2 p45.

keep on	miss	stop	avoid	**begin**	
continue	don't mind	end up	enjoy	+ verb+*ing*
finish	**hate**	keep	**like**	**love**	forget
prefer	regret	remember	**start**	try	

need	expect	manage	stop	try	
learn	**begin**	**continue**	decide	
forget	**hate**	hope	**like**	**love**	+ infinitive with *to*
plan	**prefer**	pretend	refuse	
regret	remember	seem	**start**	

help let make	+ object + infinitive
persuade allow encourage **help** ask convince expect force pay teach	+ object + infinitive with *to*
would can could had better might should will would rather	+ infinitive

V5.3 verb + infinitive with to, or verb+ing (2) (5B ❺ p50)

- Some verbs have a different meaning when they are followed by verb+ing or verb + infinitive with *to*.

  a) *forget* + verb+*ing* = looks back to memories of the past: *I'll never **forget getting** picked for the World Cup squad at only 16.*

  b) *forget* + infinitive with *to* = refers to now or in the future: *I never **forget to sit** with my head down and visualise myself scoring a goal.*

  a) *go on* + verb+*ing* = continue an action: *The biggest thing has been learning just to **go on doing it**.*

  b) *go on* + infinitive with *to* = begin a new action: *Making beats **went on to become** my life.*

  a) *mean* + verb+*ing* = involve/necessitate: *… it **means coordinating** really well.*

  b) *mean* + infinitive with *to* = intend: *Riding was just **meant to make** physiotherapy fun.*

  a) *regret* + verb+*ing* = 'I'm sorry for what's already happened': *I will always **regret losing** them.*

  b) *regret* + infinitive with *to* is a formal way of saying 'I'm sorry about what I'm just about to say': *I **regret to say** that at school I was trouble.*

TIP! • Verbs of the senses (*see*, *notice*, etc.)can be followed by:
  a) object + *ing* form when describing a repeated action/action in progress: *He **noticed me playing**.*
  b) an object + infinitive when describing a single action or a completed action: *I **saw him get** into the car.*

V5.4 Verb-noun collocations (5B ❾ p51)

do	get
a degree	a degree
English	good results
work experience	a good education
a course	work experience
an exam	a place at university
research	

go on a course
carry out* research
sit an exam
enrol* on a course
take a course/an exam
gain work experience

obtain* a degree/a good education/ a place at university/good results
have a degree/a good education/a place at university/ an exam
be awarded* a degree
achieve good results

***carry out** do or complete something, especially something that you have said you would do or that you have been told to do: *The science students carried out an experiment.*
***enrol** /ɪnˈrəʊl/ **on** put yourself or someone else onto the official list of members of a course: *I've enrolled on a pottery course.*
***obtain** get something (formal): *He obtained a first-class degree in Mathematics.*
***be awarded** be given money, a prize or qualification: *The oldest student in Britain was awarded her degree at the age of 95!*

Language Summary 5

V5.5 Expressions connected to work 5C ❶ p52

be stuck in a rut /rʌt/ be too fixed in one particular type of job, activity, method: *I've been stuck in a rut at work for over a year and it's time for a change.*

a dead-end job a job in which there is no chance of getting a promotion: *I don't want to end up in some dead-end job like my brother.*

take on too much work accept too much work: *The danger of working for yourself is taking on too much work.*

be snowed under have so much work that you have problems dealing with it all: *We need some more support before we get snowed under.*

talk shop talk about your job with those you work with when not at work: *I'm banning you and Stephanie from talking shop while we're at dinner together.*

team player someone who is good at working closely with other people: *Ann has never been much of a team player and generally prefers working alone.*

be self-employed not working for an employer but finding work for yourself or having your own business: *I'm self-employed so I tend to work on Saturday mornings.*

a pittance /'pɪtəns/ a very small amount of money, especially money received as payment or income: *She works so hard for that company and she's paid a pittance.*

a fortune a large amount of money, goods, property, etc: *Sara earns a fortune working for a Swiss bank.*

high-powered a very important job or a very successful person: *Isn't your brother a high-powered executive at a computer company?*

run-of-the-mill ordinary and not special or exciting in any way: *We just need someone to do run-of-the-mill office administration.*

work experience a period of time in which a student temporarily works for an employer to gain experience: *Lauren wants to find some work experience in the media during the summer.*

shadow sb following someone else while they are at work in order to learn about that person's job: *I shadowed a lawyer at work for two weeks.*

a deadline a time by which something must be done: *The deadline for proposals is not until November.*

against the clock If you do something against the clock, you do it as fast as possible and try to finish it before a certain time: *We would be working against the clock if we accepted the order.*

be up to your eyes in sth be very busy doing something: *I'm up to my eyes in work at the moment.*

take it easy relax and not use too much energy: *I'm going to spend a few weeks at home taking it easy over the summer.*

(climb) the career /kə'rɪə/ **ladder** the sequence of job positions through which a person progresses in an organisation: *Rob's been steadily climbing the career ladder since he joined the company a few years back.*

G5.1 Reflexive pronouns (1) Preview 5 ❶ p45

- We use reflexive pronouns (*myself, yourself*, etc.) when the subject and the object refer to the same person, thing, etc.: **She**'s teaching **herself** to swim. (she's not teaching anybody else to swim)

- There is a difference between **themselves** and **each other**. We use *each other* when we are talking about actions or feelings that involve two or more people together in the same way: *The children are allowed to read to* **each other** *before they go to bed.* (Each child is allowed to read a story to the other children.) We use *themselves* when we talk about actions that involve two or more people but do not involve the people together: *The children are allowed to read to* **themselves** *before they go to bed.* (The children are allowed to read books individually.)

- We also use reflexive pronouns to emphasise that we do something instead of someone else doing it for us: *I think I'll redecorate the house* **myself**.

- We use *by myself, yourself*, etc. to mean 'alone': *Geoff went to the cinema* **by himself**.

G5.2 Reflexive pronouns (2) 5A ❽ p48

- We can use reflexive pronouns:

  1 after *like, as well as, as (for)*, etc. instead of object pronouns, although these are possible. This use of the reflexive can show politeness: *Daniel, what makes people like* **yourself** *want to be an extra?*

  2 to emphasise a noun, pronoun or noun phrase: *I like the job* **itself**, *but …*

  3 to make it clear that an object (after a preposition) refers to the same person/thing as the subject of the verb: *She read the script to* **herself**. *(She read the script to* **her** *suggests she read it to a different person)*

We need some more support before we get **snowed under**.

Grammar

If it is obvious that the object following a preposition must refer to the subject, we use an object pronoun. *I always take a laptop with* **me**. not ~~I always take a laptop with myself~~.

- We do not usually use reflexive pronouns with these verbs: *concentrate, feel, meet*: *... unless I really concentrate* not ~~... unless I really concentrate~~ *myself*. *There are times when you feel very tired.* not ~~There are times when you feel yourself very tired~~. *It's a great opportunity to meet and have a chat.* not ~~It's a great opportunity to meet ourselves and have a chat~~.

TIPS! ● We can also use verbs *exert*, *pride* and *occupy* with reflexive pronouns: *Don't* **exert yourself**, *lifting heavy boxes*. *We* **pride ourselves** *on good service. I can* **occupy myself** *with a book for ages.*

● Some verbs, e.g. *dress, shave, wash*, are only reflexive if we want to emphasise that someone does the action themselves: *Kate can dress herself now. Do you prefer to shave yourself, or go to the barbers?*

Real World

RW5.1 Conversational strategies 5C ⑤ p53

including someone in the conversation

You look dubious, (Liz).
You're very quiet, (Josh).

adding something to the argument

Not to mention ...
And of course there's always ...

stressing an important point

That's exactly what I was trying to get at.
That's precisely what I mean.

encouraging someone to continue

Carry on, (Liz). You were saying?
What were you about/going to say, (Tracey)?

justifying what you say

All I'm saying is ...
What I'm trying to say is ...

getting the conversation back on track

Anyway, (assuming you do want promotion) ...
To get back to what (I) was saying about (promotion) ...

saying you agree with someone

I'm with (you) on that.   I'd go along with that.

conceding someone is right

You've got me there!   Well, I can't disagree with that.

disagreeing politely

Oh, I don't know about (that).
Actually, I'm not sure you can say (that).

asking someone to say more about a topic

By (provision) you mean ...?
What do you mean when you say (provision)?

Accurate Writing

AW5.1 Connecting words: time (2) ① p55

We use:

- *instantly*, *straightaway* or *at once* to mean 'immediately': *When I saw Kay at the party that summer I* **instantly** *fell for her/fell for her* **straightaway**.

- *at once* also to mean 'at the same time': *They all started talking* **at once**.

- *previously* to mean 'before the time that is referred to'. We do not use a time adverbial after *previously*: **Previously**, *I'd never had a long-term relationship*.

- *before* to talk about an event earlier in time. We can use a time adverbial (*yesterday*, *last week*, etc.) or another clause (*I met her*, etc.) after *before* if the time is not clear: **Before** *this/last week, I'd only ever seen her in photographs.*

- *immediately* to mean 'without waiting': *I* **immediately** *went up to her and introduced myself.*

- *subsequent to sth* in formal contexts to describe something happening after another time or another event: **Subsequent to** *our conversation of yesterday, I enclose the necessary forms for your enquiry.*

- *after* to mean 'following': **After** *that day, we were inseparable all through the summer. The year* **after**, *we had to go back to college.*

- *later* to mean 'after that time': *A year* **later**.

- *eventually* to mean 'in the end, especially after a long time or a lot of effort': **Eventually**, *we decided we would have to split up.*

- *at the end* to mean 'at the last point': **At the end**, *everyone applauded.*

- *lately* to mean 'recently': **Lately**, *in the last month or so, we have begun seeing each other again.*

- *finally* to mean 'after a long time or some difficulty': *They've been together for over 15 years but they* **finally** *got married at Christmas.*

- *up until* to mean 'up to the time that': **Up until** *a month ago, though, we hadn't seen each other for 20 years.*

- *prior to sth* in formal contexts to mean 'before a particular time or event': **Prior to** *meeting Bélèn, I'd never met anyone from the north of Spain.*

AW5.2 Spelling: *ie* or *ei* ② p55

- When the letters 'i' and 'e' occur together in words they are sometimes spelled 'ie' and sometimes spelled 'ei'.

- If the sound of the two letters together in a word is /iː/, we write *ie*: rel**ie**ve, f**ie**ld, p**ie**ce. (except after *c*, conc**ei**ted, rec**ei**ve, dec**ei**ve.) The exceptions to this rule include: n**ei**ther, s**ei**ze, spec**ie**s, w**ei**rd.

- If the sound of the two letters in a word is not /iː/, we usually write *ei*, e.g. **ei**ght, th**ei**r, n**ei**ghbour. The exceptions to this rule include: fr**ie**nd, pat**ie**nce.

Language Summary 6

V6.1 Words with different but related meanings
6A 6 p58

- Sometimes one word can have completely different meanings, e.g. *I commute on the train to work every day. She wants to train to be a psychologist.*

- Sometimes one word can have different meanings but the meanings are related, e.g. *The weather's fine today. I'm feeling fine now.*

- **odd** generally means 'unusual or peculiar' and can specifically mean:
  a) 'not matching' i.e. not having the same colour or pattern as something else: *She wanted to put on odd socks every day.*
  b) 'strange or unexpected': *It was odd that he didn't phone.*

- **sweet** describes people, animals or food and generally means 'pleasant'. It can specifically mean:
  a) 'charming, attractive': *His daughter is really sweet.*
  b) 'sugary': *Dark chocolate isn't sweet enough for me.*

- **top** can generally mean 'the highest point or part in distance or quality' and can specifically mean:
  a) 'the highest part': *They hopped out of the top of her sweater.*
  b) 'the most successful': *He's always top of the class.*

- The general meaning of the words in **bold** below is:
  a) a division or subdivision of something
  b) horizontally level without variation
  c) interrupt the regularity, uniformity, or arrangement of something
  d) without pattern or interesting features
  e) a great amount or weight of something

V6.2 Word pairs 6B 1 p59

take it or leave it said about something that you quite like but that you do not love or need badly: *I quite like coffee, but I can take it or leave it.*

on and off happening sometimes: *She's been working on and off for an advertising consultancy, but has never had a regular position with them.*

hit and miss if something is hit and miss you cannot depend on it to be of good quality, on time, accurate, etc: *Our recent marketing campaigns have been a bit hit and miss.*

pick and choose take what you want from a group of things or people: *They're such a good company that they can pick and choose jobs as they wish.*

make or break make something a success or a failure: *This job is so big it could make or break the company.*

each and every every thing or person in a group or category: *Each and every student must register for the exam by tomorrow.*

part and parcel of (sth) be a necessary feature of a particular experience: *A quality website is part and parcel of most successful businesses nowadays.*

sick and tired of (sth/sb) thoroughly discouraged or bored: *The chairwoman says she's sick and tired of unimaginative car advertising and wants something different.*

over and over again happening or done many times: *I've watched this advert over and over again, but I still don't understand it.*

in leaps /liːps/ **and bounds** /baʊndz/ changing or progressing very quickly: *Online marketing has come on in leaps and bounds over the last 10 years.*

(a) a **branch** of a tree

(b) Sally feels **flat**.

(c) Tom had a **break** for coffee.

(d) **plain** paper

(e) **heavy** traffic

Brighter Bank has **branches** in Bath, Swansea and Bristol.

a **flat** piece of land

break a window

plain food

a **heavy** coat

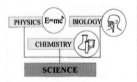
Biology is a **branch** of science.

This lemonade is **flat**.

break the law

a **plain** face

Martin is a **heavy** sleeper.

Vocabulary

V6.3 Dramatic verbs 6C **6** p63

- Some verbs are used to add dramatic effect to spoken or written language.

cajole /kəˈdʒəʊl/ (sb) into persuade someone to do something they might not want to do, by pleasant talk and (sometimes false) promises: *I shouldn't have let him cajole me into going but he was really convincing.*

leap up stand up suddenly: *When I walked into the room, he leapt up and shook my hand enthusiastically.*

grab take hold of something or someone suddenly and roughly: *He grabbed my phone from the table and disappeared.*

storm out leave a place in a way that shows you are angry: *As soon as she heard about his promotion, she stormed out of the office.*

nudge /nʌdʒ/ push something or someone gently, especially push someone with your elbow: *I didn't notice all the famous people until Sue started nudging me.*

hiss say something in a quiet, angry way: *'Shut up!' he hissed.*

drag make someone go somewhere they do not want to go: *I had to drag him to the shop but two hours later I had to drag him out!*

When I walked into the room, he **leapt up** and shook my hand enthusiastically.

Grammar

G6.1 Ways of comparing Preview 6 **1** p55

a big difference	a great deal (more successful) considerably (better) far (smaller)	than
	nowhere near as (scary) twice as (hard) not nearly as (big)	as
a small difference	slightly (more/less willing)	than
	almost as (difficult) nearly as (beautiful) not quite as (clever)	as
no difference	just as (helpful)	as
	no (longer) not any (more expensive)	than

TIPS! • We use comparatives with *than*: *The paperwork is considerably more/less complicated than I thought it would be.*

• We use adjectives with *as … as*: *To me, interviews are nowhere near as scary as exams.*

• When a comparative repeats an earlier idea or if we understand what is being compared, we sometimes don't include *than* + the noun: *Prices from the two supermarket chains, Better Buy and Price Cutter, were compared; Better Buy was found to be considerably cheaper.*

- We can use ***twice/three times/four times***, etc. + ***as … (as)*** to compare two things: *However, it's twice as hard in the winter, when the weather is bad.*

- We can use ***the + comparative/more …, the + comparative/more*** to say that one thing depends on the other: *The bigger the job, the greater the profit. The more you work, the more you earn.*

- We can use ***just*** with ***as … as*** to add emphasis: *Men are just as helpful if you do interview them.*

G6.2 Formal and informal ways of comparing 6A **2** p57

FORMAL

- The words and phrases highlighted in the text on pages 56 and 57 modify comparative forms, indicating a big difference or a small difference.

a big difference	a small difference
decidedly	somewhat
a good deal	barely (any)
significantly	marginally
distinctly	

INFORMAL

- There are also some informal phrases which can modify comparative forms to indicate a big or small difference.

a big difference	a small difference
way	a tiny bit
loads	much the same
miles	pretty much the same
not half as … as	more or less the same
not anywhere near as … as	

Language Summary 6

G6.3 Adverbs (Preview 6 ② p55)

- We usually add -ly to adjectives to make **adverbs**: surprising → surprising**ly**.
- When an adjective ends in -y, the 'y' changes to 'i' before adding -ly: unhappy → unhapp**ily**. There are some exceptions, e.g. shy → shy**ly**.
- When an adjective ends in -ble, the 'e' changes to 'y': incredib**le** → incredib**ly**
- When an adjective ends in -ic, we add -ally: scientif**ic** → scientific**ally**
- With some adjectives, we don't make the adverb with -ly: late → late, hard → hard, high (= tall) → high, good → well, wrong → wrong, early → early
- Some adverbs have two forms and there is a difference in meaning between them:

a) *late* means 'not on time' and *lately* means 'recently': *He arrived late. I haven't seen him lately.*

b) *hard* is the opposite of 'soft' and *hardly/barely* mean 'very little': *She hit him hard. I've hardly/barely spoken to you for weeks.*

c) *high* means 'a long way up' and *highly* means 'to a large degree': *The cat climbed high into the trees. He had a really highly-paid job but left to look after his children.*

d) *fine* means 'good or well' and *finely* means 'in small pieces': *I'm feeling fine. Chop the onion finely.*

- After verbs such as *taste, smell, sound, seem* and *appear*, we use an adjective rather than an adverb: *That smells good.* not *That smells well*.

G6.4 Position of adverbials (6B ⑥ p61)

- Adverbials of **place** describe where something happens/ happened: *An extremely innovative and witty example of this experimentation was at a recent whaling conference, where a German animal-welfare group fitted capsules inside the bathrooms*.
- Adverbials of **time** describe when something happens/ happened: *These days it's quite normal to regard all forms of marketing with loathing*.
- Adverbials of **manner** describe how something is done: *… by leaping out at consumers unannounced and grabbing their attention by force*.
- Adverbials of **indefinite frequency** describe how often something happens: *However, if overused or done badly, it sometimes antagonises people*.
- Adverbials describing **level of certainty** say how likely it is that something happens: *Being intrusive is probably forgivable … .*
- Adverbials of **comment** are used to express/give an opinion on what we are saying: *Interestingly, this time it's no longer what brands say that is changing*.

The average American, for example, is exposed to around 3,000 messages **every day**

- Adverbials of **definite frequency** describe how often something happens: *The average American, for example, is exposed to around 3,000 messages every day*.

Position of adverbials

FRONT POSITION

comment	surprisingly	**Surprisingly**, it worked.
level of **certainty**	maybe, perhaps, surely	**Maybe** the campaign will succeed.

- In front position, we put the adverb before the subject.

TIPS! • Adverbials of **time**, **definite frequency**, and adverbials of **indefinite frequency** are also very common in front position. In this position, the adverbials emphasise their meaning in contrast with information previously given: *The agency grew by 8% last year. Next year we want to hit 10%.*

• Some adverbials, e.g. *naturally, clearly, frankly, honestly, seriously* can be used as either adverbials of **comment** or **manner** and change position depending on their meaning. Compare:
Seriously, I don't believe you. (comment)
I am seriously thinking of leaving. (manner)

• When we put some negative adverbials of time in front position, we invert the subject and verb: *Not once have I asked you for money.*

MID POSITION

indefinite frequency	always	She's **always** right.
level of **certainty**	probably, definitely	He'll **definitely** win.

- In mid position we put the adverbial between the subject and the verb or immediately after either *be* or an auxiliary verb.

TIPS! • Adverbials of **degree** also usually go in mid position, e.g. *almost, hardly, quite, rather: I almost resigned.* Some adverbials of degree can go in mid or end position, e.g. *completely, enormously, entirely, slightly: I entirely agree. = I agree entirely.*

• Adverbials of **manner**, **place** and **time** can also go in mid position. This emphasises them more than any other position and is most common in formal written texts and newspaper reporting: *Pat reluctantly admitted defeat. The Prime Minister yesterday repeated that the economy was stable.*

Grammar

END POSITION

manner	hard	They work **hard**.
place	at the office	She's **at the office**.
time	a year ago	The advert came out **a year ago**.
definite frequency	every day	I try to exercise **every day**.
indefinite frequency	as a rule, from time to time, every so often	I work at home **every so often**.

- In end position, we put the adverb immediately after the verb or at the end of the clause: *We swim **every day** at our local pool. We swim at our local pool **every day**.*

TIPS! • Where there are several adverbials at the end of the clause, the usual order is manner, place, time: *She sang **beautifully in the concert yesterday**.*

• We usually put adverbials in end position in sentences where there is a verb immediately followed by an object: *We explored the idea **briefly**.* not *We explored **briefly** the idea.* However, if the object is long, then the adverbial can go in other positions: *We explored **briefly** the idea of starting the project in the summer.*

FOCUSING ADVERBIALS

- Focusing adverbials come before the word/phrase we want to stress.
- The position of focusing adverbials can affect the meaning of the sentence.

  1 *Jan and I **only** worked on the Volkswagen advert.* (only in mid position modifies the verb to mean that Jan and I worked on the Volkswagen advert but we didn't work on anything else)

  2 ***Only** Jan and I worked on the Volkswagen advert.* (only in front position modifies the subject to mean that Jan and I, and nobody else, worked on the Volkswagen advert)

  1 *Joe's been everywhere. He's **even** been to Tonga.* (even in mid position modifies the verb to mean that Joe's been to Tonga in addition to everywhere else he's been)

  2 *More and more people have been to Tonga. **Even** Joe's been there.* (even in front position modifies the subject to mean that you might not expect Joe to have been to Tonga but he has)

Joe's been everywhere. He's **even** been to Tonga.

Accurate Writing

AW6.1 Connecting words: purpose p65

SO AS/IN ORDER (FOR SOMETHING) + INFINITIVE WITH *TO*

- We can use *so as/in order (for something)* + infinitive with *to* to talk about the purpose of an action. We put these phrases at the beginning of a clause: *The colours need to be bolder **so as to/ in order to** make the design stand out. **In order for** the campaign **to be** a success, we must increase our budget.*

- In spoken and less formal written English we often simplify these two structures to an infinitive with *to*: *We have done research **to see** which adverts are the most popular.*

IN ORDER THAT/ SO THAT/ SO

- We use *in order that*, *so that* and *so* to talk about the purpose of an action. We put these phrases at the beginning of a clause: ***So that** we can meet our deadlines, we'd appreciate your ideas by tomorrow. I'll send you some possible slogans **in order that** you can decide.*

- *So (that)* is less formal and more common than *in order that*: *I'd like to do a copywriting course **so that** I can go into advertising.*

TIPS! • If we use a **present** verb form in the clause with *in order that / so that*, we usually use a **present** verb form or modal verb in the main clause. The present verb form or modal verb has present or future meaning: *In order that the campaign **is** a success, we **must** increase our budget.* (= so the campaign will be a success)

If we use a **past** verb form in the main clause, we usually use a **past** verb form or modal verb in the clause with *in order that/so that*. This past verb form or modal verb has past meaning: *I **warned** you, in order that you **wouldn't** be disappointed.* (= so you weren't disappointed)

AW6.2 Punctuation: colons and semicolons p65

1 We can use colons:

- to introduce lists or to indicate a subdivision of a topic: *There are three solutions: we could get an overdraft, sell the company or close it down.*

- when the second clause explains the first: *The meeting will be held in the library: the Board Room is being decorated. My father has gone into hospital: he's having a minor operation.*

2 We can use semicolons instead of full stops and commas to separate two main clauses which are connected in meaning: *I began to get a bit nervous; to calm myself down I made myself a drink. I used to live in France; I'm now based in Tokyo.*

TIP! • We tend to use full stops and commas instead of semicolons in modern written English.

Language Summary 7

Vocabulary

V7.1 Phrases with *get* (7A **2** p67)

get (my, your, our, their, etc.) own back (on sb) punish somebody because they did something unpleasant to you: *After her husband had left her, the woman got her own back by destroying his favourite shirts.*

get away with sth do wrong and not be punished: *The robbers got away with the jewel theft because there was not enough evidence to convict them.*

get round sth avoid a problem: *The government is trying to get round the problem of overcrowded prisons by releasing some prisoners early.*

get round to sth find the time to do something: *I lost my credit card a few days ago but I haven't got round to reporting it yet.*

get through to sb make somebody understand something: *My work involves trying to get through to young offenders who think that crime is their only option.*

get at sb criticise repeatedly: *The woman's colleagues kept getting at her so she reported them to her manager.*

get into sth become interested in: *My son has really got into crime novels recently.*

V7.2 Phrasal nouns (7B **3** p69)

Phrasal nouns are compound nouns formed from verbs and a particle (a preposition or adverb).

break + up → a break-up   set + back → a setback
out + cry → an outcry   on + set → an onset

TIPS! • When phrasal nouns begin with a particle, they have no hyphen (*outlook, downpour, input, onset, outcry*). When phrasal nouns begin with a verb, they may or may not have a hyphen, e.g. *kick-off, breakdown, get-together.*

• Not all phrasal verbs can be made into phrasal nouns: *They pulled down two houses.* not ~~There was a pulldown of two houses~~.

• Some phrasal nouns are made up of the same words as phrasal verbs but have different meanings: *The **intake** (= enrolment) on the course was over 100. He spoke so fast I couldn't **take it in** (= understand and remember). The tax increase caused a public **outcry** (= protest). When the dog bit him, he **cried out** (= shout because of being afraid or in pain). The drugs can only delay the **onset** (= start) of the disease. The gang **set on** (= attack) him with baseball bats.*

• Some phrasal nouns are made up of the same words as a phrasal verb but reverse the order of the verb and the particle: *set on → onset, cry out → outcry.*

• Some phrasal nouns are countable and the plural is made by adding 's' to the verb or particle at the end of the phrasal noun: *break-up → break-up**s**, outcry → outcrie**s**, setback → setback**s**,* not ~~onsets~~.

• Not all phrasal nouns can be made into phrasal verbs, e.g. *update, upshot, overkill, downtime.*

V7.3 Metaphors (7C **1** p72)

• A metaphor is a way of describing something by referring to it as something else which has similar qualities. Metaphors use a non-literal meaning of words. Compare:

The police **grilled** him for hours.   I **grilled** the meat for five minutes.

grill 1 (non-literal) to ask somebody a lot of questions often over a long time: *The police grilled him for hours about what he'd done that night.* 2 (literal) cook something by direct heat, often in an oven: *I grilled the meat for five minutes.*

warm 1 (non-literal) friendly and affectionate: *We got a warm welcome from my cousin.* 2 having a comfortably high temperature, although not hot: *The pizza wasn't warm enough so I put it in the microwave.*

storm 1 (non-literal) attack: *The police stormed the building and rescued the hostages.* 2 (literal) an extreme weather condition with strong winds, heavy rain and often thunder and lightning: *The forecast warns a severe storm is on its way.*

flood /flʌd/ 1 (non-literal) fill or enter a place in large numbers or amounts: *The market is flooded with cheap, plastic goods.* 2 (literal) cause to become covered with water: *If it rains any more, the roads will soon be flooded.*

bright 1 (non-literal) clever and quick to learn: *He's a really bright lad – I can't believe he'd turn to crime.* 2 (literal) full of light: *It was such a bright day I needed my sunglasses.*

dawn /dɔːn/ 1 (non-literal) begin to be understood by somebody: *It suddenly dawned on the inspector who the criminal might be.* 2 (literal) the first light of daybreak: *I have to get up at dawn to drive to work.*

freeze 1 (non-literal) stop moving and become completely still: *When I saw the burglar, I froze and couldn't move.* 2 (literal) lower the temperature of something below 0°C causing it to become very cold and often hard: *It was so cold that the lake froze.*

fly 1 (non-literal) pass very quickly: *The crime novel was so exciting, the time flew.* 2 (literal) travel through the air by plane, etc.: *My parents flew to Brazil last week.*

crack 1 (non-literal) become very stressed because of work pressure etc.: *Vicky is a good choice for the job because she doesn't crack under pressure.* 2 (literal) a very narrow space between parts of something: *I suddenly noticed the large crack in the ceiling.*

Grammar

G7.1 Conditionals: basic forms (Preview 7 ① p65)

Zero conditional

- The zero conditional talks about an event/situation that is a **general truth/fact**: *If you do more than 50km/h along this road, you get caught by speed cameras.*

- We make the zero conditional with: *if + subject + Present Simple, subject + Present Simple.*

TIP! • *If* and *when* have the same meaning in the zero conditional: *If/When I look after plants, they die.*

First conditional

- The first conditional talks about a **possible** or **likely** future result.

- The *if* clause talks about things that are possible but not certain: *If you get any more points for speeding, ...* (maybe you'll get more points for speeding). The main clause says what we think the result will be in this situation: *you'll be banned from driving.*

- We make the first conditional with: *if + subject + Present Simple, subject + will/won't + infinitive.*

- We can use *might* instead of *will* in the main clause to mean 'will perhaps'.

Second conditional

- We use the second conditional to talk about an **unlikely** or **imaginary** situations in the **present or future**. We often use it to talk about the opposite of what is true or real: *If you lost your licence, you'd probably lose your job.* (but you haven't lost your licence).

- We make the second conditional with: *if + subject + Past Simple, subject + 'd (= would)/wouldn't + infinitive*

- We can use *could* instead of *would* in the main clause to talk about ability or possibility: *If I won the lottery, I could go travelling.*

- We can use *might* instead of *would* in the main clause to mean 'would perhaps'.

Third conditional

- We use the third conditional to talk about **imaginary** situations in the **past**. They are often the opposite of what really happened: *If you'd hadn't gone through that red light, the police wouldn't have stopped you* (you did go through that red light so the police stopped you).

- We make the third conditional with: *if + subject + Past Perfect, subject + 'd (= would)/wouldn't + have + past participle.*

- We can also use *could* and *might* in the main clause to mean 'would perhaps'.

G7.2 Conditionals: non-basic forms (7A ⑤ p68)

- We can use a variety of verb forms in conditional sentences, not only those used in the four 'basic' conditionals.

a) The **future** with *going to* is used instead of the present to show future intention: *If you're going to commit a burglary, you'll have to be careful what you wear.* (variation of first conditional)

b) A **continuous form** is used instead of a simple form to emphasise an action in progress: *One burglar would have got away with it completely if he hadn't been sweating.* (variation of third conditional) *If I were committing a burglary, I'd be better off wearing gloves.* (variation of second conditional)

c) A **modal** is used instead of a present form, e.g. to give advice: *If a person doesn't want to leave forensic evidence, they should just slide through a window.* (variation of zero conditional)

TIP! • We can make variations of all of four 'basic' conditional forms with these future, continuous and modal forms. For example:

a) *If I'm going to be late, I always ring home.* (future used instead of the present as a variation of a zero conditional)

b) *If you're staying here in the summer, I'll leave a key to our house with you.* (continuous form used instead of the present simple as variation of the first conditional)

Mixed conditionals

- In mixed conditionals, the main clause and the *if* clause sometimes refer to a different time period. The most common combinations are second and third conditionals. Compare:

1 *If the kidnapper hadn't licked that envelope, he wouldn't be in prison now.* (mixed conditional)

2 *If the kidnapper hadn't licked that envelope, he wouldn't have gone to prison.* (third conditional)

In both conditionals we are referring to imaginary situations.

1 The first sentence is a 'mixed' conditional because the *if* clause refers to a situation in the past and the main clause refers to a condition in the present (he is in prison now). In the *if* clause, we use a standard construction for the third conditional and in the main clause we use the construction of the second conditional (*would + infinitive*).

2 In the second sentence, the *if* clause and the main clause refer to the past (he licked the envelope and went to prison) and we use a standard construction for a third conditional.

- Compare:

1 *If they weren't such good actors, most of them would have been found out much earlier.* (mixed conditional)

2 *If they hadn't been such good actors, most of them would have been found out much earlier.* (third conditional)

In both conditionals we are referring to imaginary situations.

1 The first sentence is a 'mixed' conditional because the *if* clause refers to a situation in the present (they are good actors) and the main clause refers to a condition in the past. In the *if* clause, we use a standard construction for the second conditional (Past Simple) and in the main clause we use the construction of the third conditional (*would + have + past participle*).

Language Summary 7

2 In the second sentence the *if* clause and the main clause refer to a situation in the past (they were good actors and they weren't found out) and we use a standard construction for a third conditional.

TIP! • In conditionals that refer to unreal situations, we can use other combinations of verb forms if the time in the *if* clause is not the same as the time in the main clause. For example:

a) If **I hadn't lost** my bag, **I'd be leaving** tomorrow. (*if* clause refers to the past and the main clause refers to the future)

b) If he **didn't have to** go back next week, **I would have invited** him to come. (*if* clause refers to the future and the main clause refers to the past)

c) If we **have to pay** them next week, we **would need** to get the money now. (*if* clause refers to the future and the main clause refers to the present)

d) If they **arrest** him now, they **would have** to charge him by tomorrow. (*if* clause refers to the present and the main clause refers to the future)

Formal conditionals

● We use **should** in the *if* clause in the first conditional if we want to suggest that something is very unlikely. We can use **happen to** in a similar way or combine them (*should happen to*):
… if anyone **happens to** come across a body ….
… **should** any of your listeners be thinking of committing a murder.

● We can use inversion in unreal conditional sentences when the first verb in the *if* clause is *were*, *had* or *should*. In these sentences, we can leave out *if* and we put the verb at the start of the clause:

a) **Were they to find out** the truth, we would be in serious trouble. (= If they were to find out the truth …)

b) **Had she not tried** to sell the car, they would never have caught her. (= If she hadn't tried to sell the car, …)

c) **Should you see** the man again, please call us immediately. (= If you should see the man again, …)

If a person doesn't want to leave forensic evidence, they should just slide through a window.

G7.3 Passive forms (Preview 7 **2** p65)

● We usually use the passive when we are more interested in what happens than in who or what does the action.

● We often use the passive when we don't know who or what does the action.

passive verb form	be	past participle
Present Simple	am/are/is	sent
Present Continuous	am/are/is being	blamed
Past Simple	was/were	written
Past Continuous	was/were being	encouraged
Present Perfect Simple	has/have been	stolen
Past Perfect Simple	had been	left
be going to	am/are/is going to be	announced
modal	should, could, etc. + be	told
modal + have + past participle	could, should, etc. + have + been	invited

G7.4 Impersonal report structures (7B **6** p71)

● We use impersonal report structures when we want to distance ourselves from information which is not necessarily our opinion. They are commonly found in reports and newspaper articles.

REPORTING WITH THE PASSIVE

● To make impersonal report structures we can use:

a) *it* + passive + *that* clause: **It is claimed that** even your financial records can be accessed. Other verbs which are commonly used with this structure are: *accept, agree, allege, believe, consider, expect, feel, know, predict, say, suggest, think, understand*.

b) subject + passive + infinitive with *to*: **CCTV cameras are known to operate** in more and more buildings. Other verbs which are commonly used with this structure are: *believe, consider, find, say, think*.

c) *there* + passive + infinitive with *to*: **There are now estimated to be** more mobile phones than people in many countries. Other verbs which are commonly used with this structure are: *allege, believe, claim, expect, find, rumour, say, think*.

TIP! • We use a variety of infinitive forms with impersonal report structures: She is known **to have spent** five years in India. He is rumoured **to be resigning** next month.

REPORTING WITH *SEEM* AND *APPEAR*

● The verbs *seem* and *appear* can also be used to distance yourself from events you are reporting; *seem* and *appear* are **not** used in the passive. **It seems that** they will soon become the norm … . **Opinion appears to be** divided. **There also appear to be** many hospitals using them.

● We can use a *that*-clause after *It seems/It appears*: It seems **that no one knew** about the problem.

● We can use an infinitive with *to* after *seem/appear*: The government appears **to be obsessed** with the idea of watching people.

TIPS! • We can also talk about an apparent fact using either *It + seem/appear + that* clause: It appeared that people were unaware they were being watched. or subject (e.g. people) + *seem/appear* + infinitive with *to*: In the main, people seem to support the use of CCTV.

Real World

RW7.1 Functions and intonation of questions 7C **4** p73

- Intonation patterns in English are varied and complicated. However, the following guidelines may be helpful.

- We often ask questions to find out new information (N) or check if our information is correct (C).

  What does? (N)

  Isn't this about the time George usually goes out? (C)

  How much? (C)

  So, you went on your own, did you? (C)

  How come? (N)

- We often use:
  1. a **falling** tone when asking questions to find out new information.
  2. a **rising** tone when checking information we think is right.
  3. a **falling** tone in question tags when we expect the listener to confirm that we are right.

- We sometimes have different reasons for asking questions, other than requesting 'new' or checking 'old' information. Sometimes no reply is expected and a **falling** intonation is used. For example:
  a) Giving instructions: *Could we just go over this one more time?*
  b) Aggressive/defensive response to a question: *How should I know? / So what?*
  c) Making a sarcastic comment: *Isn't that a coincidence?*
  d) A rhetorical question (expecting agreement): *He never stays in on a Friday evening, does he?*

TIPS! • We use a rising tone in question tags when we are finding out new information:
She'll be back later, won't she?
• We can use a **falling** tone when we combine a positive question tag with a positive verb form, to ask rhetorical questions or in confrontational situations: *So, you're innocent, are you?*

Accurate Writing

AW7.1 Connecting words: condition p75

- We can use **unless** in conditionals to mean *if not*: **Unless** *ex-prisoners are given help, they are likely to re-offend.*

- We can use **in case** to talk about something we do in order to be ready for possible future situations. If the clause refers to the future, *in case* is followed by a verb form in the present: *Take a sandwich **in case** you get hungry later.*

- We can use **otherwise** when we talk about an undesirable situation which would happen if something else did not happen. We usually put *otherwise* at the beginning of a clause: *We must act now, **otherwise** the prison population will double.*

- We often use **provided/providing**, **as long as** and **assuming** instead of *if* in conditionals: *Ex-prisoners should be helped financially, **as long as** there is enough money.*

- **Provided/providing** and **as long as** mean 'only if (this happens)': *Prisoners can become responsible citizens, **providing** we allow them to.*

- We can use **whether** as an alternative for **if** in conditionals when you are mentioning two or more alternatives. We put **whether** in front of the first alternative and **or** in front of the second alternative: **Whether** *the governor is right **or** wrong, there are many who disagree.*

- **Imagine** and **suppose/supposing** have the same meaning (= form a picture in your mind about what something could be like): **Imagine/Suppose/Supposing** *the prisoners aren't well enough to work, what happens then?*

- We can use **imagine** and **suppose/supposing** as an alternative for *if* in questions: **Imagine/suppose/supposing** *there was no crime, what kind of world would we live in?*

AW7.2 Punctuation: commas p75

We use commas:

- after introductory clauses beginning with *after, although, as, because, if, since, when* and *while* that come before the main clause: *If you have intruders in the house, it's better not to challenge them.*

- to separate three or more words, phrases, or clauses written in a series. We do **not** usually use a comma before the final 'and': *Avoid keeping expensive computers, handbags and wallets on view.* not *... computers, handbags, and wallets on view.*

- after introductory words such as *surprisingly, however*: *Surprisingly, she agreed to marry him. However, you should also be well insured.*

- either side of clauses, phrases and words that are not essential to the meaning of the sentence, e.g. non-defining relative clauses: *Door chains and spy holes, which your landlord will probably fit, help to reduce crime.* However, we do not use commas either side of essential clauses, phrases and words, e.g. in defining relative clauses: *That's the man who I saw shoplifting.*

- after the verb and before the opening quotation marks in direct speech: *The policeman said, "You should set up a Neighbourhood Watch scheme."*

- before the end quotation marks in direct speech when the quote is followed by the speaker: *"You should set up a Neighbourhood Watch scheme," said the policeman.*

- to separate two or more adjectives that are of the same type in describing a noun: *He's a difficult, obstinate person.* (*difficult* and *obstinate* are both adjectives of opinion. We can therefore reverse the order of the adjectives: *He's an obstinate, difficult person*). However, if the adjectives are not of the same type, we do not use a comma (and we cannot reverse the order of the adjective): *It was an expensive black wallet.* not *It was an expensive, black wallet.*

TIPS! • We also use commas in:
• geographical names: *Cambridge, Massachusetts got its name from Cambridge, England.*
• dates: *She was born on 21st August, 2002.*
• addresses: *2 Bower Road, Rainham, Kent*

Language Summary 8

V8.1 Phrases with *time* (8A ❶ p76)

have time to kill have nothing to do for a particular period of time: *If you've got time to kill, you could do some washing up.*

in plenty of time earlier than an arranged time or deadline: *If I take the motorway, we'll arrive in plenty of time.*

take (my/your/etc.) time said to mean that someone can spend as much time as they need in doing something: *There's no hurry for the report. Take your time.*

have time to spare have an excess of time to do an activity: *We arrived at the airport with time to spare so we did a bit of shopping before checking in.*

for the time being said to describe a situation that will be like that for a limited period of time but may change later: *For the time being, I'm going to stay in London.*

it's only a matter of time used to say something is certain to happen but you do not know when: *It's only a matter of time before we will experience an environmental catastrophe.*

there's no time like the present said to encourage someone to take action immediately instead of waiting: *Why don't you call him now? There's no time like the present.*

have (got) no time for sb/sth disapprove of somebody/something and not want to be involved with them: *I've got no time for people moaning about the smoking ban.*

find time arrange time to do something, see somebody, etc.: *I can't seem to find time to organise the recycling.*

give sb a hard time make things difficult for someone: *My wife gives me a hard time about buying bottled water.*

V8.2 *wherever, whoever, whatever, etc.* (8B ❷ p79)

- When we add *ever* to question words (*wherever, whoever, whenever, whatever, whichever, however*) it usually has one of these meanings:

1 It doesn't matter *where, who, when,* etc.; it can be any place, anyone, any time, etc.:

   Whoever *saw the photos identified the same emotions.* (it doesn't matter who saw the photos)

   Wherever *this experiment was carried out, the results were the same.* (it doesn't matter where the experiment was done)

   Whenever *you do this in private …* (it doesn't matter when you do this)

2 An unknown place, person, time, etc.

   Whoever *said that is wrong.* (I don't know who the person was)

TIPS! • *Whenever* can also mean 'every time': **Whenever** *she calls, I'm out.* (= Every time she calls, I'm out.)

• *Whoever, whichever* and *whatever* can be the subject or the object of the verb: **Whoever** *saw you …,* (subject) **Whoever** *you saw…,* (object)

• *Whichever* is often followed by *of*: **Whichever of** *you is last out of the house, lock the door.*

• We can use *wherever, whoever, however, whatever, whenever* and *whichever* to show surprise or to emphasise something:

a) *What's the matter?* (you look sad)

b) **Whatever's** *the matter!* (emphasises the question, for example because the person is crying)

a) *He leaves when I arrive.*

b) *He leaves* **whenever** *I arrive.* (emphasises that he leaves every time I arrive)

• We can use *wherever, whoever, however/whatever/etc.* in informal conversation as an answer to a question, to indicate that we really don't mind. *Whatever* is the most common of these expressions: A *What do you want to eat?* B *Whatever.* This use of 'whatever' can also suggest that the speaker doesn't care and therefore can seem rude.

V8.3 Word building (2): suffixes (8B ❼ p81)

NOUNS

- Some nouns and verbs have the same form, e.g. *a sound/sound, a change/change, a challenge/challenge, a plan/plan, a test/test.*

- We can make **nouns** by adding these suffixes to **verbs**: *-ance, -y, -er, -sion, -al, -ment, -ure.*

disturb → disturb**ance**	survive → surviv**al**	
recover → recover**y**	excite → excite**ment**	
ride → rid**er**	fail → fail**ure**	
divide → divi**sion**		

- We can make **nouns** by adding these suffixes to **adjectives**: *-ness, -ity.* If an adjective ends in *-y,* we usually change the 'y' to an 'i' before adding the suffix.

   happy → happ**iness**   possible → possibil**ity**

VERBS, ADJECTIVES, ADVERBS

- To make **adjectives** from **nouns** we can use *-ly, -y, -ous, -al, -ic, -ed: coward/coward***ly**, *mood/mood***y**, *courage/courage***ous**, *culture/cultur***al**, *sympathy/sympath***etic**, *talent/talent***ed**

- To make **adverbs** from **adjectives** we can use *-ly: recent/recent***ly**, *confident/confident***ly**, *final/final***ly**

- To make **adjectives** from **verbs** we can use *-ive, -ent/-ant, -able/-ible: create/creat***ive**, *depend/depend***ent**, *remark/ remark***able**

- To make **verbs** from **adjectives** we can use *-ise, -en, -ify: rational/rational***ise**, *wide/wid***en**, *clear/clar***ify**

TIPS! • Sometimes we change the spelling of the word before we add a suffix: *clear* → *clarify, create* → *creative*

• Sometimes verbs and adjectives have the same form, e.g. *dry, warm, calm: Calm down! He's always quite calm.*

• We can make abstract nouns by adding these suffixes to concrete nouns: *-hood, -ship,* e.g. *childhood, friendship.*

• The American spelling of *-ise* is *-ize: criticize, realize,* etc.

Grammar

G8.1 *Wish, If only* (Preview 8 ❶ p75)

- We often use **I wish** … or **If only** … to talk about imaginary situations. They are often used to talk about the opposite of what is true.

- We use **wish/If only** + Past Simple to make wishes about states or activities in the present: *If only I knew someone who could help. I wish Tom was/were here.*

- We use **wish/If only** + Past Continuous to make wishes about actions in progress: *I wish it wasn't/weren't raining.*

- We use **wish/If only** + Past Perfect to make wishes about past events, states, etc. These wishes are used to express regret and are often the opposite of what happened: *If only I had known you were coming.* (but I didn't know) *If only we'd been taught languages at school.* (but we weren't)

- We use **wish/If only** + *could* + infinitive to make wishes about abilities or possibilities: *I wish I could live here.*

- We use **wish/If only** + *would* + infinitive to make wishes about things other people, organisations, etc. do that we would like to change. This is often used to show annoyance or impatience about things that are outside our control: *I wish more young people would vote.* (but they refuse to do so) *If only Nancy would get her hair cut.* (But she refuses to do so).

- After constructions with **wish**, we often add a clause with *but* + subject + auxiliary verb: *I wish I could live here, **but I can't**.* (the situation now is that I can't live here). *I wish I hadn't broken up with him **but I did**.* (the situation is that I broke up with him in the past). *I wish I wasn't going to the dentist tomorrow, **but I am**.* (the situation is that I'm going to the dentist in the future)

TIPS! • We can say *I wish I/he/she/it was …* or *I wish I/he/she/it were …* : *I wish I was/were more organised.*
• We do not often say *I wish I would … .* e.g. *I wish I didn't smoke.* not ~~I wish I wouldn't smoke~~.

G8.2 Past verb forms with present or future meaning (8A ❺ p77)

- Past verb forms do not always refer to past time.
- None of these sentences refer to past time. Instead, they all tell us what the speaker would like to happen.
  1 It's time to accept the fact that everyone can make a difference. 2 It's time **we** all accepted the fact that everyone can make a difference.
  1 I'd sooner do one of the jobs. 2 I'd sooner **someone else** was doing one of the jobs.
  1 I'd prefer to get directly involved. 2 I'd prefer it if a lot more **people** got directly involved.
  1 I'd rather look at the small things I could do. 2 I'd rather **people** looked at the small things they could do.

- The verbs in pink are all infinitive forms (with or without *to*). When *it's time* and *would prefer* are followed by a verb we use an infinitive with *to*. When *would sooner* and *would rather* are followed by a verb, we use an infinitive.

- The verbs in blue are either Past Simple or Past Continuous verb forms. When *it's time, would sooner, would rather* and *would prefer it if* are followed by a subject + verb we use a past verb form.

TIPS! • We can also say *It's about time* or *it's high time* + subject + past verb form to suggest something is urgent: *It's high time we realised we can't keep using up the earth's resources like this.*
• When we talk about past situations with *would sooner / would rather* + subject + verb, we use the Past Perfect or Past Perfect Continuous: *I'd rather you'd told me before.*
• When the preference is also in the past, we can use *would have preferred it if*: *We would have preferred it if you had warned us at the time.*

Accurate Writing

AW8.1 Connecting words: comment adverbials ❶ p85

obviously in a way that is easy to understand or see: *Obviously, she was guilty.*
fortunately happening because of good/bad luck (opposite: unfortunately): *Fortunately, he wasn't hurt.*
quite honestly/to be honest in a completely honest manner: *Quite honestly/To be honest, I think he's wrong.*
surely used to express surprise that something has happened or is going to happen: *Surely, you could leave.*
in fact used to introduce something that contradicts or reinforces a previous statement: *He doesn't work. In fact, he never has.*
clearly used to show that you think something is obvious or certain: *Clearly, he didn't understand.*
amazingly used to introduce something extremely surprising: *Amazingly, Tom resigned.*
frankly used when giving an honest or direct opinion: *Frankly, I think Em's right.*
apparently used to say you have read or been told something although you are not certain it is true: *Apparently, Sy's got engaged.*
according to used to introduce something said by someone else: *According to Jo, Pam's ill.*

AW8.2 Spelling: commonly misspelled words ❷ p85

These words are commonly misspelled: *necessary, acquaint, receipt, government, succeed, address, business, accommodate, medicine, exaggerate, admitted, colleague*

Language Summary 9

sentences	meaning of verb describing state/activity
He has his own business.	possess
He's having second thoughts about the flying lessons.	experience
He appears to be fast asleep.	seem
She's appearing in a play on TV.	perform
It looks expensive.	seem
He's looking at a new car today.	go to see
This material feels very nice.	sense the texture or temperature of something when it comes into contact with your skin
She's feeling* better.	experience something physical/emotional
She comes from London.	originate
She's coming from London.	travel
He's difficult.	have a permanent characteristic
He's being difficult.	temporarily behave in a particular way
I imagine she really likes Canada.	believe something is probably true
There's nobody there. You're imagining things!	think something exists although in fact it is not real or true.
My case weighs 15 kilos.	have a heaviness of a certain amount
They're weighing all the hand luggage.	measure the heaviness of an object

TIP! • We can use both the simple or continuous form of the verb *feel* to mean 'experience something physical/emotional': *she feels/'s feeling happier.*

G9.3 *a/an, the* or no article   (Preview 9 ❷ p85)

- We use *a* or *an*:
  a) to talk about a person or thing for the first time: *… have a method for checking the identity of a VIP guest.*
  b) when we don't know, or it isn't important, which one: *They send an entry pass …*
  c) with jobs: *This is scanned by a doorman.*
- We use *the*:
  a) to talk about the same person or thing for the second/third/ fourth, etc. time: *a barcode to the VIP's mobile phone.*
  b) when there is only one (or only one in a particular place): *At a recent night at The Ministry of Sound in London …*
  c) with countries that are groups of islands or states: *Clubs in the USA …*
  d) with superlatives: *Some of the hottest nightclubs*
- We don't use an article:
  a) for most towns, cities, countries and continents: *At a recent night at The Ministry of Sound in London …*
  b) to talk about people or things in general: *… students were offered discounts if they used mobile phones to buy electronic tickets.*
  c) for some public places (*school, hospital, university college, prison,* etc.) when we talk about what they are used for in general: *I went to college in London.*

TIP! • We use *the* with public places when we talk about the building: *I went to the college at lunchtime.*

G9.4 *a/an* v *one*; *few, a few, quite a few*

9B ❼ p91

A/AN V ONE

- *A/an* and *one* both refer to one thing and can be used with singular countable nouns. However, we usually use *one* if we want to emphasise the number. Compare these examples:
  a) *It takes just a tenth of a second to complete most transactions.*
  b) *It takes just one tenth of a second to complete most transactions.* (= not two or three tenths)
- We also use *one*:
  a) when we are thinking of <u>one</u> particular day (in the future or the past), but we don't say exactly which day: *We paid that bill one day last month.* not … *a day last month. We can see the bank manager one day next week.* not … *a day next week.*
  b) in phrases with *one … other/another/the next*: *Many of us move from one means of payment to another* … not *Many of us move from a means of payment to another …*
  c) In response to the question *Have you got a five-pound note I could borrow?* we say: *Sorry, I've only got a ten-pound note.* (That's the only note I have). *Sorry, I've only got one five-pound note and I need it.* (I haven't got any more five pound notes to lend you.)

TIP! • We use *a* with singular countable nouns in exclamations, e.g. *What a big mistake! What a lovely day!*

FEW, A FEW, QUITE A FEW

- *Quite a few* means 'a considerable number': *However, quite a few American bankers are optimistic.*
- *A few* means 'some, but a small number': *If payments for a few coffees, a train ticket and a newspaper are made every day … .*
- *Few* means 'not many or not enough' (not as many as you would expect): *Few financial experts would dispute the fact that some of these methods of payment will soon become a thing of the past.*

TIPS! • *Few* is often used in more formal situations: *She has few friends.* (formal) *She doesn't have many friends.* (informal).

• *little / a little* is used with uncountable nouns in the same way as *few / a few* is used with countable nouns. *He spends little time with his children* = (not much, not enough) *He spends a little time with his children* = (some time, but a small amount)

• We can make comparatives with *fewer (than)*. We use *fewer* with countable nouns: *There are fewer reasons these days to carry cash than ever before.* We use *less* with uncountable nouns: *People carry less cash than they did in the past.*

Real World

RW9.1 **Presenting information** (9C ❻ p93)

● We usually use these phrases towards the beginning of a talk to tell our audience what we will be speaking about and to give them an idea of the structure of the talk.

I'm going to divide the talk into (three sections).
First of all, (how economics is related to real life).
Then I'll go on to (the intellectual challenge)
And finally I'll (discuss future careers)

to make the first point

First of all ...
Let's start with/by ...

to refer to a point made earlier

As I said before ...
To go back to ...
To return to something I mentioned earlier ...

to signal a new point

Now I'll talk about ...
Let's move on to ...
Leaving that aside for a moment ...

to summarise what's been said so far

So to sum up ...
Just to recap ...

to signal the last point/bring the talk to an end

In conclusion ...
Last but not least ...
And finally ...

Let's start by looking at some statistics

Accurate Writing

AW9.1 **Connecting words: reason and result** (❶ p95)

● We use ***because/because of*** to give the reason for something. They go at the beginning of a clause of reason.

I lent Mary my racket **because** *hers was broken.*

reason clause

● ***Because of*** is followed by a noun phrase:
  1 ***Because of poor visibility***, *there were several road accidents.* not ~~Because of visibility was poor, ...~~
  2 ***Because of terrible floods***, *they lost all their crops.* not ~~Because of there were terrible floods ...~~

● We use ***as/since*** to mean *because*: ***Since/As*** *you don't want to help, I'll do it myself.*

● We use ***so***, ***as a result***, ***therefore*** and ***consequently*** to introduce the result of a situation. We usually use *as a result, therefore* and *consequently* at the beginning of a sentence. *As a result, therefore* and *consequently* are mainly used in formal contexts.

My Spanish is really bad. **As a result***, he didn't understand me.*

Mary's racket was broken, **so** *I lent her mine.*

There were terrible floods. **Therefore***, they lost all their crops.*

Visibility was poor. **Consequently***, there were several road accidents.*

● We use ***due to*** and ***owing to*** at the beginning of a phrase to introduce the result of a situation. If an event **is due to** something, it happens as a result of it. These phrases are followed by a noun phrase.

Due to/Owing to *bad weather yesterday I didn't go climbing.* not ~~Due to/Owing to the weather was bad yesterday, ...~~ In formal, written English, we don't usually use ***owing to*** after the verb **be**. *The road accidents were* **due to** *bad weather.* not ~~The road accidents were **owing to** bad weather.~~

TIPS! ● We use 'cos' /kəz/ in informal speech to mean 'because'.
● If we put a verb after phrases like *as a result of, due to* or *because of*, we use a verb+*ing* after the subject. This type of structure is more common in formal contexts: *As a result of my Spanish* **being** *really bad, he didn't understand me. Because of the visibility* **being** *poor, there were several road accidents.*

AW9.2 **Spelling: -*ible* or -*able*** (❷ p95)

● The adjective suffixes -*ible* and -*able* are often confused.
● We usually use:
  a) -***ible*** if the root (= the word to which the suffix is added) is not a complete word, e.g. *ed* + -*ible* = **ed**ible, **vis**ible, **destruct**ible, **incred**ible. Exceptions include: *contemptible, digestible, flexible, responsible, sensible*
  b) -***able*** if the root is a complete word, e.g. *understand* + *able* = *understandable*, *do* + *able* = *do***able**: *notice**able**, *believ**able**.

TIP! ● If a root word ends in -*e*, we usually replace the -*e* with the suffix, e.g. *believe* → *believable*. However, there are many exceptions to this rule: *love* → *loveable, notice* → *noticeable*.

Language Summary 10

Vocabulary

V10.1 Antonyms p101

- Adjectives must collocate with the nouns they are describing, the opposite of *a clear idea* is *a rough idea*, but the opposite of *a clear sky* is *a cloudy sky*.

- ≠ means 'is the opposite of'

a)
a clear idea	≠ a vague/ a rough idea	
an easy decision	≠ a difficult/ a hard decision	BUT
a sweet guy	≠ a nasty guy	

a clear glass	≠ an opaque glass
easy-fit jeans	≠ slim-fit jeans
a sweet drink	≠ a sour drink

- Other common antonyms include:

b)
a rough surface	≠ a smooth surface
a light colour	≠ a dark colour
a gentle wind	≠ a strong wind
an old person	≠ a young person
a tall building	≠ a low building
a dry wine	≠ a sweet wine
plain food	≠ rich food
a strong coffee	≠ a weak coffee

a rough sea	≠ a calm sea
a light meal	≠ a heavy meal
a gentle person	≠ an aggressive person
an old building	≠ a modern building
a tall person	≠ a short person
a dry day	≠ a wet day
a plain shirt	≠ a patterned shirt
a strong possibility	≠ a faint possibility

BUT

Grammar

G10.1 Subject/verb agreement p97

- A verb usually 'agrees' with its subject (i.e. a singular subject has a singular verb and a plural subject has a plural verb):

  *Horses, too, **have** powered the information superhighway for thousands of years.*

  *Further north, **mail was** being delivered to the icy corners of the world by huskies.*

- We use a **singular** verb:
  a) if the subject of the verb is a clause: *Having cats **is** now a thing of the past.*
  b) with nouns which end in -s but are not plural: *News **comes** via email these days.*
  c) with expressions of quantity, measurement, etc.: *2,000 miles **is** a long way to travel.*
  d) after words such as *everyone, anything*, etc.: *The information that everyone **was** so anxiously waiting for.*

- We use a **plural** verb:
  a) for nouns which don't end in -s but which are not singular: *The police **were** using a pigeon service.*
  b) after words such as *both of, all of, plenty of, a number of, a couple*: *Only a couple **were** recruited.*

- Some collective nouns and names can take either a **singular** or a **plural** form:
  a) When focusing on countries which are a group of states, an institution or organisation as a whole, the verb is usually **singular**: *The USA **has** fifty states; The British army **was** also dependent on pigeons; the team **was** a financial failure.*
  b) When focusing on a collection of individuals, the verb is usually **plural**: *The public **were** fascinated by the Pony Express.*

Grammar

TIPS! • When the subject is two or more nouns linked by *and/or*, we use a plural form: *A letter **and** a parcel **were forwarded** to our new address.*

• In clauses with *what* as subject, if the following noun is plural, the verb is either plural (in more formal contexts) or singular (in more informal contexts). *What surprised me **was/were** the sheer numbers of pigeons used in the war.*

• In complex sentences, the verb agrees with the main noun: *During the four-month siege, **more than a million letters were delivered** to the citizens of Paris.*

• We use a singular verb with **the** number of (but a plural verb with **a** number of): *The number of applicants always **exceeds** the number of places.*

G10.2 Modal verbs (1): functions
Preview 10 ① p95

- We talk about ability using *can* and *could*: *Unfortunately she **can't** touch-type. My brother **could** surf when he was eight.*

- We ask or give permission using *can, may* and *could*: *You **can** use my phone. **May** I use your phone? **Could** I leave early today, please? When I was young, I **could** only watch TV at the weekend.*

- We talk about obligation using *must* and *have (got) to*: *Ben had an eye test and he's **got to** wear glasses. You **must** get your brakes fixed, they're dangerous.*

- We give advice using *should* and *ought to*: *You **should** return this as it doesn't work. He **ought to** change his accountant.*

- We talk about repeated/typical behaviour using *will* and *would*. We often use *always* or *often* with *would*: *She'll come home and immediately turn on the TV. He'd **always** stop for lunch at noon.*

- We refuse using *won't* and *wouldn't*: *I **won't** let her use my car. She **wouldn't** give me a lift last night.*

- We criticise people's past behaviour using *ought to have/should have* + past participle: *They **ought to have told** you. She **should have gone** to university.*

- We talk about prohibition using *can't*: *You **can't** smoke on any public transport.*

SEMI-MODALS

be allowed to

- We use **be allowed to** to say we have permission to do something: *We **were allowed to** wear whatever we wanted at school.*

manage to

- We use *manage to* to say that we succeed in doing something, often after some difficulty: *I lost my key but I **managed to** climb in through the window.*

be able to

- We use *be able to* to talk about ability or possibility. We also use *can* to talk about ability and possibility but *can* only has two forms: *can* and *could*. Therefore, we sometimes need *be able to*: *I might be able to come.* not *I might can come.*

- If we say someone **was able to** do something, then we usually mean they had the ability to do something <u>and</u> they did it. We cannot use *could* for this meaning. If we are talking about a single achievement rather than a general ability in the past, we usually use *be able to/managed to* instead of *could*: *I **was able to** meet him last Friday.* not *I could meet him last Friday.* However, we can use *couldn't* to talk about a specific situation in the past: *I tried to start the car but I couldn't.* We can use *could* with verbs such as *see, hear, feel,* etc. to talk about specific situations when we were able to do something: *I could see a car in the distance.*

needn't/don't need to

- We use *need to* to talk about things that are necessary for us to do. In positive sentences we use *need* + infinitive with *to*: *I need to buy some stamps.*

- In negative sentences we can say both *don't need to* and *needn't* with no change in meaning. *I don't need to/needn't go yet.*

didn't need to/needn't have done

- In negative sentences referring to the past we can say *didn't need to/needn't have done*.

- However, these two structures have a difference in meaning: *I didn't need to change planes, there was a direct flight.* (= it was not necessary for me to change planes so I didn't) *I needn't have changed planes; there was a direct flight.* (It was not necessary for me to change planes, but I did.)

G10.3 Modal verbs (2): levels of certainty about the past, present and future (10B ③ p99)

- Modal verbs are auxiliaries which express our attitude to, or assessment of, an event or situation and roughly divide into two groups; a) functions such as obligation, advice, permission, prohibition, etc. b) levels of certainty.

LEVELS OF CERTAINTY

We use:

- *will, won't, can't, must, would(n't)* when we think something is definite:
  1 *... I'm sure he'**ll be working**.* (present)
  2 *He's certain he'**ll find** a buyer for his next animation film.* (future)

  3 *Tang Yun, for example, you just know it **won't have been** easy for him as a kid.* (past)
  4 *... It **can't be** easy having Martin as your partner.* (present)
  5 *My father says it's obvious that I **can't have wanted** it badly enough ...* (past)
  6 *Clearly, he **must enjoy** what he does; why else would he put in so many hours?* (present)
  7 *He **must have devoted** most of his childhood to practising.* (past)
  8 *My father says it's obvious that I can't have wanted it badly enough or I **wouldn't have given** up.* (past)

- *should* when we think something is probable: *People are just starting to notice his work, so it **shouldn't be** long before he gets the recognition he deserves.* (future)

- *may, might, could* when we think something is possible:
  1 *I **may have had** some natural talent, who knows.* (past)
  2 *He **might be creating** a new animation character ...* (present)
  3 *... or he **could be working on** his next short film.* (present)

- When modal verbs refer to the present we often use: modal verb + infinitive or modal verb + *be* + verb+*ing*: *He **must enjoy** what he does. It is Saturday night and I'm sure he'**ll be working**. It **can't be** easy having Martin as your partner.*

- When modal verbs refer to the future we often use: modal verb + infinitive. *... **shouldn't be** long before he gets the recognition he deserves. He's certain he'**ll find** a buyer ... .*

- When modal verbs refer to past certainty we use: modal verb + *have* + past participle: *Tang Yun, for example, you just know it **won't have been** easy for him as a kid. He **must have devoted** most of his childhood to practising. I **may have had** some natural talent, who knows. My father says it's obvious that I **can't have wanted** it badly enough or I **wouldn't have given up**.*

TIPS! • ***Ought to / ought not to*** has the same meaning as *should/shouldn't*, but it can sound more formal: *She shouldn't be too much longer. She ought not to be too much longer.*

• We don't use ***can*** to talk about levels of certainty. We use **may**, **might**, **could** instead: *He could be at home now.* not *He can be at home now.*

• We use ***couldn't*** or ***can't have*** + past participle to mean certainty about the past: *It couldn't/can't have been easy.*

• We don't use ***can*** or ***mustn't*** when we speculate. We use **can't**, **could**, **might**, **may** or **must**: *He can't have known about it.* not *He mustn't have known about it.* *He could have been at home at that time.* not *He can have been home at that time.*

It **can't be** easy living with him.

Recording Scripts

AMY So, Ann, why did you suggest this book?

ANN Well, I've bought quite a few self-help books over the past few months and I suggested this one for the book club because my brother's been telling me to read it for ages. Apparently, it's sold over 16 million copies and it's still selling well, which surprised me because it's pretty basic stuff, really. I mean, you know, smile at people – that's a bit obvious, isn't it? Or, make the other person feel important. That's pretty obvious, too. But as my brother said, if what Carnegie's saying is that self-evident, then why don't people do it? And he's got a point.

SY Yeah, I agree with your brother there. And OK, even if some of the points he makes in the book seem basic, I mean, I still find it fascinating. Actually, I think people are getting fed up with me talking about it! I've told at least ten people about it at work this week. To be honest, it's the first time I've read a book like this, and even though I haven't quite finished it yet – I mean, I've, I've read about 150 pages so far – I totally agree with what he's saying. I mean, the bit where it says "as a rule we aren't good listeners," I mean, that's so true. I mean we're usually just waiting to speak. If someone's talking about something that's happening to them, or happened to them, then most people are just waiting to butt in, aren't they, with, you know, "Same thing happened to me," and off they go, you know, wittering on about themselves. I mean, I think Carnegie's right when he says that if you want people to like you, you've got to learn to really pay attention to what they're saying. Yeah, I mean, actually encourage the other person to talk about themselves, by asking questions, I mean, showing that you're interested in them. Anyway, I've been trying to be a more attentive listener and not interrupt, but it, I tell you, it takes some self-discipline, I can … Soon as you've finished reading it, I mean, I'm going to give it to my brother, because he's got no social skills whatsoever! I mean, it's true! What about you, Dean. Did you like it?

DEAN Yeah, I did, and to be honest, I wasn't expecting to. Like Sy, I agree with a lot of what it says, like the bit about how important it is to remember people's names. Never thought about that before, but a friend of mine, John, he's brilliant at that. And it works, especially when he's chatting up girls. For instance, last night we went out for a pizza. I went to the loo. I hadn't been gone for more than a minute, but by the time I got back to the table, he'd introduced himself to the three girls at the table next to ours and learnt their names. There he was, saying stuff like "So, Clare, how are you enjoying London?" You could see Clare was thinking "What a nice guy." And I'm sure it was just because he'd called her by her first name. Actually, since Ann suggested this one I've read a couple of his other books.

ANN Yeah, I bought one of his other books recently, too.

AMY Well, during the last couple of weeks I've actually been trying out some of Carnegie's suggestions, as well, you know, like the one where he goes on about how powerful a smile is.

ANN Yeah, but that's true, though, isn't it? I mean, most people walk around with a scowl on their face. So, that when someone actually does smile at you, it really makes an impression.

AMY It does! You know he suggested smiling at everyone you come into contact with for a week and note what happens. Well, I did and it really does make a difference. Like, I've been going to the same train station for years and up until now, I've never really had any contact with the guy in the ticket office other than, "Return to Richmond, please." So, I started with him. You know, a smile and a bit of eye contact and it was amazing! He's been really chatty ever since. Much nicer way to start the day. And remember the bit where Carnegie says, even if you don't feel like smiling, force yourself to, 'cos smiling actually brings on a nice feeling. Well, I've been trying to do that too, and it works!

ANN Yeah, it's a different mindset, isn't it? And I loved that quote – that, the Chinese proverb, "A man without a smiling face must not open a shop!" I know, I know a few shop assistants who could learn from that, especially …

DAVE I do go out and see friends on a fairly regular basis. It's usually based around squash, or playing sports or something, and we'll end up with a drink and talk afterwards. What we talk about isn't deep and meaningful, though – far from it! It's usually about current affairs, something like that, and it usually degenerates into a list of five best cars, or old films, or whatever. I think the whole issue of friendship between men isn't, sort of, based around the emotional bit, it's much more to do with common interests, and the fact that someone is sort of into something that you are. I think if it was something serious, something close and emotional you'd tend to go with and talk to older friends – people that you were at college with, someone that you think you could unload everything on to. The problem with men is that they don't do that – what usually happens is we sort of bottle things up, and don't use friends as well as women do.

HELEN Well, if something major happened, it would probably be my parents I'd talk to first – they'd be the first people to know. But, I do confide in my friends a lot on a day-to-day basis. We tend to meet about once a week – and we we meet in a café. We always meet in the same place, actually, and the reason we meet there is that they put up with all our noise. We try to snatch about half an hour, but – that's what we say – but it usually goes on. We just relax and giggle and I always end up saying much more than I'd intended to. So, yeah, friends are a really big part of my life and they have to put up with a lot from me, but I hope I'm able to give them a little bit back, but most importantly we do manage to have a really good laugh about things.

ANDREA OK, a person who I tend to confide in is my hairdresser, funnily enough. I think the reason I confide in him is precisely because I don't want to unburden all my worries on my family, so the hairdresser's is a neutral ground if you like, where I can just go and talk and I know what I say won't go any further 'cos it's of no interest to my hairdresser. We've got a set routine, I suppose. We sit down and he's focusing on, on my hair, and we have a quick "how are you?" and he tells me very briefly, and then I launch onto, onto what I've got to talk about. It was great, but it wasn't until he broke up with his girlfriend that my hairdresser started to confide in me, which really changed the dynamic of our relationship. Suddenly, he became this person who had needs and who wanted to unburden himself onto me. I mean, if it wasn't for the fact that he gave me such a good haircut, I'd definitely think about moving to another hairdresser.

ALEX I mainly talk to my friends, usually on MSN or by text, because they're my age group and they're the most interesting people to talk to, and we talk about a lot, like what's happened at school, and the latest sports results, and a lot of things like that. If there was a problem, I'd talk to my friends because they'd be more likely to understand what I was going through, or maybe my sister, because she's also young and she'd know. I probably wouldn't talk to my parents, because my mum would get in a flap, and I don't think they'd really understand.

1 The reason Lucy's coming is to help me out. | 2 It was after leaving my last job that I began to work freelance. | 3 What you should do is write a letter and refuse to pay. | 4 It's Tim who's the problem, not Jo. | 5 The person I wanted to speak to was Ben. | 6 What happened was I forgot the map.

CLAUDIA Well, my favourite saying is "Let's cross that bridge when we come to it". It's probably not very exciting for British people, but for me as a non-native speaker I thought it was really, really nice. It basically means that you can't always plan ahead and you can't control everything. Well, to put it simply you can't really worry about things that are way in the future. The first time I heard it was from my then boyfriend, Ben, and nothing has influenced my life more than that saying actually. Well, Ben and I are now married, so I reckon it worked out alright!

CHRIS My favourite expression is "You pay peanuts, you get monkeys," which kind of basically means that the less money you pay the worse the service. It's an expression I've always wanted to tell my boss but never really had the courage to do that.

CLAIRE One of my favourite sayings is "If you fly with the crows, you'll get shot with the crows". I can remember my grandmother saying it to me when I was growing up in Scotland. And, what it means is that if you hang about with the wrong crowd, and what she was saying to me is, at school, that if people who be, behave badly you'll get punished with them, even if you were (weren't) wrong. I've not heard the expression in years, but recently I've heard it quite a lot in the news and political contexts.

LYNN Well, my favourite saying is something I, I picked up from my mum and I use it because I'm not a very practical person. The saying is

"Why have a dog and bark yourself?" And this basically means there's no need to bother doing something difficult if someone around you can do it better than you. So, for example my boyfriend's fantastic cook, and people say to me "Do you cook?" I can say "Why have a dog and bark yourself?" because, because there's really no need for me to bother.

PETE Well, I grew up in a horsy family and everyone in my family rode horses, except for me. And as a result of that, I picked up quite a few expressions involving horses. One of my favourites is "Horses for courses". Basically, different horses are involved in different kinds of races, and the horses are suited to its particular course. So, in real life every person is suited to a particular job, every machine to a particular job and "Horses for courses" basically sums up that connection between the thing and the job it should do.

R1.5

COMPERE OK, Peter will you please tell us the definition of the Australian expression 'She'll be apples'?

PETER Lovely expression, isn't it, 'She'll be apples'? Or should I say 'She'll be apples'? Well, what this basically means is someone is going to be really pleased, or surprised, or really thrilled with something. For example, if you show me a present that you've bought for your mother and I say "She'll be apples," – this simply means I think she'll love it.

C Naomi, your definition is?

NAOMI Peter's pronunciation is very good, but of course that's not the real definition of 'She'll be apples'. Let me explain the real meaning to you. As you know, apples are nice, they're sweet, they're good. So if a person is frightened or worried about something, then Australians try to comfort that person by saying, "Ah, she'll be apples". In other words, everything's going to be fine so don't worry – she'll be apples.

C And finally Ralph.

RALPH Actually, neither of those definitions is true. 'She'll be apples' basically means you think someone is perfect for a particular job – if at an interview, let's say, the person applying for the position is fantastically well-qualified and the best applicant, then you'd say 'she'll be apples'. Or to put it another way, you have a lot of confidence in the person.

C OK, Shirley's team. Which do you think is the true definition of 'She'll be apples'? Does it mean someone is going to be really pleased, or surprised, or is it a way of saying 'don't worry everything will be fine', or does it mean someone is perfect for a particular job?

R1.6

COMPERE OK, Shirley's team. Which do you think is the true definition of 'She'll be apples'?

SHIRLEY Well, they're all convincing. But we think Ralph's definition is true. We can imagine after a job interview, the interviewers choosing someone saying, 'He'll' or 'She'll be apples', meaning they'll be the best person for the job.

C Ralph?

RALPH Sorry. Wrong!

C And the true definition is?

NAOMI It means 'don't worry, everything will be alright'.

C So Peter's team is in the lead with two points to one.

R2.1

PRESENTER Walking into Tommy McHugh's semi-detached home, you're overwhelmed by a cornucopia of shape and colour. Everywhere you look – on every wall and ceiling – there is a mass of abstract designs, animals and faces. Until he hit his 50s – only six years ago – Tommy was a Liverpool builder, with a bit of a rough past as a street fighter, and no apparent interest in art. Nowadays though, he's a man with a passion – full of emotion, driven to create. He describes his mind as a volcano exploding with bubbles, each of which contains a million other bubbles full of unstoppable creative ideas. He spends his days – and most of his nights – painting, sculpting and carving.

TOMMY When you walk into my house, you walk into my brain. I've got that much going on in me brain, I have to let it all out or it overloads. I can't switch it off.

P The transformation in Tommy has been quite remarkable. So, what happened six years ago to bring it about? The extraordinary answer is a brain haemorrhage. One day Tommy was in the bathroom, when he remembers something "popping in his head". By the time he reached hospital, his eyes had turned bright red and he was in agonising pain. Two arteries in his head were leaking blood, and a delicate life-saving operation followed. Tommy's ex-wife describes what happened next.

JAN A few days later, he was sent home with a bag full of tablets. I didn't know what to do – he couldn't walk, or feed himself, or do anything really. Sometimes he didn't even know where he was. It was awful. He was totally frustrated, angry, and in pain. So, he took it out on me because I was the only one there. We didn't have any aftercare whatsoever.

P Jan was desperate to find anything that might give her husband an outlet. She'd always painted as a hobby, so she handed him a pen and a piece of paper and suggested he tried drawing. When she turned back from cooking the tea only a minute or two later, he'd filled the whole page with tiny faces – all different. Not surprisingly, Jan was unnerved, but this was only the beginning of it all. As soon as he was fit enough, Tommy started on the walls and also began to melt candles to sculpt heads of wax. At this stage, he didn't enjoy his manic creativity and wrote cries for help to doctors around the world. Most ignored him but two letters hit home, including one to the artist Marion Kalmus, who recognised in him an extreme version of what many artists feel.

MARION I told him I couldn't stop the bubbles exploding in his head, but I did know a lot of people who felt like that. It's called being an artist.

P This was a turning point for McHugh – it gave him a new name and a new identity and he began to enjoy his work. The other letter, meanwhile, had reached Alice Flaherty, a neurologist from the US, who has a special interest in this field. Flaherty has corresponded with McHugh for several years and recently came to the UK to meet him. Cases such as his, she says, are rare, but not unknown.

ALICE Tommy's manic creativity is extremely likely to be down to changes in his temporal lobe, the part of the brain responsible for understanding meaning. Van Gogh almost certainly had temporal lobe epilepsy, and at times of great creative output, he not only painted but would write constantly, which is not uncommon. Tommy does it, too.

P Flaherty strongly believes that the increased creative output may be partly because the brain is becoming less self-critical, and stresses that creativity is not necessarily a guarantee of quality. Indeed, McHugh's early paintings are nothing to write home about, but some of his recent work, now that he's had some practice, is wonderful – in particular his stone carvings. And even though there is no way of knowing how much longer Tommy will survive, he's not in the least bit depressed any more. His life has become an adventure, and he loves every minute of it.

R2.2

BRUCE One of the places I remember most are the Galápagos Islands.

PAT Oh, yes.

B This group of islands about 600 miles out from Ecuador.

P I've heard of them, yes.

B Yeah, fantastic place. We went to see some friends in Ecuador and then they organised this boat trip for us which lasted about a week.

P And were they exotic, sun-kissed, tropical islands as the brochures would have you believe?

B Not at all, actually. They were quite grey, I just remember greyness, sort of volcanic rock, bit of vegetation, very cold, forbidding sea and a lot of, yeah a lot of cloud. Even though we went in August, it was quite cloudy.

P Oh, did you get to see a lot of animals and birds?

B Oh yeah, it's brilliant for that. Absolutely brilliant, you know. I was really excited – they have these giant land tortoises, you know the famous tortoises. They've got albatrosses, which are unique to the island, marine iguanas, blue-footed boobies.

P What are they?

B Oh, they, they're great. They're sort of rather stupid-looking, clumsy birds with blue feet and long necks and they're about the size of a goose and do really strange, flappy dances.

P And are they tame?

B Yeah, all the animals are absolutely tame. You can walk right up to them, you can walk through them they, they don't run away at all, they're absolutely fantastic.

P Oh, incredible.

R2.3

MELISSA I'm not sure I've told you about my trip to Ireland, have I?

BRENDAN No, no, you haven't.

M No, well this was last summer. I haven't seen you for a while. We were expecting, sort of two weeks on sandy, beautiful, sandy beaches …

B OK.

M … and we were expecting the lush, green hills of Ireland. I mean, I'm American so you know, all the clichés of Ireland apply to me and, we all love to go there. Anyway, we were expecting a beautiful lodge that, that we'd rented from some friends of friends. After we got there, there was sort of 18 hours travelling in this driving, pounding rain – we stopped off, our first stop, when we got near to the house, was to buy the toughest waterproof gear that we could find.

B Right.

M We then arrived very late at night at the house which turns out to be not a beautiful lodge but a very stark, modern …

B Right, OK.

M … log cabin.

B No rustic charm then.

M Primitive …

B Oh, OK.

M … is, more than rustic I think, the word there. And the thing that we decided to do the next day was get up and explore our surroundings. Instead of a sandy beach what we had was a very thin strip of gravel.

B Oh, dear.

M And the owner had forgotten to tell us that the beach was actually half an hour, sail away in a very small dinghy.

B Which is something that you don't want to be doing in bad weather.

M Not really in the choppy seas that we were surrounded by. So, I have to say it wasn't our best holiday.

R2.4

INTERVIEWER Can you tell us how many overseas visitors come to England each year?

KATE Oh a lot. On average well over 27 million a year. Last year 27.4 million overseas visitors came and they came from all over the world.

I Can you give us some statistics of the breakdown of nationalities?

K Well, Americans top the list. The latest statistics I've got for that show that about, they, they account for about 3.5 million of the 27 million that I was talking about. And then the French and Germans come next, about 2 million overseas visitors each – Spain, 1.7 million and Italy, 1.2 million. So those are the most frequent visitors we've had in recent years, anyway.

I And where do they head to when they get here?

K Overwhelmingly, they go to London. It's by far our most popular destination. Last year, there were over 15 million overseas visitors to London. And it's a shame really because many people don't venture very far away from the capital. But you know, England has much, much more to offer. It has great diversity, really.

R2.5

INTERVIEWER So, where would you suggest people go to find this diversity?

KATE Well, it depends what people want really. We like to think we've got something for everybody. Most overseas visitors probably wouldn't think of England as the obvious place for a beach holiday, but if you think about it we are an island and there are hundreds of miles of coast, staggeringly beautiful coastline. And for families, I suppose you can't do better than Cornwall, really, in the Southwest of England. You can get surfing, lots of water sports – really good for family holidays, as are the Norfolk Broads, which is in the East of England. You could hire a boat, meander through more than 125 miles of waterways, passing the most peaceful countryside. And if you're into getting away from it all and climbing and hiking, then go to the Lake District. That's a place of breathtaking scenery. If you're into quaint villages and rolling countryside, you're really spoilt for choice. Go to Northumberland or the Cotswolds. You can really escape the masses and at the same time see fantastically picturesque villages with

typical thatched cottages and of course the traditional country pubs. Wonderful place to go.

I And, of course, England is steeped in history.

K Yeah. If it's history you're after, then again you're spoilt for choice. There are lots of historic towns other than London. For example, there's York, dating back to before Roman times. A walled city, tiny, cobbled streets, a delight really. And then, York Minster is a fine example of gothic architecture. In fact, it's Europe's second largest gothic cathedral. And if you happen to be there on a Sunday, well you're really in for a treat because the magnificent bells ring out all over the city. I mean, it's fantastic.

R2.6

KATE If you're into nightlife, or if you're what we call a 'culture vulture' then well, any of the cities really – Liverpool, Manchester, Leeds. There's a wealth of music venues, clubs, museums, galleries, theatres – I mean, there are really many, many vibrant cities in England and all of them of course are very, very cosmopolitan – as is the food, actually. We get a lot of stick for our awful English food, but really if eating out is one of your pleasures, then every imaginable style of cuisine is available in England. No longer are we the country of fish and chips. I mean, the most common food we eat these days is curry. As I said, a country of great diversity.

R2.7

ANSWERS 2 shoulder 3 remember 4 twists
5 turns 6 falls away 7 remain 8 slide 9 shine
10 turn 11 heart 12 wash away 13 feel

R3.1

INTERVIEWER Have you heard of 'impostor syndrome'? No, it's not someone trying to steal your identity. It's the nagging feeling that even though, to everyone else you are supremely successful and capable, inwardly you are convinced that you are just bluffing your way through and that at any moment now you'll be found out. Sound familiar? I interviewed people about the latest syndrome to hit the psychiatrist's couch …

R3.2

INTERVIEWER Valerie, had you heard of impostor syndrome before?

VALERIE Yes, I had actually, it's interesting 'cos you read a few, sort of bi, biographies of famous people and they start, a lot of them all start talking about it, but I didn't actually put those words to it, but I understand what, what it's about and I feel that, perhaps I am a bit of a sufferer.

I And your profession is?

V I am a garden designer. But I've come late to that, I used to be a teacher. And I think having come late to something you begin, you're kind of feel a bit more of an impostor because you've lived so long as a teacher. You can't possibly be a real garden designer. Because, I think the more you learn about something, the more you know that you don't know, so of course, you know, your confidence begins, you're sort of not totally confident.

I So, do you think that your clients are going to, sort of, rumble to the fact that, you sense this within yourself or?

V Well, I don't think they do because I think years of teaching have taught me that you, I

can overcome that, but I do feel it inside.

I And, did you have it when you were a teacher?

V Yes, I think I'm the sort of person, doesn't matter what I do, I'll always feel I don't know it all, and I will be, you know, somebody's going to catch me out one day.

I Richard, had you heard of the term 'impostor syndrome' before?

RICHARD No, I hadn't, not until you explained it to me.

I And you do think you've personally had experience of it?

R Why, no. I don't want to sound arrogant but, but it's not something I recognise.

I And what in fact do you do for a living?

R I'm a cameraman. I work in television.

I So, you have all these directors and producers expecting rather wonderful images from you, and in general you feel quite self-assured that you can give them what they need?

R Well, I'm not saying I'm perfect, but I, I think I'm good enough that most of the time when I make a mistake, only I realise I've made one.

I I see. And, in the media in general do you think there, there are people out there who have this sort of nagging self doubt?

R No, I don't think so. The media is famously full of probably overly self-confident people. No, nobody, nobody likes to show any doubt in the media.

I Miranda, had you heard of 'impostor syndrome' before?

MIRANDA Well, well, I hadn't and then I kind of put the idea of 'impostor' and 'syndrome' and, and, and then I read about it and thought well, actually, I feel a little bit like an impostor because I've been incredibly lucky. I've had an enormous amount of good fortune in, in, in being given this privilege of, of being, of having a place at this wonderful university and a fully funded PhD, which is not only fully funded for all my fees, but I'm also being paid to travel the world to go and collect my data. So, how could this happen? How could this happen to me? And when I go and see my supervisor, I keep thinking that he's going to say, "I'm sorry Miranda but actually, that, it was all a trick, it really wasn't what you thought it was and we've found out that you are not who you say you are."

R3.3

1

NAOMI What do you do then Rachael, to cheer yourself up?

RACHAEL Well, when I'm feeling really down about things and maybe feeling a little bit lonely, or anything especially when you've just moved to a new place, I've got, I've kept all the letters that people have sent me over the years and photographs and, just odd loose photographs and tickets from plays and, concerts that I've been to, in lots of shoeboxes marked with the year when I did those things, and sometimes I'll open one of those and go through things and it kind of reminds me that, the friends that I've had. and the good times I've had, and that there will be some more to come.

N That's lovely. That's really nice.

R What about you?

N Well to be honest, sometimes I do that as well. I have some lovely photos of when I've travelled. And it's lovely to look at them, but then it always makes me think I haven't seen these people for ages I want to see them, and then I start planning something sociable to do, or something fun, so actually it really does take you out of your, your down moment, doesn't it?

R Yeah, because sometimes you get too stuck in the moment that you're actually in, and you forget you, you lose perspective. So, I think that gives me a bit more perspective.

2

HELEN So, what's your preferred pick me up then, Alex?

ALEX Oh, it's always been perfume ever since my grandmother let me play with her beautiful art deco, glass and silver atomiser that she had, it smelt of violets, it was wonderful. And I've always found that perfume seems to go straight into my brain, and lifts my mood, and I can choose perfume to suit the occasion, and of course I can, I can do it anytime I like. What about you, what do you do?

H Well, I need some kind of physical release really. I really like going for a really fast bike ride at top speed with the wind whistling in my ears. It's impossible to feel stressed when you're zipping around like that.

A I suppose that's true.

3

FRAN So, Ian how you do cope when you're feeling a bit down?

IAN Well, I have a couple of tricks really if I just need cheering up, I like to go kite flying because it's, it's just great fun and it's colourful and it's quiet and peaceful, and I'm on my own, but if something is threatening to get a little bit too serious, that it's perhaps bothering more, me more than it really should, then I try to be cynical about it to get it in context.

F Oh, right!

I And I think about what I do when I'm cynical, and when I'm cynical about something, I raise one eyebrow so I, find that if I just raise an eyebrow and thinking about something it, it brings out the cynicism and it all goes away.

R3.4

IAN How about you?

FRAN Well, generally if I, um, if I'm not feeling, um, too happy then, um, I need something to work towards, so, um, I try and make contact with friends that I don't really see very often and, um, and I find that if I'm, I'm with them then I kind of forget about what's going on at the time and just remember the things I, you know, used to do with them, and, um, they just kind of, er, accept my personality so I don't have to, you know, that, that trivial thing that's usually making me not very happy. Doesn't really mean very much to them so …

I Yeah, good memories always help.

F Exactly.

R3.5

1

BOSS Oh, hi Al. I've been looking for you everywhere! Listen, would you and Lisa like to come round tomorrow evening for a bite to eat?

a)

AL Well, actually, we were planning to go to the cinema tomorrow, so … But yes, we must all get together some time.

b)

AL We can't tomorrow. We're going out.

2

MARY Do these look OK?

a)

LIZ I don't like bright colours on you. And they're too tight round the hips.

b)

LIZ Well, I think darker colours suit you better. I'd go for black instead if I were you. And they could do with being a bit looser around the hips.

3

GREG That was great, wasn't it? Did you enjoy it?

a)

KAREN No, I didn't. Most of it was really slow and the woman who played the main role was rubbish.

b)

KAREN Well, it was sort of interesting in parts. But quite honestly, I've seen better performances.

4

WAITER Did you enjoy your meal, sir?

a)

MAX It could have been a bit hotter. And unfortunately, the steak was on the tough side, too.

b)

MAX It was stone cold and the steak was tough.

R3.6

We were planning to go to the cinema tomorrow. | I'd go for black instead, if I were you. | We must all get together some time. | I think darker colours suit you better. | And quite honestly, I've seen better performances.

R4.1

DAN So, what were you watching on telly last night, Sue?

SUE Oh, *Big Brother*, you know, you know I like that.

D Oh, reality TV. It's just everywhere you look on the television, reality TV, it's rubbish.

S It's just relaxation, sometimes you just want to put your feet up and let it wash over you.

D It's not. It's intellectually bankrupt and it's just rubbish.

S Well, I think it's fun and actually, sometimes you need to keep in touch with the youth of today, don't you, and they like this sort of thing, so reality TV is fine by me.

D Well, it's a sad indictment on society, frankly.

S Well, it's fun to see people outside their normal environment testing themselves.

D But they're not though, are they? They're not.

S Why not?

D It's aw, it's a tired template that's been used, that's provocative, it's there to create conflict, it's to see the worst in people. It's actually, it's poking fun at people, at their misery.

S Well they know what they are letting themselves in for, what's the problem?

D Well, more fool them frankly. Most of them are trying to get fame a shortcut way.

S What would you rather watch then?

D Well, I'd like to watch more sport and more comedy, frankly.

S There's enough sport on TV as it is. It's on all the time. What about some costume drama?

D Oh, that's a bit dull though isn't it, that's a bit heavy.

S Well, you say you want to be intellectually stimulated by the television, that's exactly what you want.

D No, actually, what I want is some good comedy for me to relax. And laugh.

S See, relaxing, just like reality TV.

D No, no, no, no, something that involves, you know, creativity. Something that's in, innovative, something that makes you laugh. That's not reality TV. Reality TV, as I said, it's poking fun.

S Well, each to their own.

R4.2

Was *Star Trek* the inspiration for cell phones? Apparently so. Dr Martin Cooper is considered the inventor of the first portable handset and the first person to make a call on a portable phone, in April 1973, much to the bewilderment of passers-by in a road in New York. The first call he made was to his rival, Joel Engel, who was the head of research at Bell Labs. Cooper was later to reveal that watching Captain Kirk talking into his communicator on the TV show *Star Trek* had inspired him to research the cell phone. The first phones weighed over a kilo compared to most modern phones that weigh a hundred grams or less.

Did *Star Trek* inspire Voyager 1 and 2 which were launched in 1977? Well, Dr Marc Raymon was five years old when he first watched *Star Trek* and became fascinated by the idea of space travel. He wanted to know how far into space we could go and he dreamed of being a science officer on the *Starship Enterprise*. Instead, he would become a senior science officer for NASA and was involved in the Voyager probes. Voyager 1 is now at the edge of the solar system and heading for interstellar space. Interestingly, following a letter campaign, NASA agreed to name its prototype space shuttle after the *Starship Enterprise*.

And was *Star Trek* the inspiration for MRI and CT scans? It probably was. Dr John Adler, professor at the Stanford University Medical Center, acknowledges that the non-invasive diagnostic technology used by *Star Trek*'s medical officer, Dr McCoy, helped inspire a medical revolution. Medicine in the 1960s and 1970s was a world away from *Star Trek*. It involved messy, dangerous, exploratory surgery where surgeons would cut through tissue to discover what the problem was. The idea that diagnosis could be done the way Dr McCoy did it, quickly, painlessly and without a surgeon's knife, was something to strive for. In fact, Dr Adler has invented the 'CyberKnife' which can destroy cancerous cells by passing hundreds of beams of radiation through them.

Was *Star Trek* the inspiration behind the iPod? Well, *Star Trek* certainly inspired Steve Perlman who, back in the late '80s, was an employee at Apple Computer, Inc. While watching an episode of *Star Trek: The Next Generation* he saw something that fired his imagination. The robotic character, Data, was able to call up any music he wanted from his computer. Steve would later be part of a team that invented Quick Time technology which can select, store and play movies and audio files. It was this software that helped pave the way for the iPod.

R4.3

ANSWERS 1 into their reality 2 inventors 3 modern technology 4 entertainment

R4.4

INTERVIEWER Could you tell us, Andrew, is there still a difference between the tabloid newspapers and the so-called quality press in Britain?

ANDREW Oh yeah, there's a huge difference. I mean, physically you'll see the difference straightaway because a tabloid paper is smaller, the so-called quality press, otherwise known as broadsheets or the heavies, have, up to now tended to be bigger. Recently, because of the problems people have had, say on trains, on buses, opening newspapers that are too big, they've become smaller. *The Times*, for example, has gone into a tabloid format but the tone of the paper hasn't changed – they still use more serious language, they still use smaller headlines, they still present the news in a more sober kind of fashion. Whereas, a tabloid newspaper tends to shout at you a bit more, tends to direct your eyes more across the page, huge pictures, huge headlines – it tells you what to think and how to react. Also, the tabloid papers tend to have a a much bigger circulation – they sell, they sell in the millions whereas the broadsheets sell in the hundreds of thousands, and that's, that's a sort of reflection of the kind of, the way society breaks up, you know – of the way society is constructed. The more intellectual end of the newspaper market, would, they maybe sell between 3-, 400,000 and 800,000 and the biggest selling papers sell about 3 million, and they're the furthest downmarket.

I Can you tell us, Andrew, what kind of stories really sell newspapers?

A Well, it depends what newspaper you're talking about, the, you have to – as a journalist – think about who's reading your paper when you're deciding how to prioritise your stories. The broadsheet newspapers tend to focus on the more serious stories – political stories especially are a great favourite for them to lead on. If you go right to the other end of the market with the downmarket, so-called red-top tabloids, they like TV stories, they like stories about film stars, they like stories about royals, they like crime stories, something with a much, sort of brasher, instant appeal. Our newspaper, the paper I work for, is somewhere in the middle of the market, so sometimes we'll splash – the splash is the main story on the front page, it's a term that journalists use – sometimes we'll decide that the splash should be a political story, sometimes a crime story. We like family stories, we like stories that relate to the kind of people that are buying our paper, the middle-class families that we think are at the heart of our circulation.

R4.5

INTERVIEWER Clearly, the stories in different sorts of newspaper are written in different ways. Could you explain to us how the journalists know what kind of language to use?

ANDREW As I mentioned earlier, the pictures are bigger, the headlines are bigger. But what you find when you get to read the actual story is that the language in a tabloid newspaper tends to be snappier, shorter words, shorter crisper sentences, what we call a sort of 'crash bang wallop' style, a sort of a straight to the point without any elaboration, without any flamboyant sentences, without words that are too long. Most paragraphs – if you, if you look at a tabloid newspaper – most paragraphs are about 20 words, very few paragraphs are longer than 30, and some are as short as about 10. It means the story is easier to read, it has a faster pace, it's, it's more in tune with the kind of audience, with the kind of readership that the paper has. And if you see, if you read a story from a from a heavy paper, the paragraphs will be much longer to look at on the, on the page and much harder work to get through. So, that's a, that's a really discernible difference.

R4.6

INTERVIEWER Could you describe for us the process of deciding on the story for the front page of a newspaper?

ANDREW Yes, I mean, this is probably the most exciting part of the job, deciding what the best story of the day is and how to present it. Every reporter wants to get his or her story on the front page, so they'll be trying their hardest to convince the news editor of the paper that theirs is the best story and that's where it should go. So, reporters are trying their best to get the, to get everything they can out of a story to write it in the most exciting and accessible way and then the news editor himself will try to convince the editor that that's where the story should go.

I Thank you very much Andrew

R4.7

ANSWERS 2 neck 3 Been 4 a shadow 5 half dead 6 Walking 7 world 8 a girl 9 dance 10 heat 11 pity 12 can't 13 Cool 14 pretty 15 cat 16 look 17 wheezing 18 meet

R5.1 **R5.2** **R5.3**

INTERVIEWER When you go to the cinema or watch telly and see all the people in crowd scenes, the chances are you never give them a second's thought. And yet for many people this is their job – they're extras, like Daniel and Kate, who are with us today. Good morning.

DANIEL Hi!

KATE Hi.

I Daniel, what makes people like yourself want to be an extra?

D Good question. Well, I guess I've always been keen on amateur dramatics and so, I suppose it's a way of keeping in contact with the acting world. Luckily, the working hours for my normal job are quite flexible, otherwise, I wouldn't be able to do it. You never know when you'll be needed on set.

I I suppose there's a lot of hanging around?

D Yeah, they're long hours, but I have no problems amusing myself. I'm a writer, so I always take my laptop with me and, well, just get on with my work.

I Now, you've appeared in some big films, haven't you? What's it like seeing yourself on the big screen?

D Well, half the time, I can't even spot myself, unless I really concentrate, but I'm usually in crowd scenes as a wedding guest, or a person in the street – you know, that kind of thing.

I Are there ever jobs when you are more than just a face in a crowd?

D I get given short scenes from time to time, when I'm a postman or a taxi driver, or whatever. Sometimes, I have to react to what someone says. I mean, you often find out that you've been edited out later, which can be disappointing, but it makes a change and you get paid more, so that's always welcome. The money's not bad at all really, for what you actually do.

I Do you have any hope you'll break into film acting yourself?

D No chance. It would be like being given wings and asked to fly.

I Kate, how did *you* end up being an extra?

K Well, I kind of fell into it. I once knew somebody who'd done it and I thought it would be a way of supplementing my income and enjoying myself at the same time.

I You do mostly TV work, don't you?

K Yes, you know, lots of soap operas, period dramas, that sort of thing.

I And what kind of people become extras?

K Oh, all sorts, from young drama students to solicitors on their day off, bored housewives, whoever. We do all share a common interest so it's a great opportunity for us all to meet and have a chat and a good laugh.

I Do you ever get the chance to meet the principal actors?

K Well, we're actually actively encouraged *not* to interact with them – they have a job to do. But we sometimes bump into them on set. The stars themselves are quite friendly on the whole – it's the minor actors who tend to be a bit standoffish.

I And are you treated well in general?

K Mostly. I think the money is reasonable. There's a lot of standing around, though, and there are times when you feel very tired.

I Is there a lot of stress on the set?

K If there are delays, nerves do get frayed as there's a sense that time and money is draining away. We aren't really affected though – we're not important enough!

I Are there any rules about how you treat the actors?

K Not really, other than it's understood you let the crew and principals help themselves first in the canteen at lunchtime. But that's fair enough – it's common sense – they need to get back to work.

I Right. And do you enjoy it?

K I like the job itself, although the unpredictable hours can be a bit of a pain.

I What do you like about it?

K It's good being able to dip in and out of different worlds, like last week I was in a fire on an 18th century ship.

R5.4

INTERVIEWER Good morning. With us in the studio today are three young people about to leave sixth-form college. We talk to them about the difficult choices they have to make as they decide which university course to follow, or which job to go into. So, Claire, do you know what you want to do when you leave college?

CLAIRE Not really – it's something that I've struggled with for a long time, what I want to do with my life. The problem these days is there's so many possibilities out there, so many opportunities, and I think it's quite hard for people to decide, and to find out what the real world the, the real working world is like.

I So how are you trying to come to a decision?

CLAIRE Well, recently, I've been trying to do lots of work experience in lots of different fields and talk to people in those different areas to try and gain an insight. I've looked into teaching, publishing, I've done some charity work, so just basically trying to gain some experience.

I Is this working?

CLAIRE Yes and no, I've certainly found some things that I don't want to do. And I've really enjoyed doing some work experience in a small publishing firm, so I'm thinking about that.

I So, Will, you're taking a gap year before going to university. Was that an easy decision to take?

WILL Not really, I had – when I finished my GCSE's I didn't know really what I wanted to do for A Level let alone at university. So, I kind of chose, I chose four subjects that I enjoyed for A Level and then chose to have a gap year because I thought that would give me an extra year to work out what I wanted to do. And I just wanted a gap year to have a, a bit of time out really because things have been, a lot of, been a lot of pressure, for a lot of years so I wanted to take the time out to work out completely what I wanted to do.

I And do you think you'll be using this year to look at your options?

W Absolutely, I've, I've now found, found a place at university to do sports science so I'm really glad I've got that sorted in the end.

I So, Charlie, do you know what you want to do when you leave college?

CHARLIE I do now, I, I want to do law at university and I've applied and, luckily got a place, but that decision came after a lot of change with me because I wanted to do English originally after GCSE, but after my A Level in English, it was a much bigger step up from English at GCSE, very different course than what I thought it would be, and I felt a little bit out of my depth, and I looked round universities thinking of doing English and it didn't click, it didn't feel right, and that's when I thought law is what I wanna do.

I And you're confident in your choice now?

CHARLIE Yeah, it feels, it, this feels a lot better and more right with me than, than English did. I've done a lot of research into it and I've gone to places like the Old Bailey in London and looked at law cases, and I found it very interesting. I've gone on law courses and, yeah it, it, it's a bit daunting but it, it definitely feels right.

R5.5 R5.6 R5.7

1

JOSH It's totally ludicrous, isn't it really, I mean, the salaries these company directors and corporate lawyers and financial people in the City get paid, don't you think? I mean it's completely out of proportion to what they actually do, for one thing.

TRACEY Yeah. Not to mention the astronomical sum that footballers and film stars and so on get, too. I suppose it's all about market forces but it does seem very unfair.

J Well, it is, you know, when you consider that someone like a nurse or an ambulance driver gets paid a pittance – relatively – you know, for what they do and, I mean, how could we get along without them? And what about all these jobs nobody wants to do, but have to be done?

T Can you imagine having to clean the streets, or collect the rubbish or …

J That's exactly what I was trying to get at. I mean, they're horrible jobs, so … what I think is that anyone who has really, you know, a hard job should expect to get paid well for it. You look dubious, Liz.

LIZ Well, it's a difficult one, because well, historically people expect to get paid less if they've got no qualifications.

J But how come, though? Is it their fault if they're no good at exams, or financially they couldn't afford higher education, or if, you know, …

L Yeah, no of course not, but I don't understand how would it work in practice …

2

T Does what job you have matter that much anyway? I mean, there's a whole world out there beyond work. It's only a means to an end, so you can eat and stuff.

J For you, maybe. But for some people it's the be all and end all to earn a lot and get on.

T Yeah, but surely it's an interesting job that's the main thing, not …

J Well, yeah, I'm with you on that, but all I'm saying is many other people – for them, their job is the main thing in their life, it's how they define themselves.

T Well, they're saddos, if you ask me. They should get a life – find some interests. Well, that's why people get so stressed out and have to take so much time off work – because they work too hard and get things out of proportion.

L But, for some people they love their work and anyway, when you're young if you want to get on, you know, you have to put …

T Climb the career ladder, whoopee!

J Hang on. Carry on, Liz. You were saying?

L … well, you have to work long hours and put a lot in, or people think that you – well, you know, they, they won't give you promotion.

T Well so what?!

J You say that now, but wait until you want a nice house or a flash car or …

T Er, excuse me? It was you saying that what mattered was interest.

L Anyway, assuming you do want promotion, you usually have to …

3

L What I do feel strongly about is that employers make provision for working mothers.

J By 'provision' you mean … ?

L Well, for example so they can have flexibility, so if they have to, have to drop kids off at school or if one of them is ill they can work at home or if they …

T And allow more women to work part-time or, or job share.

J … or men of course!

L Yeah, right. How many men do you know who work part-time so that they can look after the kids?

J Ah. You've got me there! Well, perhaps they would if it was more accepted.

L That's just what I was going to say. It's a kind of chicken and egg situation. Until employers offer people more flexible hours, parents – well, mothers really – are stuck because they feel guilty working full-time but need to work for whatever reason and often, they have no choice anyway – they need the money.

T The problem is, people with no kids might turn round and say "Well, why should we cover for you? It's your choice to have children," and they might resent it if working mothers …

L Or fathers.

T … or fathers have special treatment.

J Oh, I don't know about that. I mean, after all, as a society we're all responsible for the future

generation, aren't we? But it'd certainly be a hassle for employers to organise.

L Which is why it would have to be law that they did it. After all …

R5.9

Listening Test (see Teacher's Book)

R6.1

PETE I have a friend called Martina and she owns two rabbits. Not so strange in itself but she's got a habit of taking them everywhere she goes. So, a typical afternoon round a friend's house will consist of people crawling around in a neighbour's hedges looking for them. And then there's the chicken wire over her bookcases to stop the rabbits eating her books. And the thing that I will never forget is the first time I met her. She came to the pub, dressed very glamorously – long coat and high heels, opened her coat and there hopping out of the top of her sweater were the two rabbits.

NATALIE Really! Blimey. I commute on the train to work every day and, on the way back home, there's a guy that gets on the train and he starts at one end of the platform. He, he hops on the train at the back end, and he patrols all the way up the carriages, through to the, the front of the train and then patrols back again until he finds the perfect seat. I think, I guess that's what he's looking for, I mean, I've been travelling for two years now. And, I've sort of…

KEITH He's not a ticket inspector then?

NATALIE No, no he's not a ticket inspector …

ALEX Undercover.

N … he's, you know, he does the same thing, day in day out and the only thing that I can put it down to is that he's just trying to find the best seat on the train. I thought that was quite bizarre.

A That is very bizarre. I used, I used to commute to Liverpool Street for ten years and you've just reminded me actually, there was a couple, who used to get on at King's Lynn and go all the way down to Liverpool Street, and she – the woman – had extraordinary eyebrows that were painted on with very, very heavy eyebrow pencil. But they used to have a, a bag of toy animals. Stuffed, you know, children's toys …

N Oh, OK.

A And they used to get them out and line them up. I've only just remembered this.

K How very strange.

A Yeah, and they used to line them up, so that the, the toys could look out of the window.

N That is very, very bizarre.

A It was extraordinary.

K Very odd behaviour.

A We all used to sit there just, ignoring them and nobody, you know, nobody, 'cos we're British, nobody would say anything.

N No.

A Like, why are you lining up all these toys? You're a grown-up couple.

N Gosh.

K My daughter does that but she's six, so I think it's more understandable.

A Yeah, quite.

K But she does, she does strange things, I mean she can, she, she collects pebbles which really winds us up, 'cos we've, she's just got her this really nice coat and she always like, she comes home from school and she's always got pockets and pockets full of pebbles. Grubby pebbles that just, make holes in the pockets and so on, you, you take, you know help her off with her coat and it's so heavy … We empty them every day we've got this great heap of pebbles in the garden. She collects them with her friends.

A You can get her to make a path one day.

K She collects with her friends, I think, and sort of compare them. And the other thing actually, recently, she went for a week and she insisted on putting on odd socks every morning.

N Really?

K Yeah, she wanted to put on different colour socks. It's obviously the height of fashion …

N Oh, wow.

A It's sweet though isn't it?

K … in her class at school.

R6.2

GRAHAM Well, I've worked in advertising and marketing for about 20, 25 years, mostly on the copy-writing side. So, when we've come to plan campaigns, I've always been thinking about the words more than anything else. And I was particularly impressed, it's a few years back now, but particularly impressed with the Coca-Cola campaign, which focused on the words 'It's the real thing'. At the time when it came out, I wondered how this would work but they used that phrase across TV advertising, billboards, on commercial radio, and I was particularly impressed, as I say, by the campaign because of the words 'It's the real thing'. The word 'it's' just implies that's part of everyday life. Coca-Cola, you don't have to use the name, in the actual slogan or the strapline they're using. Then you have 'the real thing'. The 'real' implying, well it's genuine, it's the real article, it's not, of course, their main opposition Pepsi Cola, it's, maybe it, it even suggests it's healthy and good for you. So 'the real thing' and then 'the thing', well, an everyday item, something that's part of your life. I just felt this worked so well, and people would say 'it's the real thing' and you just thought of Coca-Cola and you didn't need to say "Coca-Cola, the real thing", you just thought of the product when you saw the strapline or the phrase. And that did work for a number of years, and I think there's still a lot of people around, if you say to them, "It's the real thing" they will think 'Coca-Cola' and they won't think about anything else. Even though that's a phrase, of course used generally in society and in language, in an everyday kind of way.

R6.3

LINDSAY A successful advertising campaign that springs to my mind are the iPod ads that have been around for a few years now. I'm thinking particularly of the ones where you've got the dark silhouette of a young, probably attractive, really trendy, urban person who's listening to some great funky music. And they're throwing themselves around, really enjoying themselves and it's set against a really vivid background, kind of bright purple, bright blue, almost neon. And they've got the iPod in their hands with the white earphones going into their ears. And the, I think that the thing with the iPod is that it's really a design icon. It's such a simple design, but it's something that people recognise, almost instantly if you see their, someone wearing the earphones walking around the street then you know what product they have. And I think the

adverts really recog, really complement this because they, they show a lifestyle they don't actually give any information about the product itself. It's more an image that people want. They want the product, they want this lifestyle and, you know, I love my iPod and for me, I may not be that young anymore but, you know, I want that kind of fashionable lifestyle and this wonderful fashion accessory. And I think advertising campaigners in the future will probably look at this as a really good, simple, effective advert that people remember and they'll use design in the future to promote their own products.

R6.4

JOHN A good story has to have several standard components – it's got to have a beginning, it's got to have a middle, and it's got to have an end. And the way that works is you have something that sets the story in its situation and context, and you can call that the premise, and the character is speaking, or the narrator is telling you about the character, and then someone else maybe comes in and the situation gets complicated. This is known as the development, and whatever then happens makes the story even more interesting, that's a complication and then something gets sorted out and you have the ending – the resolution. And these elements can be mixed up in any length and shape, and a joke can be a story, or a narrative can be a story, or just someone telling something that happened to them that morning can be a story. Anything can be a story, but if you're putting it on the radio it needs to hook the listener in straight away. So, you've got to have something to catch their attention, and that is where the interest is struck up and you've got to maintain the interest, build up the tension until somewhere along the line, the reader is ready for the story to come to an ending – positive, negative, happy ending, sad ending or even a laugh – because a joke is a story as well.

R6.5

"Are you James?" he asked. I nodded uncertainly. "Kirsti asked me to give you a lift. She's at another place."

I tried to be cool about this turn of events. Sure, it was unusual that Mr Universe's better-built brother was chauffeuring me to a date with Miss World's better-looking sister, but I wouldn't let it ruin what I hoped would be the start of something special. Finally, we arrived at some expensive-looking building in the mountains. Kirsti was outside, waving to me.

"Quick, James, go through there." I protested, but she frowned, shooing me along. "There's no time!" I found myself in a large room, filled with rows of chairs. Only about half were occupied, mainly by middle-aged couples. It took me a full ten minutes to realise where I was. Me at a time-share presentation? Do I really look the sort of person who would buy a share in a holiday home overseas? Humiliated, I stormed out. Kirsti was waiting, and dashed after me.

"We're miles away from anywhere. Please, give it a chance," she cajoled. "We can go for a meal afterwards."

"I'll call a taxi," I said.

"You won't get one. I can take you back, but only when the presentation is over."

"Then I'll walk."

It took me six hours. I swear, I intended to confess all to my mates, but I couldn't face telling them the truth.

The next day, we were back in the same club again when Mike nudged me. "Here comes your missus." Kirsti was indeed walking very determinedly towards me. Horrified, I leapt up to intercept her before she reached our table.

"I need a sale, James, and I need it today."

"Sorry, I just don't have that sort of money."

"It's only a £200 deposit."

The lads were watching us like hawks, trying to work out what was going on. Kirsti smiled maliciously.

"They think we're going out together, don't they? What if I go over now and tell them the truth?"

"No!" I blurted out. "Please, I'm a student. I …" She started towards them. I capitulated. "OK, OK, I think I can make a withdrawal on my credit card."

Her relief made me feel bolder. "But first you have to kiss me. Here, now," I said, bravely. She snorted. I raised an eyebrow. "I thought you needed that sale, Kirsti?"

She sighed, and then grabbed me. All I remember is my heart thumping and hearing my friends cheering, until, after a glorious eternity, the most gorgeous woman I'd ever met came up for air.

"Right, so now we go to the bank," she hissed, pulling me towards the door. "And then we'll go for that meal."

My friends looked on in amazement, as this beautiful woman dragged me away.

Time-share scams are a thing of the past these days … A bit of a shame, really.

R6.6

JOHN When you're telling a story on the radio, the first and most important thing is to get the listener involved. Get the listener listening, and you do that with various tricks and techniques and pauses and rhythm and stress. And you've got a range of words: adverbs, adjectives, even the verbs, to keep the story moving, to keep it lively. The livelier your choice of words, the more interested the listener is going to be and you've got to vary the pace, you've got to vary the stress, you've got to build up the tension, perhaps make it scary, or perhaps hold something back to surprise the listener with a twist in the tail if the story is going to go in that direction. The tone of the story is going to be judged by the listener from your tone of voice as you tell the story. So, is it going to be gripping and exciting, or is it going to be light and frivolous? Is it going to be serious, is it going to be scary? What kind of atmosphere do you want to create with your voice and with the range of vocabulary that you are offering in your telling of this story? You've got to make it sound as if it has the elements we mentioned earlier – the beginning, the middle, the end – but you also have to give it a flow to make sure the listener is carried along with your telling of the story, and make sure that the listener enjoys it.

R6.7

ANSWERS 2 a) 3 c) 4 e) 5 d) 6 f) 7 h) 8 g) 9 i) 10 l) 11 k) 12 j) 13 n) 14 o) 15 m) 16 r) 17 q) 18 p) 19 u) 20 s) 21 t) 22 x) 23 w) 24 v)

R7.1

INTERVIEWER Good morning! In the studio with us today we have Zoë Powell, a freelance science journalist. Zoë has recently been working on a TV documentary in which potential criminals try to outwit a forensic scientist and get away with it. Zoë, I'm sure our listeners would find it very useful to hear how they did it!

ZOË Interesting, rather than useful, I hope! Well, at one time, if someone committed a crime, you didn't have as much to go on. These days, of course, techniques are much more sophisticated. Recently, for example, there was the famous case when a kidnapping was solved 20 years later, after the seal of an envelope was re-examined and the tiniest trace of dried saliva found there.

I So, if the kidnapper hadn't licked the envelope … ?

Z He wouldn't be in prison now, exactly. You have to be so careful not to leave any trace of yourself at all.

I Which is easier said than done, presumably, since our DNA is in virtually every cell in our body.

Z Indeed. If a person doesn't want to leave forensic evidence, they should just slide through a window because any broken glass, or other damage for that matter – scratched paint, for example – comes in very handy to forensic scientists. One burglar, who was found recently through his DNA, would have got away with it completely if he hadn't been sweating at the time.

I And if I were committing a burglary, I'd be better off wearing gloves, of course, so as not to leave fingerprints.

Z Yes, providing you didn't leave fibres behind as these can also be traced fairly easily. It's the same with socks.

I So, best to go barefoot, then?

Z Ah, but even the tiniest fragment of skin is enough to match you, so you'd actually be better off covering up as much as possible!

I But can't you can get round the problem by wearing smooth clothes like silk?

Z Absolutely!

I No woolly gloves and socks, then.

Z And needless to say, if you're going to burgle a house, you'll obviously try not to draw attention to yourself. Don't stagger out with a huge television, or whatever. Do it quietly. And avoid the temptation to rush out and sell whatever you've stolen right away!

R7.2

INTERVIEWER And what does a would-be murderer have to bear in mind?

ZOË Well, what's similar about most killers is they are cool, detached sort of people. They seem to be able to carry on as if nothing's happened, behaving perfectly normally. In fact, if they weren't such good actors most of them would probably have been found out much earlier.

I So, a lot of it comes down to personality?

Z Yes, and you obviously need a water-tight alibi, too. And having a few maggots to hand to confuse the scientists might help.

I Maggots?

Z Yes, forensic scientists use creepy crawlies to help them work out the time and place of death. By counting how many maggots are on a body, and how mature they are, you can have a pretty good idea of when someone died. Unless the murderer has put them there themselves, of course!

I You're joking!

Z It has been known. And flies are useful, too. The kind of place you're in will attract different kinds of flies, so if you found a body in the countryside with urban flies on it, the murder would probably have been committed in the city.

I That's incredible!

Z Then obviously, you also have to destroy your weapon, or at least get rid of any distinguishing marks.

I If you'd used poison, there wouldn't be a weapon as such, would there?

Z Yes, but the thing with poison is it's actually quite easy to find out where it was obtained and trace it back to the suspect. Actually, the ideal weapon is one which destroys its own evidence.

I Such as?

Z Well, for example, you could use an icicle, which of course will then melt.

I So, if anyone happens to come across a body next to a small puddle of water, you'll know what's happened!

Z Thankfully, violent crimes are still relatively rare. But should any of your listeners be considering committing a crime, be careful – scientific advances are making the likelihood of detection more and more probable every day!

I Indeed. Anyway, if you tune in to our programme …

R7.3

INTERVIEWER In your opinion, how much state intervention should there be in people's everyday lives?

STEFANO I think that, basically, if the state intervenes, for example, to ban smoking from enclosed public places, that's, that's a good idea. It's been proved that passive smoking is harmful for people and so, it's important that the government prevents this. People are free to smoke outside. And, so, there's no unexcessive limit in their liberties. I do agree when smoking is banned from enclosed places, but of course, I wouldn't agree if the government ruled that people are not allowed to, for example, to smoke in a public park – that would be definitely too drastic.

HILTRUD In the case of rubbish, there clearly has to be more state intervention because, rubbish is piling up and landfill sites are running out. So, we need to do something and, charging for rubbish seems to me a good idea. It is fairer because people pay for what they throw away, and it is also effective.

JUSTYNA I also agree with a certain degree of state intervention in areas like health or environmental issues. However, when it comes to the state intervening in people's lifestyles, for example, promoting marriage over other types of partnership, I think it is highly unfair and, for example, in England, there is a debate going on about tax exemptions for married people, which I think is a terrible example of bias against other partnerships and relationships. This basically means that people who want to benefit from tax exemptions will have to forsake their choice of lifestyle, and for example, get married. I think this is a state intervention gone too far.

R7.4

POLICEMAN Right, Mike, could we just go over this one more time?

MIKE When are you going to realise it's useless to keep grilling me about this? I've told you everything I know. I went round to a friend's. I got back home late. There'd been a break-in and police were swarming all over the flat. End of!

PM You see, it all strikes me as very odd.

M What does?

PM Well, that it's on that particular night you suddenly take it into your head to go and visit your ex-girlfriend.

M So what? Can't people stay friends?

POLICEWOMAN A convenient alibi, though, isn't it? Her living just opposite, right on the doorstep, and all.

M If you say so.

PW Anyway, you say you went out at about 7.30. Isn't this about the time George usually goes out? He never stays in on a Friday evening, does he?

M How should I know? We're not joined at the hip, you know.

PW Well, that's not what we've heard. We've heard you're always out together. Anyway, just by chance that's the night you decided *not* to go out with him. Isn't that a coincidence? Wouldn't have had anything to do with the £2,000 in cash he'd been paid that day for a building job, by any chance?

M *How* much?

PM Oh, come on, Mike. We weren't born yesterday! You knew he'd stashed it away somewhere. And who else would have known his secret hiding place under the stairs?

M You tell me, since you obviously know all the answers.

PM Anyway, you're still saying that you stayed at Emma's the evening the money was stolen?

M Apart from when I nipped out to get a pizza.

PW I? Right, so you went out on your own, did you?

M Is that a crime? Emma had already eaten.

PW How come? You said she was expecting you.

MIKE Dunno. Ask her.

PM And when was it you went out, exactly?

M Around eight – give or take five minutes.

PM Took the opportunity to go back to your flat, did you?

M Are you serious? Why would I want to do that?

PM Well, that's what we'd like to know. But your neighbour swears she saw you going in around 8.20. Her dog was barking, so she looked to see what was going on.

M She would! She's a nosy old bag, and as blind as a bat at the best of times.

PM So, you're saying you didn't go back?

M That's right.

PW So, it's just a coincidence that we found most of a pizza in the bin at your flat, is it?

M Must be.

PM And, when you got back to Emma's, what did you do then?

M Watched the end of that new soap opera *Hospitals*.

PM Oh yeah? I saw a bit of that. But I missed the end. What happened?

M Er, well, E, Emma was going on about something so I lost track of what was happening.

PW Stayed late at Emma's, did you?

M Quite late. Time flies when you're having fun.

PW Mmm. Expensive phone you've got there.

155

Recording Scripts

M It was a present from my mum.

PW No fun, is it – being unemployed? Especially for a bright kid like you. Must have hit you hard, losing your job. Must be tempting to get money when you can.

M Look, you've got nothing on me and you know it! Why don't you just leave me alone?

R7.5

1

POLICEMAN You see, it all strikes me as very odd.
MIKE What does?

2

POLICEWOMAN Anyway, you say you went out at about 7.30. Isn't this about the time George usually goes out? He never stays in on a Friday evening, does he?

3

POLICEWOMAN Well, that's not what we've heard. We've heard you're always out together. Anyway, just by chance that's the night you decided *not* to go out with him. Isn't that a coincidence? Wouldn't have had anything to do with the £2,000 in cash he'd been paid that day for a building job, by any chance?
MIKE *How* much?

4

MIKE Apart from when I nipped out to get a pizza.
POLICEWOMAN I? Right, so you went out on your own, did you?

5

MIKE Is that a crime? Emma had already eaten.
POLICEWOMAN How come? You said she was expecting you.

R7.6

1

POLICEMAN Right, Mike, could we just go over this one more time?

2

POLICEWOMAN Anyway, you say you went out at about 7.30. Isn't this about the time George usually goes out? He never stays in on a Friday evening, does he?
MIKE How should I know? We're not joined at the hip, you know.

POLICEMAN Well, that it's on that particular night you suddenly take it into your head to go and visit your ex-girlfriend.
MIKE So what? Can't people stay friends?

3

POLICEWOMAN Well, that's not what we've heard. We've heard you're always out together. Anyway, just by chance that's the night you decided *not* to go out with him. Isn't that a coincidence? Wouldn't have had anything to do with the £2,000 in cash he'd been paid that day for a building job, by any chance?

4

POLICEWOMAN Anyway, you say you went out at about 7.30. Isn't this about the time George usually goes out? He never stays in on a Friday evening, does he?

R7.7

1

A I haven't got any money on me!

B Isn't that a surprise?

2

A So we're meeting at nine, are we?

B Yes. Sorry, I've forgotten already. Where are we meeting?

3

A Could you put everything in the dishwasher, please?

B Why should I always do it?

4

A Thank goodness it's arrived at last!

B What has?

5

A I heard from Terri last night.

B Oh, so she finally decided to phone, did she?

6

A I believe 200 people are coming to the wedding.

B Are you sure?

7

A I need some money.

B Oh you do, do you?

R8.1

EDDY CANFOR-DUMAS One person that I think is very inspirational, is a woman called Hazel Henderson and the reason her story has struck me so strongly is because she was an ordinary person who did something extraordinary. She was born before the Second World War and she had a very typical upbringing for a, a young girl. She went to school and hated school – couldn't wait to leave. She left as soon as she could without any qualifications and she got a job in a local dress shop – she was born in Bristol and brought up in Bristol. And she enjoyed that for a time but then started to think that the world held other possibilities. So, she took a job in a hotel as a receptionist, enjoyed that, and then realised that because hotels are around the world she could get a job elsewhere. So, she applied for and got a job in New York and enjoyed that very much and met an American man, fell in love, married had a family. And one day she noticed that her, her young child who would play everyday in a, in a local park in New York was covered in soot and in fact it was quite typical that she would come home very dirty, and she'd have to put her in a bath and scrub her to, to get this dirt off her. So, she went to investigate where the soot was coming from and saw that all of the equipment in the, the playground was covered in soot. And the reason for this was because the, the quality of the air in New York was so poor from the pollution of the cars and also there were lots and lots of incinerators that burnt rubbish. So, she started to talk to some of the other mothers whose children played in the park and they also saw this was a, a problem. But she did some investigating and discovered that the, the, the town hall in, in New York used to measure, every day, the quality of the air. She'd written to the, the mayor of New York about pollution in New York and he said actually the pollution wasn't pollution it was mist rolling in from the sea, but she didn't take this for the answer. So she did this investigation and she found that,

that the, the air was measured and she asked that this information be made public as part of the, the daily weather forecast. But she then did some more research and found that there was a federal law about information, that you know, about public health and so on. So, she used this to persuade ABC, one of the, the networks to, to take this. Eventually, they, they agreed 'cos they saw that there was a, a need. And very soon every media outlet in New York City was carrying this information. And of course once it started in New York it travelled across the country to all sorts of other cities, and eventually it travelled around the world. So the, the daily pollution in, index that you have in, in weather forecasts all comes about because of one woman. The great thing about Hazel Henderson is that she didn't stop there. She's an advisor to governments and organisations in 30 countries around the world, and her articles appear regularly in 400 newspapers around the world. So again, this all comes about through one ordinary woman deciding that she wasn't going to put up with what her daughter was experiencing in the local park and taking it on, and deciding to make a, a real difference.

R8.2

ANNOUNCER And now, *Science Today*, introduced by Simon Grey.

PRESENTER Today we are looking at emotions and with me in the studio are our resident scientists Dr Aaron Palmer and Dr Marion Bates. First Aaron, we hear people refer to basic emotions. What are they exactly?

AARON Well in the 1970s a Dr Ekman from the University of California devised a list of six basic emotions, which are: anger, disgust, fear, joy, sadness and surprise.

P And are these emotions common to all human beings?

A I think it's fair to say most members of the scientific community agree that, yes, basic emotions are universal.

P But men don't experience the same emotions as women, do they?

A Whoever said that is wrong. All human beings experience the same basic emotions. They may choose to express their emotions differently.

P OK, so can you explain how Ekman arrived at this list?

A Well, initially he based his theory on cross-cultural research done on a tribe in Papua New Guinea. It was a completely isolated tribe; they still used stone to make tools and weapons. And Ekman found that the people from this tribe could reliably identify six facial expressions of emotion. To do this he used photographs of people from around the world. And they could identify all the basic emotions from the photographs, even though they'd had absolutely no contact with any other culture before.

MARION Yes, in fact, wherever this experiment was carried out, the results were the same. Whoever saw the photos identified the same emotions. Ekman's discovery showed that the facial expressions associated with these basic emotions are universal. He therefore concluded that humans are born with the ability to recognise them in others.

A Of course, our ancestors relied on these basic emotions to stay alive. The survival value of emotions like fear, disgust and joy are still obvious. Whenever you come across something

The survival value of emotions like fear, disgust and joy are still obvious.

that frightens you, run away from it; whenever you come across something that disgusts you, don't eat it; whatever gives you pleasure, do more of it, etc. But beyond these basic emotions there are others which are referred to as 'higher emotions'.

P And they are?

A Well, these are not as well defined as the basic ones but they include such things as guilt, embarrassment, shame, pride, sympathy. These are emotions which are thought to be confined to, if not humans alone, then to a subset of large-brained mammals, several of whom are related to humans.

P So, what do these 'higher emotions' have in common?

M Well, with these emotions it isn't just what the person experiencing the emotion actually feels. For example, in the case of fear, the person's body reacts, the heart starts pumping faster, you might start sweating, etc. Higher emotions, on the other hand, are triggered by what other people might be thinking about you.

P Can you give an example?

M OK. Well, let's take embarrassment and, let's take a situation like, say, spilling coffee all over yourself. Now, whenever you do this in private, say, in your own kitchen, and however many times you do it, it's unlikely to cause embarrassment. But if you spilt coffee all over yourself in a very public place, you might well feel embarrassed.

P So, you're saying there isn't embarrassment in the act itself, but in what others might think of you?

M Yes, exactly, and that's the difference between higher and basic emotions.

P OK, I can see that with embarrassment, but is it the same with guilt or pride? Do we only feel guilty or proud when someone else witnesses the act and … ?

R8.4

INTERVIEWER Do you think that being a man or a woman has ever stopped you from doing something you wanted to do? And if you could live your life again as a man or a woman, which would you choose and why?

EM So far in my life, being a woman hasn't stopped me doing anything that I've wanted to do. An experience that springs to mind was when my boyfriend and I were travelling around Italy and we ran out of money. So we needed to find work, and we found work on a building site. So Toby was building and I was Toby's labourer. And that's not a typical role for a woman, but it was a really good experience. If I could live my life again, I would definitely come back as a woman, for the simple fact that I've really thoroughly enjoyed my life so far. And I hope it carries on to be as much fun as it already has been – as a woman.

BOB I've never really thought about it. Everything I've sort of wanted to do has always been from a male perspective. So, I don't know any other way of behaving other than being a man. No, all the things like sport and work and that, I've never had any problems with – it's all flowed probably from being, well, a man, I guess, so no, I don't think it's hindered me at all. Definitely, I'm happy staying a man, I real, you know, I really enjoy it. But if for a day or two I could come back as a woman, just to gain, gain a greater understanding or empathy, then I

could probably do that. As long as I could revert back to being a man … at will.

MICK Well, yeah funnily enough the one thing that I cannot do and probably will never be able to do unless science progresses far beyond I imagine it will, is give birth. It's something that biologically, obviously I can't do. And it is something I do think about. I have lots of female friends that have got babies and have given birth and have said that it's the hardest thing but it's also the most rewarding thing they have ever done in their life. And like I say, it's something that I will never ever be able to do. In some aspects I wish I was a seahorse, 'cos seahorses are the only mammal where the male gives birth. But having said all that, if I were to come back, I think I probably still would be a man.

KAY Well, when I think about my childhood I was at a huge disadvantage being a girl 'cos I was brought up in a house of brothers and I desperately wanted to join in with the football. And I think I would have been really rather good at it, but I wasn't allowed. They wouldn't, they wouldn't let me join in ever and I ended up doing ballet, which of course I wasn't good enough at. But I think I would have been a, a pretty good footballer one way and another. And, and I love the game; I really enjoy it. So that's, that would have been a, a good reason to be a fella. And if I was to live my life again, I think, I think I probably would try it as a male. One reason being that you wouldn't have to queue up in the toilets. And they only have to, they only have to think of one thing at a time – men.

JOEY It hasn't ever stopped me from doing anything I've wanted to do, but being a woman makes life harder and more complicated in that you're trying to do a job and you're also having to look after your family. And I have definitely seen with women that I work with, trying to juggle those two things can be quite difficult and it can hold up their careers or make them feel that they're not successful at doing both things at once. I'd quite like to be a man to see what it's like, but I think I'd choose to be a woman because I think women are better communicators and they have richer lives with their friends. And they can have it all really if they, they work at it.

DAN Being a man has been, you know, been a wonderful experience. I've, I've not felt restricted being a man. I felt that actually doors have been opened for me. And I've been very conscious of the fact that being a woman at times, in, in this present society, has been difficult for women, but that, it's, it's worked out, it's been all right for me. If I could live my life again, I don't think I'd, I have a particular preference of coming back as male or female. I, I'm, if I think of the answer to that question, would I come back as male or female? I just think, yes, I'd come back as male or female. What a wonderful thing.

R8.5

ANSWERS 2 holds 3 tears 4 fears 5 said 6 read 7 you 8 view 9 you 10 pain 11 to 12 face

R9.1

CATE 'Money can't buy you happiness' is actually a statement I think I would have to agree with. I recog, I mean, I recognise that we need

money, we do need money for our basic needs, but money is not the route to happiness. I think there are, there are other factors that play far more important roles.

MAUREEN I know a lot of people say that, Cate, but then they're thinking of possessions and things, and sure possessions can't ultimately buy you happiness. But maybe it's the opportunities that, that having money give you that makes me think money *can* buy you happiness. You know, it can buy you time to do the things you want to do: travel, learn something new, spend time helping people, whatever. So, in that way, I think money really can buy you happiness. I'm not saying it always does.

C You mean, if you don't have to worry about money, that in itself allows you to do some of the things that might contribute towards your happiness. Is that what you're saying, Maureen?

M Sure. I think, yeah, you know, you could really become whatever you wanted to be if you have plenty of money. You know if, if rich people aren't happy then I don't have any sympathy for them 'cos they haven't used the opportunity they have to find what it is that *would* make them happy.

PETE Well, what about things that don't necessarily take a lot of money but still make you happy? One of the happiest moments in my life was when the football team I play for, we, we won a cup in an amateur tournament.

C And I expect you had a brilliant time.

P Yeah, that happened a few years ago, it was one of the happiest times I've ever had, and I shared it with 12 other people. *And* it didn't cost us a penny. It doesn't matter how wealthy you are, you can't buy that kind of feelgood factor. I mean, it's like what you say, Cate, I know a guy who worked in the City, you know, in the money markets and he worked all hours, and I mean all hours just to be able to buy some amazing home-entertainment system. That's all he dreamed of. And finally he got it, and he wasn't any happier.

M Yeah, but I wasn't saying that. That's back to possessions – I was saying money can let you do what you want to do and that could include, you know, giving it away like Bill Gates – you could become a better person, if you like.

C As I said earlier, I think we need *some* money. I would agree with that. Yeah. And not having money can really make you miserable, but …

P Yeah, I've been there, worrying about where the next penny comes from. It's no joke. So yes, money can free you from worries, but the question was, can it buy you happiness? That's different.

M For me it isn't. And it's like when they say money can't buy you health – well, that's not true, either. You just have to look at how long people live in poor countries. I can't remember where it was, but I recently read about a place where the average life expectancy is 40-something.

P I'm with you on that one.

M And when they say money can't buy you love? Again I think it can sometimes.

C Oh, I don't know about that!

P Well, I'd like to have loads of money just to check all this out.

M You mean, do some research?

C Yeah. Hear, hear!

157

Recording Scripts

R9.2

ANNOUNCER And now *Spotlight* introduced by Kate Conrad. The subject of today's programme is Satish Kumar.

PRESENTER Back in the early 1960s in Europe, the UK and the US, there were many community-led campaigns against nuclear weapons, and Satish Kumar wanted to be part of this peace movement. So he and a friend planned to leave their native home of India and walk round the world for peace, visiting the heads of state in Moscow, Paris, London and Washington. Before they left India, one of Satish's teachers told them not to take any money with them on their journey. His reason was this: at the end of each day after they had walked 20 or 30 miles Satish and his friend would be exhausted, and if they had money, they'd look for a restaurant and a bed for the night. If they did this, the teacher said, they wouldn't meet anyone and they wouldn't pass on their message. However, if they had nothing at all, they would be forced to rely on the kindness of strangers, who were bound to ask them why they were making this journey. So the two men, who weren't particularly money-minded anyway, set off without any means of paying for anything whatsoever, which meant their journey was totally unpredictable.

R9.3

PRESENTER And, as we might imagine, their 8,000 mile walk certainly wasn't entirely stress-free. It took Satish and his companion through deserts, mountains, storms, snow and blazing heat. They were thrown into jail in France, they faced a gun in the US, but nothing put them off their mission for peace. In fact, their determination was made even stronger when, on their way to Moscow, they met two women who worked in a tea factory. After Satish explained why they were doing the walk, one of the women gave them four small packets of tea, one to be delivered to each of the leaders of the four nuclear powers with this message: "When you think you need to press the nuclear button, stop for a minute and have a fresh cup of tea." Satish and his friend did eventually deliver 'peace tea' to the leaders of the four nuclear powers and their journey is chronicled in Satish's book, *No Destination*. They began their journey at the grave of Gandhi in India and the journey ended at the grave of John F Kennedy in the US. And it's noteworthy that apart from crossing the English Channel and the Atlantic by boat, they really did walk all the way.

R9.4

PRESENTER That journey taught Satish a great deal. In particular, he said he learned that if he travels as an Indian with an Indian flag he'll meet a Pakistani, or a Russian, or a US citizen carrying their flags. If he goes as a socialist, he'll meet a capitalist. If he goes as a brown man, he'll meet a white man or a black man, but if he travels through life as a human being, he'll meet only human beings. So, Satish concluded that if people could forget boundaries of country, religion, language and culture, then they could begin to understand that basically, we are the same, and as such we can learn to live with one another in peace.

R9.5

TEACHER Right, settle down please … OK, OK, a show of hands here, how many of you are considering studying economics next year? Ah, two. I promise you those people are not related to me in any way. Right, so why should anyone want to study economics? After all, it's often referred to as 'the gloomy science,' but believe me it isn't. And I've got three minutes to convince you that rather than being gloomy, it is in fact optimistic – it could save your world. So, **I'm going to divide the talk into** three sections. **First of all**, how economics is related to real life. **Then I'll go on to** the intellectual challenge. **And finally I'll** discuss future careers.

R9.6

TEACHER **Let us start with** world issues. How many of you would like to make the world a better place? Ah good, three of you this time! Let's take poverty. The current rise in world food prices is likely to lead to a serious outbreak of famine in less-developed countries which rely on rice and wheat. We hear a lot about this from politicians, yet its roots and consequences are economic. In fact, most of the world's problems can be understood in terms of economics. Obviously, it won't provide easy answers to these problems but it does clarify the issues. For example, we exploit the earth's resources, trees, oil, etc., in order to create economic wealth, but we don't realise the real cost of doing so. What do we make plastic from? Oil, right, right. So, what is the real cost of, let's say using a plastic bag? It isn't just the cost of producing it, you have to think about the cost of disposing of it when you throw it away. Economists can do that, they can analyse the full social costs of our actions, so we can make better choices like, should we have more airports or more railways? Should we use nuclear power or renewable energy? What are the real costs and benefits of each? **As I said before**, economics won't provide all the answers but it will help you form balanced and informed opinions and with those you may find solutions. **So, to sum up** this first section, if you have a wish to really understand and analyse the background to world issues and not just have an emotional response to them, then economics is absolutely essential. **Let's move on to** the intellectual challenge involved in economics. It's a subject that suits people who are logical thinkers and who enjoy serious debate. It's for those who like creating and testing theories. I'm not saying it's easy. It does need a good understanding of mathematics and you do have to be able to communicate clearly in writing. But if you have these skills, then economics might just put them to the best use. And even if you aren't interested in the business world as such, because economics is related to most other subjects it will give you a deeper understanding of anything you want to study from politics to rocket science to fashion. **And finally**, there's the small matter of how you're going to earn a living. Well, careers in business, finance and management obviously all have economics at their heart. However, careers in architecture or engineering also need an understanding of what we call opportunity cost, the building block of economics.

Perhaps you're interested in agriculture, overseas aid, politics or journalism? Whatever your ambition, the study of economics provides a good grounding for these and many other careers.

So **in conclusion**, if you want to study an interesting and interdisciplinary subject, which provides relevant knowledge and skills for your future career, go for economics. It's not gloomy at all. It is, in fact, a lively and exciting science; challenging and deeply satisfying. Right, let's have another show of hands, see if …

R10.1

PRESENTER Everything has to start somewhere, and some things which are a matter of course in our everyday lives have some interesting, not to say very strange origins.

MAN The first idea for ice cream, for example, can be traced back to the 1st century AD, when the Roman Emperor, Nero, ordered buckets of snow to be sent from the mountains in the north down to Rome, where it was mixed with red wine and honey and served at banquets. It's probably the Chinese, though, at around the same time, who invented the first form of the half-frozen fruit-flavoured ice cream we know today. When Marco Polo returned from the Far East in the 13th century he was a mine of information about how to make ice cream from snow, fruit juice and fruit pulp. As a result, it became popular in Europe, although it wasn't until the end of the 19th century that ice cream became a treat for ordinary people.

WOMAN Turning to drinks, tea is something we'd find very difficult to do without in Britain, and this has an even stranger origin. According to ancient myth, in 2737 BC, a handful of dried leaves from a bush blew into a pot of boiling water, into which the Chinese Emperor was staring. There is no record as to why the water was boiling, why the leaves were dried, or why the Emperor was staring into the pot, but the resulting brew was to be known henceforth as 'tchai'. Is there an element of truth in this story? Nobody really knows, but what we do know is that it was to become China's national drink during the 1st century AD.

M And how many of us realise that coffee was originally eaten, not drunk? Before 1000 AD, it appears that a tribe in Ethiopia began to eat ground coffee beans mixed with animal fat for extra energy. Rumour has it that a goatherd, Kaldi, had noticed his goats jumping around with more energy after chewing berries from wild coffee bushes, so he tried them and found the same happened to him. Whether this rumour is true or not is a matter of opinion but what we do know is that news of Kaldi's magic beans spread rapidly and coffee consumption became a national habit, later spreading throughout the world as a popular drink.

W Moving away from food and drink, skyscrapers are very common these days, and yet it wasn't until 1885 that the first one became the centre of attention in its home town of Chicago. Nowadays, the term 'skyscraper' is only applied to over 40 storeys. The Home Insurance Building in Chicago, with its ten storeys was to revolutionise urban life. Its construction set off a train of events, because higher buildings led to larger numbers of people living and working in the same areas.

M The first escalator actually started off as a ride in an amusement park near New York in 1891. Jesse Reno pioneered a kind of moving ramp built at an angle of 25 degrees, which was a novelty for the 75,000 people who rode on it during the two weeks it was at the park. Another American inventor then developed a moving stairway with wooden steps and both were displayed at an international exhibition in Paris in 1900, where the word 'escalator' was coined. Ultimately, the two designs merged, a stroke of genius which created the escalator that is commonly used today.

P So, as you can see every invention tells a story! More on this can …

R10.2

ADELA My brother Martin's a good example of someone who sticks with it. He's amazing. He's really bright. He actually studied Latin and Greek at Oxford University, but his real love is animation. Ever since he was a kid, he's always drawn funny little characters. And now that's his job. He's naturally talented, but he still puts hours and hours into every little animation film he does. Like, here it is Saturday night and I'm sure he'll be working. He might be creating a new character, or he could be working on his next short film. Clearly, he must enjoy what he does, why else would he work so hard? But I feel sorry for his girlfriend, it can't be easy having Martin as your partner. She has to be so patient. I mean, like for example, whenever they are about to go out, he always says, "Just need to finish this bit. It shouldn't take me long," and of course it always does. But when I see Martin giving his all to a project, it makes me realise if you want to be really good at something, then you've just got to work at it. People are just starting to notice his work so it shouldn't be long before he gets the recognition he deserves. Another thing, he's always so positive; like he's certain he'll find a buyer for his next animation film. So yes, being positive and sticking with it are important.

LOUIE Some famous golfer said this, it might have been Tiger Woods, I'm not sure. Anyway, when whoever it was was asked if he thought luck came into the game he said, yes, but he noticed that the harder he practised the luckier he became. I like that. And it's obvious, isn't it? Take world-class performers, Tang Yun, for example, you just know it won't have been easy for him as a kid. He must have devoted most of his childhood to practising. And though I'm no Tang Yun, I've got some idea of what his childhood must have been like because I went to a school for gifted kids and I remember practising for hours every day. I may have had some natural talent, but who knows? But, I did practise six hours a day – at least – sometimes more. We all did at that school. I remember hearing a programme about gifted kids once, it said that 'the gift' seemed to be they just didn't mind spending hours practising. And that's true. It's not that we just picked up an instrument at the age of two and started playing Beethoven's violin concertos or anything. But, I'm afraid I didn't stick with it – well, not enough to earn a living as a soloist. My father says I can't have wanted it badly enough or I wouldn't have given up. I guess he's right.

R10.3

MARIA PIA I think I had different strategies for different levels, really. At a very low level, I started off by memorising a lot of vocabulary and only after that I actually started looking into how the sentences built – so the grammar side of things – that was clearly supplemented with an awful lot of grammar exercise, which is always very important. But, it's quite interesting 'cos it wasn't, the memorising's always worked for me, and not only in learning English but also learning other languages – Russian, for example. But at a higher level, I think things change quite a lot. The thing, the things I've always done are, for example, reading the papers. I think that's very, very important – it just not only helps you to learn new words, especially if you start reading the big, the big newspapers, but you can also keep up with what's going on in the country, you know, where the language you're learning is spoken. But, in addition to normal newspapers, I think it's quite important to remember that language is changing at all times. So, for example, you know, reading the classics has always been one of my passions, which is absolutely, you know, it's absolutely brilliant and you can learn so much from those books, but you have to remember that you run the risk of using words which are terribly out-of-date, and you end up speaking like Jane Austen, which I almost did at some point in my language learning! So, just reading magazines, for example, is a perfect way to keep up-to-date with the current language and new terminology, and so is using the Internet. I found the Internet very, very useful at a higher level. Also, the other thing is, to be honest, watch television and listen to the radio. In England, there's so many local and regional accents, and so you just learn to hear the different ways of pronouncing words. And the other thing when you learn new words, I've always tried to use them and in conversations always bring them up, and for me it was a very easy way to remember new words. I used to have – I don't do this any more – but I used to have a little, like little notebook, with an alphabetical order, it was like one of those booklets you buy for telephone numbers, and every time I came across a new word, I would just jot it down in my little book, and just maybe writing it would help me memorise it … a little bit, a little bit quicker, little bit faster so at the end of this, my period of studies, I ended up with my own little dictionary. But I suppose the main thing is, just try and speak as much as you can. You can do a lot of grammar work, you can do a lot of lang, take a lot of language lessons but I think it's very important to try and put into practice what you've learned on the books and maybe just depends, it's just the kind of person I am, but I'm a very gregarious learner I think, so going out, meeting people, even, you know, find myself an English husband, you know, just try and interact with other people as much as possible and, the more you speak, the better the language skills will be, I think.

R10.4

BRUCE Yes, I, I've tried to learn various languages at different points of my life, including French, Italian, Mandarin and Arabic, all with rather different levels of success. I think when starting out, I found the classroom experience very helpful. I enjoy the sort of, the sociable nature of learning in a group, and being instructed by, by you know, a professional. However, as I move up into, sort of, intermediate, good intermediate level, I prefer to work more independently. What's been really useful for me is, is reading – anything from trashy magazines to crime novels to love stories, even actually things in, in translation have been quite good, because translators tend to simplify the original language, also reading newspapers. Because I think in this way, you, you acquire language a bit like a sponge acquires water, so you absorb new vocabulary, you consolidate your knowledge of grammar, you just get a feel for the right word in the right place.

I also like to listen a lot, so I buy CDs occasionally or download stuff to my iPod so I can listen in the car, or when out for a walk. I go and see foreign films when, when possible – I *hate* anything that's dubbed, you know, I really think that spoils it. But it all takes effort and I think people tend to underestimate the amount of time it takes to, to learn a language. Yeah, having said that, you know, I do feel I ought to do more grammar exercises 'cos I'm still a bit woolly about some of the grammar. I do like to learn new vocabulary and I often put a, I look up words in a dictionary and I put a tick next to the word when I look it up so if I have to look it up *again* and I already see a tick, I know I really have to have to learn it because it's a high-frequency word. And, you know, you just have to go for it. I think people are actually quite tolerant of you, when you try to speak their language. They don't mind you making mistakes, so yeah, just go out and be creative with the language, even. There was a great Irish writer called Samuel Beckett and he used to write in English, and then he switched to French as he found it gave him more freedom to express himself away from the, the constraints of the English language. Now how amazing is that?!

I think once you've got to an advanced level, you need to leave the classroom behind, really. I mean, language learning doesn't stop there, there's a whole load of things to learn, but you have to go out and do it by yourself and interact with people and do all these things like reading and listening by yourself.

R10.5

Listening Test (see Teacher's Book)

CD-ROM Instructions

Start the CD-ROM

- Insert the *face2face* CD-ROM into your CD-ROM drive.
- If Autorun is enabled, the CD-ROM will start automatically.
- If Autorun is not enabled, open **My Computer** and then **D:** (where D is the letter of your CD-ROM drive). Then double-click on the *face2face* icon.

Install the CD-ROM to your hard disk (recommended)

- Go to **My Computer** and then **D:** (where D is the letter of your CD-ROM drive).
- Right-click on *Explore*.
- Double-click on *Install face2face to hard disk*.
- Follow the installation instructions on your screen.

What's on the CD-ROM?

- **Interactive practice activities**

Extra practice of Grammar, Vocabulary, Real World situations and English pronunciation. Click on one of the unit numbers (1–10) at the top of the screen. Then choose an activity and click on it to start.

- **My Activities**

Create your own lesson. Click on *My Activities* at the top of the screen. Drag activities from the unit menus into the *My Activities* panel on the right of the screen. Then click on *Start*.

- **My Portfolio**

This is a unique and customisable reference tool. Click on *Grammar, Word List, Real World* or *Phonemes* at any time for extra help and information. You can also add your own notes, check your progress and create your own English tests!

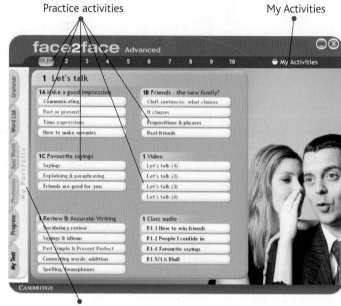

Practice activities   My Activities

My Portfolio

System specification
- Windows XP or Vista, Mac OSX 10.4+
- 256MB RAM for XP, 1GB RAM for Vista

Support

If you experience difficulties with this CD-ROM, please visit: www.cambridge.org/elt/cdrom

---

Acknowledgements

The authors would like to thank everyone at Cambridge University Press for all their support and hard work during this project, in particular: Dilys Silva, Verity Cole and Karen Momber (Editorial team); Andrew Reid, Sue Ullstein and Brigit Viney (Freelance editors); Ian Collier, Alison Greenwood and Nicholas Tims (CD-ROM team) and all the team at pentacor**big**.

As always, many thanks go to Chris Redston and Nicholas Tims for their invaluable contributions. The authors would also like to thank their family and friends for keeping them sane.

The authors and publishers would like to thank the following people for their contribution to the recordings:
Angelo Acanfora, Stefano Antonini, Will Atkinson, Eddy Canfor-Dumas, Sue and Dan Clark, Claire Cole, Verity Cole, Ian Collier, Hiltrud Collison, Pam Connelan, Andrew Cook, Fran Disken, Lynn Dunlop, Richard Gibb, Rachael Gibbon, Valerie Goldman, Melissa Good, Katherine Gregory, Miranda Hamilton, Amybeth Hargreaves, George Harris, Helen Harrington, Laurie Harrison, Graham Hart, Charlotte Judd, Helen Kenyon, Pat Lodge, Naomi Long, John McRae, Alex Milne, Bruce Milne, Sue Mohamed, Helen Norman, Pete Northcott, Justyna Matwiejczyk, Claudia Payer, Elmer Postle, Alex Priestley, Marie-Claire Raphael, Helen and Dave Riches, Beth Rigby, Maria Pia Salcito, Keith Sands, Cate Shields, Maureen Street, Anne Szabo, Lindsay Warwick, Claire Thompson, Brendan Wightman, Chris Willis.

The authors and publishers would like to thank the following teachers for the invaluable feedback which they provided
Dorota Adach, Poland; Michaela Bojarova, Czech Republic; Allan Dalcher, Switzerland; César Elizi, Brazil; Madeline Hall, UK; Iris Grallert, Germany; Alison Greenwood, Italy; Lorraine Mollica, Italy; Margarita Navarro, Spain; Alejandro Naveas, Chile; Joanna Pawlak-Radziminska, Poland; Susana Perez del Sastre, Spain; Antoin Rogers, Turkey; Ruth Taylor, UK; Claire Wood, Switzerland.

The authors and publishers are grateful to the following contributors:
pentacor**big**: cover and text design and page make-up
Hilary Luckcock: picture research, commissioned photography
Trevor Clifford: photography
Anne Rosenfeld: audio recordings
Richard Gibb: authentic recordings
Mark Found: authentic recordings
Hazel Henderson: for up-to-date information on Hazel Henderson's work, see www.ethicalmarkets.com
Sarah Kedge: for tourist information about Great Britain, see www.enjoyengland.com
David Burgess: for sharing his expertise on economics

The authors and publishers acknowledge the following sources of copyright material and are grateful for the permissions granted. While every effort has been made, it has not always been possible to identify the sources of all the material used, or to trace all copyright holders. If any omissions are brought to our notice, we will be happy to include the appropriate acknowledgements on reprinting.
For the text in 1A: adapted from 'Fake Nice' by Harriet Lane, *Independent*, 29th April 2006 © Independent News & Media Limited; for the text in 1B: adapted from 'Friendship Overload' by Mary Killen/Shane Watson, *Express Saturday Magazine*, 17th September 1999; for the text in 2A: adapted from 'The Cleverest Man on Earth' by Helen de Bertodano, *Sunday Telegraph*, February 2005 © Telegraph Media Group Limited; for the text in 2B: adapted from 'I lost my heart' by Claudia Winkleman, interview by Tim Wapshott, *Guardian*, 22nd June 2002; for the text in 3A: adapted from 'Born to lose' by Anjana Ahuja, *The Times*, 31st August 2008; for the text in 4B: adapted from 'The world goes to town' by John Grimond, *Economist*, 5th May 2007 © The Economist Newspaper Limited, London; for the front-page image and article in 4C: 'Hero Pilot Saves Flight BA038' by Martin Fricker and Rebecca Evans, *Daily Mirror* 18th January 2008© Mirrorpix 2008; for the front-page image and article in